The Problem of Plurality of Logics

Also available from Bloomsbury

Advances in Experimental Philosophy of Logic and Mathematics, edited by Andrew Aberdein and Matthew Inglis
Knowledge and the Philosophy of Number, by Keith Hossack
The History of Philosophical and Formal Logic, by Alex Malpass and Marianna Antonutti Marfori
Using Questions to Think, by Nathan Eric Dickman
Why Did the Logician Cross the Road?, by Stan Baronett

The Problem of Plurality of Logics

*Understanding the Dynamic
Nature of Philosophical Logic*

Pavel Arazim

BLOOMSBURY ACADEMIC
LONDON • NEW YORK • OXFORD • NEW DELHI • SYDNEY

BLOOMSBURY ACADEMIC
Bloomsbury Publishing Plc
50 Bedford Square, London, WC1B 3DP, UK
1385 Broadway, New York, NY 10018, USA
29 Earlsfort Terrace, Dublin 2, Ireland

BLOOMSBURY, BLOOMSBURY ACADEMIC and the Diana logo are trademarks of
Bloomsbury Publishing Plc

First published in Great Britain 2021
This paperback edition published 2023

Copyright © The Institute of Philosophy of Czech Academy of Sciences, 2021

The Institute of Philosophy of Czech Academy of Sciences has asserted its right under the Copyright, Designs and Patents Act, 1988, to be identified as Proprietor of this work.

Pavel Arazim has asserted his right under the Copyright, Designs and
Patents Act, 1988, to be identified as Author of this work.

For legal purposes the Acknowledgements on p. vi constitute an extension
of this copyright page.

Cover image: Laura Chiesa/Pacific Press Media Production Corp/Alamy Stock Photo.

All rights reserved. No part of this publication may be reproduced or transmitted in any form or by any means, electronic or mechanical, including photocopying, recording, or any information storage or retrieval system, without prior permission in writing from the publishers.

Bloomsbury Publishing Plc does not have any control over, or responsibility for, any third-party websites referred to or in this book. All internet addresses given in this book were correct at the time of going to press. The author and publisher regret any inconvenience caused if addresses have changed or sites have ceased to exist, but can accept no responsibility for any such changes.

A catalogue record for this book is available from the British Library.

Library of Congress Cataloging-in-Publication Data
Names: Arazim, Pavel, author.
Title: The problem of plurality of logics : understanding the dynamic nature of philosophical logic / Pavel Arazim.
Description: London ; New York : Bloomsbury Academic, 2021. | Includes bibliographical references and index. | Identifiers: LCCN 2021006722 (print) | LCCN 2021006723 (ebook) | ISBN 9781350146754 (hb) | ISBN 9781350146761 (epdf) | ISBN 9781350146778 (ebook)
Subjects: LCSH: Logic.
Classification: LCC BC50 .A73 2021 (print) | LCC BC50 (ebook) | DDC 160.1--dc23
LC record available at https://lccn.loc.gov/2021006722
LC ebook record available at https://lccn.loc.gov/2021006723

ISBN: HB: 978-1-3501-4675-4
PB: 978-1-3502-5822-8
ePDF: 978-1-3501-4676-1
eBook: 978-1-3501-4677-8

Typeset by Deanta Global Publishing Services, Chennai, India

To find out more about our authors and books visit www.bloomsbury.com and sign up for
our newsletters.

Contents

Acknowledgements		vi
1	Logical dynamism	1
2	The issue of the plurality of logics	11
3	Kant's view of logic	21
4	The holistic view of logic	35
5	Model-theoretic demarcations of logical constants	61
6	The role of logic	95
7	Proof-theoretic demarcations of logic	133
8	Pluralism or monism?	151
Conclusion		177
Notes		179
References		187
Index		195

Acknowledgements

There are many people and ideas which inspired me during the time I was writing this book and I cannot possibly name them all. Yet some of them stand out. I would like to express special thanks to my beloved wife, Zuzana, for the love and support she gave me, particularly at times when I was doubtful about the outcome of my work. Furthermore, I thank Jaroslav Peregrin, who supervised my dissertation on which this book is based. From the text it should be obvious how much I owe him. This book was supported by the grant of The Czech Science Foundation (GAČR) 20-18675S *The Nature of Logical Forms and Modern Logic*, led by Vladimír Svoboda, my colleague from Czech academy of sciences.

1

Logical dynamism

The plurality of logical systems is one of the peculiar features of the modern development of logic. While it certainly is worthwhile to investigate not only the mathematical properties but also the philosophical credentials of specific logics, here the focus will be on the very plurality itself rather than on the virtues and vices of specific logical systems. The phenomenon of plurality challenges philosophers of logic. So far, it seems to have led them to two kinds of stances. On the one hand, there are *logical monists*, who argue for a particular system as being the true one or at least in some important sense privileged. On the other hand, lots of authors argue that more logics are correct in some sense and various flavours or elaborations of this tendency bear the title of *logical pluralism*. Given how complex this issue is and how much intellectual effort was already invested in its clarification, it may well seem pointless to try offering yet another view of it. Many ingenious forms of both logical monism and logical pluralism have been offered, as well as arguments for them. If one wants to, one can just review the broad offering of positions and choose the one that feels the best according to his or her individual philosophical and logical tastes.

While I discuss some of the accounts which have been proposed recently and which can be seen as rivals to mine in the last chapter, in this section I want to briefly present at the outset my own view on the plurality of logics. It should be noted that this book is not intended to only be an investigation of this view. It is not limited to my own thesis and its alternatives, and, in general, I want to present what the problem of the plurality of logics consists in and also display its broader philosophical implications, as well as provide an overview of the history of addressing it. But now let us start with my promised take on the plurality of logics.

1.1 Why dynamism?

I call my view *logical dynamism* because it is based on observations pertaining to the dynamic nature of logic. I will briefly explain why it cannot be straightforwardly identified either with logical monism or with logical pluralism. When we ask which logic is the right logic or which logics are the right logics, we should also ask what should the logic or logics be right *for*. If we were not to learn something about the nature and purpose of logic by investigating the issue of the plurality of logics, it would hardly attract so much attention. My approach to the plurality of logics is based on inferentialism and the related logical expressivism of Robert Brandom, as he presented these doctrines in *Making It Explicit*.[1] Yet here I will limit myself to more general observations to give the basic flavour of my view.

I take logic to be constituted by rules. In fact, any human affair is closely related to rules, lots of them being constituted by rules. This general remark does not oblige me to much as of yet. It might seem that in advance I am unfairly preferencing proof-theoretical approaches to logic over the model-theoretical ones. But in a weaker sense, even model theory and model-theoretical semantics, including its account of logical consequence, is based on rules, for example, on the rules of assigning elements of the model to expressions of a certain specified kind. Ultimately, I believe that logical expressions are constituted by inference rules, but there will yet be occasions to discuss this particular point. For the moment, let us focus on rules in general.

1.1.1 Some remarks on rules

Two features of rules will be of particular import for us here. For one, rules develop and are dynamic in their nature. This point, I believe, is fairly obvious to anybody who considers them without prejudice due to peculiar philosophical preferences. You can take any kind of rules and you will find not only a possibility of development but the actual development which they have undergone in the course of some time. The rules for passing an exam at university change, as the university wants to become more or less demanding, all kinds of laws keep being novelized as there is a political will to do that (hopefully for good reasons), even mathematical notions change all the time and with them the rules for doing mathematics. Before the advent of negative numbers it was correct to assert that adding a number never diminishes the number you start with, yet this changed with the advent of negative integers. Practically any expression can change and typically does change its meaning over some decades. Of course, some expressions might be more prone to such changes than others, but the tendency for them to develop is quite general.

1.1.1.1 Identity of rules

An obvious criticism can be raised here. When a given rule or system of rules changes, should we not say rather that new rules were accepted and not that the old ones have developed? In other words, what are the criteria of identity of rules across time and context? When the rules for, say, addition in mathematics change with the advent of negative integers, should we not say that the old rules were replaced, so that we do not have to do with rules A, B, C and so on anymore but rather with X, Y, Z and so on, and furthermore, with a new operation, which is different from the original addition, though it might be very similar? Well, my claim certainly is not that we always have to interpret the rules as remaining the same, despite all the changes. How they should be judged depends on the specific cases. On many occasions, both the claim that we are dealing with the same rules, though in a changed form, and the opposite claim that these are in fact really new rules can be equally warranted. Then the choice is just optional. What I, nevertheless, claim is that in general we have to reckon with the ability of rules to develop. In some cases, we have to say that it is still A, B and C that we are dealing with.

1.1.1.2 The real, clean shape of a rule

Those who believe that every rule is precisely identified with only one specific shape rely, I believe, on an illusion of something as the real and clean shape of rules. The same holds for meanings. It is tempting to think that there is something like a real, definite shape of, say, the conjunction, though we may struggle to pin it down exactly – to sufficiently disambiguate and differentiate it from other related meanings. But tempting as this is, such reasoning gets it wrong.

Every rule makes real sense only in the context of many further rules with which it interacts and which are also necessary if we are to understand the rule. As Robert Brandom puts it, understanding only one rule is a sound of one hand clapping.[2] But as we know from Wittgenstein, not all the rules can be explicit.

Wittgenstein goes yet further by showing that for any rule which we make explicit, we rely on many others which have to remain implicit in the context of explication. And because understanding a given rule fully and explicitly would also mean understanding in the same way the other rules which have to remain implicit, it is simply impossible to get to a fully definite and specific shape of a rule. Explication and, consequently, explicitness is always partial.

Furthermore, we have learned also from Wittgenstein and Kripke[3] that when we focus on a given rule, it is always open to a plurality of interpretations. On some level, this is no big issue in everyday life but it still undermines the notion of there being something like clear-cut definite meanings and rules which we just try to pick as precisely as possible by our language. The point is illustrated even by Bertrand Russell, who in his article 'Vagueness'[4] admits that even in mathematics, vagueness of terms can be at best reduced but never fully eliminated. In accordance with Russell, I by no means intend to say that a request for more disambiguation and clarification of what one means by a given utterance are illegitimate. Only that they are always dependent on the context and never fulfilled in a perfect, definite way. If anyone wants to consider definite rules and meanings as useful fictions or regulative ideas, I can agree with the proviso that their usefulness is limited and has to be adjudicated in every specific case. Sometimes the pursuit of as great a clarity as possible can be even harmful.

I think we were taught not only by Wittgenstein and Kripke but also by Quine and Davidson that all the rules, as well as meanings, always fail to be fully definite. Both the considerations pertaining to rule following, in particular Kripke's example of impossibility to definitely distinguish addition from some kind of quaddition and the considerations pertaining to radical translation or interpretation, show this, each in a specific way.[5] All these authors typically seem to speak of an intended interpretation and how we fail to pick just it and nothing else. Addition clearly seems preferable to any kind of quaddition. *Gavagai* seems more naturally translated as *rabbit* than as *an undetached rabbit-part*, yet all the attempts to distinguish them are short-lived. Their success is easily overcome by new distortions of the same kind. Now, it seems we have two options of how to interpret both the quaddition and the gavagai considerations.

In all of those examples, one obviously seems to be confronted with unequal alternatives. On the one hand, there is an obviously natural interpretation, which understands the + sign as denoting addition and *gavagai* as determining rabbit. The other interpretations just seem strained. From this perspective, it would seem that all those examples purport to say is that it is difficult, maybe even impossible, to pin down the correct interpretation. Yet I plead for learning a stronger lesson from them, namely that there is no definitive interpretation. There is always something open-ended and undecided. We may opt to go in one direction, which may also seem much more natural, yet we will have to make similar decisions later. All specifications of meanings remain partial and fail to be definite. Any specification is only provisory and will have to be revisited in new contexts.

This all means that both meanings and rules cannot be as clean and definite as they are often conceived. Let us focus once again on meanings. It is common to speak of propositions as of meanings of sentences and of concepts as meanings of predicates. A given sentence may fail to pick up exactly one proposition, though we can try to come closer to full clarity and the pinning down of a single proposition. This is the way that the orthodoxy goes. I think, however, that it is incorrect. The notion of a proposition or concept completely detached from actual language use is a fiction: sometimes, perhaps, a useful one but often harmful.

1.1.2 What about formal languages and formal logics?

It is in our practices that our rules and also meanings reside, not somewhere beyond. But it should be added that these practices are by necessity dynamic and always developing, perhaps not always for the good, but developing nevertheless. But still, is it not different in the case of formal languages? And what is dynamic about formal, mathematically defined logical theories, such as classical propositional logic, propositional intuitionistic logic, first-order logic, modal propositional logics and others?

Let us remind ourselves that already in 'Two Dogmas',[6] Quine saw this objection coming and still chose to bite the bullet. I basically follow his lead. When we speak of the dynamic nature of meanings and rules and their constant development, this pertains to formal languages, as well. First of all, we understand formal languages only by means of the natural ones. When a student attending a logic course gets acquainted with conjunction, she has to understand that any formula of the form $A \wedge B$ is true exactly in those cases in which *both* A *and* B are true, which amounts more or less to understanding conjunction. The boundary between the realm of the allegedly messy natural language and the allegedly neat formal one is thus at the very least unclear and the latter is strongly dependent on the former. On the other hand, it should be noted that the *naturalness* of natural language should also not be overrated. Obviously, it is regulated quite explicitly; it is not constituted only by our spontaneous linguistic behaviour but also by decrees on the part of linguists. It is thus codified though obviously less so than formal languages.

This leads us to further considerations about the relation between rules and their expressions. We normally distinguish between sentences we utter or write and what they state. The sentence *There is a dog over there* is certainly distinct from the dog itself. On the other hand, in the case of rules it seems that this distinction cannot be drawn so clearly; the rule and the sentence which expresses it appear to be intimately related. This impression is only partially right and in important respects misleading. While expressions of a rule can influence the rule much more directly than descriptions of a dog can influence the dog itself, they are still not the same thing.

1.1.2.1 Rules and their expressions

A given rule truly holds only if it is in some way acknowledged by the society or social group for which it is supposed to hold. This cannot always happen by means of explicit acknowledgement; at least sometimes it must be a mere tacit approval manifested in action, as we know from Wittgenstein. The rules thus have to live in our society and cannot be equated with their expression. When someone formulates the rule and wants it to be followed, his proposal has to be accepted by the members of the respective community.

A rule is thus a living social phenomenon. It lives in the mutual recognition of the members of the community and in their behaviour. If the rule holds, they typically act on it, though they also sometimes break it. Yet more importantly, they assess each other and themselves by the rule and act correspondingly, by encouraging one another to follow it and discouraging one another from breaking it. But what about the expressions of the rules? How does a statement such as 'It is prohibited to trespass this line' relate to the very rule that this line should indeed not be trespassed? The relations can be manifold. Let us review some of the forms can take.

If the given rule has not been established, uttering this statement or a similar one can lead to it. If the person uttering it has a particular authority, maybe the utterance can indeed establish the rule. Typically, though, the situation is not so clear and the utterance is more likely to just initiate a discussion about whether the rule should be adopted.

If the rule already holds, the utterance at least expresses it. This can be done for various purposes. We can merely remind ourselves of the rule. In more interesting cases we can be unsure about its actual shape. Remember that not all rules which we accept have to be explicitly formulated, and even if the given rule was expressed, we might be unsure how to interpret it. Furthermore, we can initiate a debate about what to do with the rule, whether to uphold it, modify it or withdraw it completely. Overall, we can thus see that an expression of a rule can cause or contribute to the rule's coming into existence or to its modification. Yet, they still are not the same.

When we review the issue of formal languages and formal logics, I claim that the impression that their rules do have the definite and clear-cut shapes arises from the interchange between rules and their expressions. As the formal languages are typically regimented and much more perspicuous than natural languages, we are tempted to interchange the difference of degree with the difference of kind. Formal languages are dependent on natural languages though they can also influence them. When someone learns how to work with, say, classical logic, that person will probably also use her natural language differently, perhaps with greater caution. Similarly, the rules of any formal logic cannot be understood and are thus dependent on analogous rules which hold for informal reasoning.

1.1.2.2 *Explicit and implicit rules*

We have already mentioned the division of rules into explicit and implicit ones (which is strongly emphasized, for instance, in Peregrin and Svoboda (2017)). This distinction, though, should be taken as at best auxiliary. Every rule makes sense only in connection with other rules, in some ways only in connection with all the other rules. And because it is impossible that all rules be explicit at the same time, even those which were expressed remain to some degree beyond our reach and sight. In this sense, I take them to be implicit. Maybe the rules of chess are particularly clear and explicit, yet even they are dependent on our understanding of words such as *move*, *position* and others.

Though they have their specific, artificial meaning in the context of chess, this meaning still could not be understood without the standard meaning these words have in English.

But more importantly, this holds also for the rules which define formal logics. As clear as the behaviour of logical connectives appears to be, we can still discover new facts about it by proving new theorems. As unlikely as it might seem, the study of even such a simple system as that of classical propositional logic may bring us into situations when we will be forced to decide which rules really hold about it. I think the situation is similar to that of geometry. As I will explain in more detail in one of the following chapters, the advent of non-Euclidian geometries indeed showed that some important aspects of our geometrical notions were much less clearly established then they had seemed.

1.2 The rationale of formal systems

I thus claim that both the rules of our reasoning in natural language and those of formal logical systems are dynamic and open-ended, though perhaps to different degrees. While we obviously use something as a conditional or negation, quantifiers and other logical elements in natural reasoning, these concepts, just as the extra-logical ones, keep developing and adapting to new contexts and situations. But when the formal logics and our everyday reasoning differ so little in this essential aspect, why do we develop formal logics at all?

I believe there might be many reasons to do that. Obviously, logicians who develop them can have various motivations. Yet I believe that the main rationale of these enterprises is to exhibit how the concepts with which we reason could develop. When someone gets acquainted with classical logic, it can influence the way she reasons, though perhaps only slightly. The same holds for intuitionistic logic and all the other systems. Besides this, getting to know the various systems, and seeing how none of them can be said to exactly correspond to the way we normally reason, leads us to see this very potential to change and develop which lies in our concepts.

The various formal logics point to the possible directions of development of logical concepts. Logical concepts we actually use develop anyway even if we do not want them to, as the whole of language is a dynamic and living entity, yet we can at least partially get this development under our control. As the dynamic character of rules, even the logical ones, is at the core of my account of the plurality of logical systems, I like to call my account *logical dynamism*. Later on, I will show why and how I link it with logical expressivism, which, I hope, will add to the plausibility and attractivity of my approach. But for the moment, let us forget this preliminary sketch and start with the philosophical problem of the plurality of logics, as it were, from the beginning. I intend to show how this problem could historically arise and show a path which leads to my account. I believe that this should not only illustrate how this account is related to historical development and perhaps other accounts which are current. It should also give it more content, put more flesh on the bones of this sketch.

2

The issue of the plurality of logics

There are many logics. Or are there? The plurality of logical systems we can encounter in literature today makes one unsure what can yet be cogently maintained about the nature of logic. Because of the sheer number of logics it becomes less clear how to recognize what still is a logic and what is not logic anymore but instead, for instance, mathematics, abstract linguistics or some other discipline. And more importantly, the plurality of logics raises the question whether and how can multiple logics be correct. Furthermore, does the plurality entail that we can in some sense choose a logic we use and can we then under some circumstances change it? Such a supposition, I believe, cannot be avoided if we accept that multiple logics can be correct. But at the same time, at least according to some understandings, logic seems to be so fundamental for our reasoning that any idea of stepping outside the logic we use in order to change it would lead only to absurdity. Stepping outside our logic is thus understood as a failure to reason and be rational at all.

    I have undertaken the search for an explication of the nature of logic which both renders logical pluralism acceptable and yet does not water down the significance of logic for our rationality. My search has been done partly from a historical perspective, yet eventually I end up mostly inspired by contemporary authors and the gist of my account is a development of ideas introduced by Robert Brandom in 1994 and subsequently refined and clarified both by himself, Jaroslav Peregrin, Giacomo Turbanti[1] and others. The historical background which offers at least a part of my outlook is provided by Kantian epistemology, though taken rather selectively, as I did not want to dedicate the whole book just to historical questions. Why is Kant so important? I take him as a figure who clearly defined the account of logic which lies behind the monist intuitions, that is behind the intuitions which make us think that logic has to be only one and cannot be changed.

The way Kant saw logic as fundamental resembles in important aspects the way he saw geometry. I thus briefly review how the development of plurality of geometries was discussed, as I hope to gain useful insights regarding logic as well. I take the more holistic view of geometry as the most important result of the debates about the conflict between the plurality and the fundamentality. We have to understand geometry not as an isolated discipline but rather as communicating and even continuous with physics. This leads to a natural analogue with the case of logic, as the possibility of such a holistic shift in understanding logic was offered, though rather indirectly, by Frege and his logicist programme. I take its basic idea to be that logic is better understood in its relationship with mathematics and not as an isolated discipline. It was thereafter natural for me to focus the next chapter on model-theoretic demarcations of logic which have a logicist background. These attempts reach back to Tarski and form one of the two main approaches to demarcating logic in the face of plurality of the logical systems. The other approach is proof-theoretic and will be discussed later.

I find the model-theoretic approach, though certainly respectable and conductive to fascinating mathematical results, unconvincing, as it, at least as far as I know, lacks an account of the pragmatic role of logic. What do we actually want logic to achieve? And what properties must logic possess in order to fulfil this role? By considering how we define logical constants, I come to doubt that logic should be seen as a tool for the expansion of knowledge, which is maybe the most natural supposition one can have and which is indeed still maintained in literature by many. I find Brandom's logical expressivism to be the doctrine which explains the importance of logic convincingly. Not only is the fact that logic does not expand our knowledge in a straightforward sense consistent with logical expressivism, this fact actually enables logic to fulfil the role attributed to it by logical expressivism, namely rendering our inference rules explicit.

As logical expressivism is based on an inferentialist understanding of meaning in language, including meaning of logical expressions, it is natural to investigate the proof-theoretic approach to demarcating logic. Unlike the model-theoretic approach, this approach also straightforwardly suggests itself to accompany logical expressivism. I discuss a few, according to me, of the most important proof-theoretic demarcations and discuss their merits and drawbacks.

In the final chapter, I place my approach on the map of the important views on the plurality of logics available today. My view is ultimately neither straightforwardly pluralist nor monist. The pluralist and monist tendencies should be rather reconciled in a view of logic which stresses the capacity of logical notions to develop. I find the term *logical dynamism* to be an adequate title for the doctrine proposed.

2.1 Which logic is this book written in?

There is an immediate worry regarding any attempts to discuss the plurality of logics. What logic are these discussions and considerations done in? Any direction one goes, whether one decides to be a monist claiming there is only one true logic or whether one opts for a pluralist view, it seems impossible to remain really fair when adjudicating the credentials of all the formal logics that have been developed or could yet be developed later. Logic, the line of thought goes, should be at the bottom of all reasoning; reasoning outside logic is just nonsense. Therefore, all the considerations about the plurality of logical systems and deciding about which of them are genuine logics have to be done by means of one of these logics. This logic will then most likely have an unfair advantage over all the others.

What I will offer here is only a preliminary response to this concern. Only when we are equipped with the notions I will explain later and with the doctrines which make use of them can we hope for more thorough answers. I will come back to the issue at an appropriate point. For the moment, though, let us note that a similar worry is sometimes raised in more technical settings. Namely, when any logic is presented, one can ask, 'How is it that we can understand this very presentation?'

In a typical curriculum, a student of logic gets first acquainted with classical propositional and first-order logic. Let us say the student then encounters intuitionistic logic and learns its Kripke semantics or its axiomatic system. For example, the clauses for satisfaction of complex formulae seem to be comprehensible only if we interpret the (meta-)language in which they are formulated as classical. Thus, when our student learns that the negation is satisfied in a given possible world (no implications are intended by the use of the term *possible world*, the reader can substitute any other term such as *point* or *information state*), if and only if the negated formula is not satisfied in any of the accessible worlds, she needs to understand this somehow. Among other expressions, *if and only if* and *not* have to be understood. And as it is yet unclear how to understand them intuitionistically, we have to understand them classically. Is such reasoning correct?

2.1.1 Proving too much?

If we apply this reasoning only one level higher, its limits immediately emerge. Our logic student learned classical before intuitionistic logic, and we can ask how this first form of learning could succeed. If some logic was needed in the next step, then the same applies to the first step. Which logic had the student used in order to understand classical logic?

It would simply not be acceptable to claim that it was classical logic, and by learning classical logic, the student merely recalled the logic she had been always using. Besides being hardly verifiable, this claim is falsified by a few obvious historical and psychological points. The historical point is that classical logic obviously was not with humanity from the beginning but had to be developed only during the first half of the twentieth century, though the conceptual equipment which had to be put together stemmed already from the nineteenth century. The related psychological point is that although classical logic is particularly user-friendly when compared with most of the other logics, students typically also need some time to get used to reasoning within the system. Classical logic contains lots of counter-intuitive features. The list is long, but let us confine ourselves to recalling how unpalatable the behaviour of the classical conditional is to many.

It appears that the claim that we have always been using classical logic and cannot really reason without it cannot be defended. But what reasoning were we using when getting to know classical logic? By analogous arguments, it will not help very much to claim that it had to be Aristotelian syllogistic logic. Although it probably shaped the way people reasoned, there must have been a way to learn even this system. There is no escaping the conclusion that one can reason in some cogent way without having the reasoning founded in any particular logical system.

We will get back to the issue of ascribing a given logic to someone according to the way he or she reasons. But for the moment, we will return to the question about the logic this book is written in. I claim that it is not written in any particular logic, just as almost any other book besides very technical books which are focused on the mathematical study of a selected formal logic.

Does it mean that my reasoning and its conclusions are free of the suspicion of bias in favour of some systems and perhaps also of failing to be charitable enough towards others? Clearly, I cannot deny that I am writing from a certain perspective and that I could not come to my conclusions if it were not for various important authors who have appeared during the history. But it would be rather problematic if the opposite were the case, as any philosophy has to be in a dialogue with a certain tradition. But putting this historical point aside, my position, which I have already called *logical dynamism*, does not rely on preferring any of the formal logics that are on the market nowadays. The charge of bias thus appears to be ill-founded.

No doubt more explanation will be needed concerning the possibility to reason cogently without relying on any particular logical system. I hope, though, that the following chapters (especially the final one) provide exactly this explanation.

2.2 Roots of the issue

It is a simple fact that there is a plurality of abstract systems which are called *logics* by most logicians. Consequently, if we suppose that these logics somehow relate to real reasoning and that we can see the formulae as placeholders to be filled by sentences of, for example, English, then there are cases in which different logics give different verdicts as to an argument's logical correctness; that is one logic diagnoses the given argument as being logically correct while another as being logically incorrect. It is certainly wise to be on one's own guard when it comes to naive intuitions, but it is equally wise to at least consider them and understand where they come from, as this can lead us to retain the healthy part of them, if there is one.

Now one of the strong intuitions regarding logic is that what does and what does not hold in logic (understood now not as the specific system of, for example, classical propositional logic but rather as a logic of real argumentation) should be rather definite, perhaps more definite than anything else. The modern plurality of logics is thus something that provokes consideration, as it is in a radical contrast with some basic intuitions about logic.

The importance of this issue, I believe, can be illustrated also by some fairly simple and obvious historical points. First of all, the very idea of the plurality of logics is very young and the phenomenon of there being more competing logics is not much older. That is, when the Fregean revolution was taking place, it was meant to find the one true logic and replace the one which – according to Frege and similarly minded contemporaries – only seemed to be such. The same can be said of the attempt at an intuitionistic revision of this revolution.

Today we can certainly still find logicians and philosophers who strongly favour one or another logic, in most cases probably the classical or the intuitionistic, but overall it is much more common to see the various logics as somehow equally good or perhaps good for different purposes. Thus the common stance, if there is one, is that there are many logics.

2.3 Where to look for the criteria?

Can we, then, look for some reasonable criteria to decide about the correctness or otherwise of the various logics? Indeed, the very number of them threatens to rob such an undertaking of any hope for success and therewith any motivation whatsoever. One cannot even realistically hope to get an overview of all the systems that are called logics. Not only because there are so many of them today but new ones are almost certainly going to keep surfacing in the time to come.

This was observed by Jean-Yves Bezieau in the following, somewhat hyperbolic, manner:

> Logics were proliferating: each day a new logic was born. By the mid eighties, there were more logics on earth than atoms in the universe. (Beziau 2007, p. vii)

Now, these logics can be seen simply as various sorts of mathematical structures. Clearly, some structures are more important than others, but basically it is always good to study as many such structures as possible. We never know whether some of those which appear to be rather parochial will not turn out to be very useful for some purpose. Thus, what happens when new logics emerge is something to be welcomed from the mathematical point of view, even though this plurality of systems of course makes it difficult to have a good overview. It is thus natural that mathematical methods have been developed to systematize the various logics, as to their mathematical properties. Beziau, in an introduction to a collection of papers presenting these various approaches, thus gives this collection the following unsurprising rationale:

> It will help those who are lost in the jungle of heterogeneous logical systems to find a way. Tools and concepts are provided here for those who want to study classes of already existing logics or want to design and build new ones. (Beziau 2007, p. viii)

Nevertheless, we will strive to obtain a rather philosophical understanding of the existing plurality. From the philosophical point of view the matters look much differently, though. The development of various logics is a serious challenge for the philosophy of logic. This immense plurality awakens a suspicion of a lack of insight into the essence of logic. A widening of the breadth may in part be happening as a substitution of an analysis which goes into depth.

This does not mean that the philosophical and mathematical points of view have to be seen as conflicting. The philosophy of logic clearly does not have to stop the development of mathematical investigations. Nevertheless, it should not uncritically accept some philosophical views which are easily suggested by mathematical developments.

2.3.1 Relativism

One of the views which surely is suggested by the mathematical development of logic is some sort of relativism. Clearly, given that there are so many logics, it probably just depends on your point of view what you take to be logic. Those who study the properties of classical logic probably typically mean classical logic when they speak of logic. The same holds for those who study intuitionistic logic and so on. And it is not just the intimidating number of logics which suggests this view, but also their mathematical character. By being defined mathematically, the meanings of the constants of these logics seem to be absolutely specific. It would therefore seem that when people speak of there being different logics, they probably do not understand what they are saying, as a difference of logic means simply a change of meaning of the logical constants. We will get back to this argument, which was presented by Quine;[2] yet for the moment, however, let us remind ourselves that Quine himself warned us not to succumb to the false impression of definite meanings, arguing in 'Two Dogmas of Empiricism' (Quine 1951) that an idea of definite meanings of individual expressions is false even if we consider formal mathematical languages. The indefiniteness of meaning permeates all the layers of our discourses.

And even putting the indefiniteness aside, such a view would clearly cause the mathematical logics to lose a lot of the interest that is there in them. Clearly they can be regarded from an internal perspective, but they are also here to model something outside them, something pertaining to reasoning and the norms for its evaluation.

On the other hand, it is often suggested that the natural language counterparts of logical constants are just too vague and therefore the logic of a natural language cannot be definite. This cannot be completely false, but as it holds that there is some indefiniteness even in the realm of mathematical meanings, there must be some degree of definiteness outside of mathematics as well. The practices of judging some inferences as correct or otherwise must give us some guidance as to their correct formalization. Indeed, the vagueness, or rather implicitness, of the rules of inference which underlie our very rationality is out of question, but it cannot prevent us from giving an account of the respective merits of various logics. The implicitness of what we may call natural logic makes us reflect on why we make logic explicit and why we develop such systems as the classical or intuitionistic logic in the first place.

When we speak of logic at all, we have to have some idea or, better, a concept in mind, though perhaps a vague one. Maybe even an incoherent one. It is true, though, that speaking about logic we do not speak about a specific mathematical system, but rather about an informal concept, which we just tentatively entitled *natural logic*. Yet, even informal concepts can be, of course, doubted as to their coherence. I do not want to adjudicate here in these extralogical matters but there is no absurdity in the idea that, say, the idea of god or of tolerance may turn out to be incoherent, even if they do not appear to be such from the outset. Perhaps some of our naive ideas about logic conceal contradictions of their own and should therefore be adequately revisited.

Nevertheless, were the concept of logic transcending that of the very specific mathematical logics incoherent (which I believe it certainly is not, as will be clear later), this fact would be something to be discovered through philosophical reflection. And it is hardly imaginable that the mathematical logics would attract the attention they attract should they be wholly self-contained, not pointing, as it were, to something outside them which they somehow spell out or make explicit. Thus, it makes sense to ask what logic is and expect that we can find some better answers than that it just depends on which logic we mean by the word *logic*, whether classical, intuitionistic or some other one yet.

2.3.2 A developing concept

A very first and naive formulation of my main question might therefore run thus: Which logic is the true logic? Such a formulation presupposes that it is somehow given independently of us what the correct answer is. And yet we obviously have some significant leeway in choosing what we mean by the word *logic*. We can choose to mean, for example, the classical logic or perhaps the psychological laws of our judgement and so on. Given this, it appears to be absurd to ask which of these concepts is somehow correct or true.

Yet, such a stance rests on an abstraction. A concept can develop. Frege probably meant by logic something else than Kant did and Kant something else than, say, Aristotle. Yet their importance consists in the fact that the concepts they used were not chosen by chance, but rather organically grew out of the ones they inherited into the new respective contexts.

A non-mathematical concept does not have an exact definition and this aspect partly constitutes its depth and importance. Thus changing such a concept does not have to be tantamount to just arbitrarily changing a definition. Frege's rejection of psychologism surely was not done by a mere fiat, as it makes sense to question it and examine its cogency.

The modern context which, I believe, requires a new development in the concept of logic is characterized, perhaps more importantly than by anything else, by the existent plurality of mathematical logics. The continuing development of new logics thus moves the very concept of logic in a new direction but at first only implicitly. It has to be philosophically explained what exactly has happened with logic(s) in recent decades. Thus, while this mathematical development towards plurality has to be respected, it does not avoid the need of philosophical reflection to question it and perhaps also to come to the conclusion that some of the so-called logics are not actually logics at all.

Answering the question as to what logic is, we have to both find and create the concept of logic. We have to develop the concept so that it illuminates the present context. And it would not be extremely surprising if there were additional different and interesting options of how to modify the concept. I do not intend to provide anything like an overview of such options, just what I believe to be one of them. I do not undertake such a complete overview not only for reasons of space but because I will argue that ultimately no such overview can be given. As I take the concept of logic to be dynamic, I cannot reckon with there being a definitive set of possibilities given in advance. Rather than saying which logic is the true one, I will be aiming at a fruitful explanation of the very possibility of a plurality of logics.

The fact that concepts develop is surely not particularly new and I do not claim to have presented any particular insight by saying it. However, I believe that the interconnectedness of logic and mathematics and the fact that in these disciplines people are used to working with sharp, exactly defined concepts cause people to underrate the ability of logical concepts to develop.

The idea of the development of logic is in and of itself somewhat unpalatable, as logic appears to be something which has to build the very basis of any knowledge and therewith also remains rather the same, thus forming the stable ground on which the flux of other disciplines can happen. Stewart Shapiro (1991) calls this and similar views opposing the possibility of development in logic *foundationalism* and is very critical of it. Though there is much to agree with in his criticism, first let us spell foundationalism out and see what makes it prima facie so plausible. For this purpose a historical detour will be useful, namely revisiting Kant's view of the essence and role of logic.

3

Kant's view of logic

First of all, the choice of Kant as a figure to discuss in the context of the controversies between logical monism and logical pluralism is something that itself has to be justified. Why exactly should we talk about Kant?

To forestall possible misunderstandings, I will focus mainly on Kant's view of what he called *formal logic* rather than on *transcendental logic*, even though the connection of these two is of considerable importance. Kant did not himself contribute to the development of formal logic, being content with its Aristotelian status quo.[1] From this perspective, he seems to be too recent to be a substantial figure for logic. On the other hand, he lived before logic changed radically in the nineteenth century. Thus he might seem to be outdated.

Yet I am inclined to see him as an important figure of logical monism – in a way, maybe as the first substantial logical monist. I suppose that the idea of logical pluralism or relativism had not been taken into consideration before the twentieth century. Development of various kinds surely happened in logic during the many centuries between Aristotle and Frege, despite the famous Kantian dictum.[2] Yet when someone proposed some correction or change in logic, this change was considered rather as a change inside the one logic, rather than as a proposal to create a new logic.

In fact, logical monism was something so common that it was hardly worthy, perhaps even hardly capable, of being stated. Kant was an author who stated it or at least came close to stating it. He did not defend it from its opponents, as there were none, but nevertheless endeavoured to substantiate it and show exactly why we cannot abandon the logic we have. Nevertheless, because the possibility of logical pluralism was not open yet, it has to be admitted that even logical monism could not have been actually maintained in the way it can be today because, as Wittgenstein reminds us, we can hardly be said to know something we could not meaningfully be said not to know:

> Wird 'Ich weiß etc.' als grammatischer Satz aufgefaßt, so kann natürlich das Ich nicht wichtig sein. Und es heißt eigentlich 'Es gibt in diesem Falle keinen Zweifel' oder 'Das Wort *Ich weiß nicht* hat in diesem Falle keinen Sinn'. Und daraus folgt freilich auch, daß 'Ich weiß' keinen hat. (Wittgenstein 1984 [1969], aphorism 58)[3]

In a way, Kant did not overrate the importance of logic in the manner other authors did and still do. According to him, logic cannot be very instrumental in gaining new knowledge, it typically just tells us what we already knew. In this he comes close to those who despised logic, for example Descartes (see paragraph 6 of chapter 2 of Descartes 1965). As an example of the opposite extreme we could mention Leibniz with his idea of *calculus ratiotinator* but also contemporary authors such as Gila Sher.[4] We will dedicate more space to the issue of the importance of logic and discuss the stances of the authors just mentioned later.

Yet logic, according to Kant, is, nevertheless, very important and actually reveals something quite essential about our very rationality. It delimits the very area in which rationality can happen. When we leave the realm of logic, we leave the realm of thought. This point can be difficult to track down in Kant. Therefore, I would like to make it more apparent by demonstrating an analogy with Kant's views of geometry.

3.1 Geometry in Kantian epistemology

In Kant's epistemology, geometry is given the pride of a similarly central place as logic. According to him, knowledge has two basic sources, namely intuition and intellect.[5] Just as logic is basic for the conceptual element of knowledge, so is geometry for the one stemming from intuition. They both mark the arena in which all knowledge can happen. It should be added that they do so typically together, despite their being two distinct sources of knowledge. Kant does not claim that a specific piece of knowledge has to stem from just one of them; indeed true knowledge arises from the interplay of the two sources.

We can use various concepts according to all the possible rules that we find convenient to introduce. Yet all those concepts have to obey the laws of logic. In the same way we can perceive lots of different things by our senses, yet our perceptions cannot contradict the laws of geometry (and even less those of logic). Both the disciplines delimit the boundaries of cognition. And they delimit it, so to speak, *from inside*.

Any idea of pluralism in logic or geometry thus seems to be inadmissible within the Kantian framework. If we can change logic and geometry, then we have to somehow move beyond their dominion. Thus we have to be capable of some rationality and cognition which is contrary to either logic or geometry or both. Some essential revision has to be done in order to reconcile the conflict between the Kantian conception and the existent plurality. Let us now review the Kantian view of geometry and the development which put it into question.

3.1.1 What is geometry about?

Geometry is obviously somehow related to space. Now it should be clarified what space is supposed to be and what the nature of the relation between geometry and space is.

According to Kant, space is neither an entity which simply exists outside of us in a way, for example the trees do, nor something we created by abstraction from the spatial relationships between objects.

The first option would suggest that space is a thing in the same way in which the material objects are. Yet all these objects obviously are *in* space, rather than space being one of them. Of course we talk in a way suggesting that space is a kind of thing we can study as to its specific properties. But then it is a thing of a special kind or, better, of a special order. We can think of an empty space but not of material things not being situated in it.[6]

The second option Kant refuses to endorse is that space is something we abstract out of the relations we perceive among objects. This option implies that the spatial objects are prior to the space. Yet, as we just noted, there is a dependence of the material objects on the space and not vice versa. Space is thus prior to the things which are in it, as it is not an object of the same order as the others, as the first option suggested, and it is even less of a lower order, being just derivative of them, as the second proposal suggests.

This strong priority of space means that it has to be investigated by quite different means than the material objects, that is, not empirically. The knowledge of its properties has a peculiar character. Just like the knowledge of the properties of time, of which Kant held an analogous view, it is *synthetic* a priori.

3.1.2 Away from synthetic a priori

Synthetic a priori cognition is something rather peculiar to Kant's philosophy. And given that arithmetic and geometry are the only disciplines which normally produce this kind of knowledge, it might seem somewhat ad hoc to countenance this category. Moreover, as there are not so many clear examples of synthetic a priori knowledge, it also seems somewhat mysterious. True, it enables Kant to highlight some essential differences between geometry and arithmetic on the one hand and other kinds of knowledge on the other hand, but still lots of authors felt the need to explain it away.

Thus, they had to argue either that these sciences are merely analytical or that they are a posteriori. We will consider the cases of geometry and arithmetic and then come to a comparison with logic. We have to begin, though, with a short review of how the non-Euclidian geometries emerged in order to understand the relevant debates about the synthetic a priori.

What later developed into non-classical geometries, that is the hyperbolic geometry and the elliptic geometry, was in the beginning considered just as a set of axioms or better an intentionally wrong set of axioms. The departure from the classical geometry in fact happens by saying that it does not hold that, given a line and a point outside it, only one new line can go through this point which does not intersect with the original line. Hyperbolic geometry is based on the claim that there are more such lines (actually, there have to be then infinitely many), while elliptic geometry that developed later claims that no such line runs through the point.

For many centuries it was thought that such systems must necessarily contain a contradiction and that it was only very difficult to prove their inconsistency. Nevertheless, their systematic development by authors such as Lobachevsky or Gauss was putting this conviction into question. It appeared still less and less probable that these systems would actually turn out to be inconsistent, that is that a contradiction would be derived from them by means of logic.

However, this development would not yet genuinely challenge Kant's epistemology. According to the Kantian view, geometry does not have to be just consistent, it also has to be true. It is here to describe space as a condition of experience. The new geometries were thus for Kant possibly consistent, but false at the same time, as it appeared that the pure intuition of space shows us that Euclidian geometry with the fifth postulate was true, while both alternatives were false.

To fully legitimize the new geometries as alternatives to the Euclidean one, it had to be shown that they can describe space as well. And this indeed happened. Eugenio Beltrami presented a model of the non-Euclidean geometries (see Beltrami 1868), and later, on the basis of this model, Hermann van Helmholtz successfully showed that we can think of space as curved and then better described rather by the new geometries than by the old one. He did this by presenting thought experiments about the ways the world and our experience could be which would lead us quite naturally to consider rather the non-Euclidean geometries as adequate descriptions of space.[7]

Helmholtz actually considered the possibility that we might discover the actual space to be curved after all. He often speaks of this as being a matter of fact which simply has to be verified empirically.[8] Geometry would thus be testable in the same manner physics is. The very thought experiments conceived by Helmholtz, nevertheless, suggest that the curvature of space is a matter of perspective rather than a fact independent of us. We can choose to regard space as curved basically as much or as little as we want, if we adapt also some parts of our physics, particularly mechanics, correspondingly. Helmholtz thus contains traits of a view much more subtle that mere empirization of geometry, namely of the conventionalism which Henri Poincaré advocated later in Poincaré (1902).[9]

Philosophical reflection thus came with the result that we are in a way free to consider the space to have different properties and thus to correspond to different geometries. The Euclidean geometry appeared to be the only possible one merely because we did not realize this freedom we had vis-à-vis space. Geometry obviously has to be somehow linked to our spatial perception, yet there are more possible geometries which enable us to model it. Adopting a certain geometry has got consequences for other disciplines, particularly for physics. The development thus leads us to a holistic view of the role of geometry in our overall conceptual schemes. A view which does not correspond straightforwardly either to seeing geometry as analytic, a posteriori or synthetic a priori.

3.1.3 Formalism

As we mentioned, Kant thought that not just geometry but also arithmetic is based on our pure intuition and its truths are synthetic a priori. An attempt at a radical attack at this thesis was undertaken by Frege with his logicist programme. Frege wanted to examine whether the arithmetical truths cannot be actually shown to be analytical.

And speaking of the status of arithmetic, we already have to turn our attention to logic as well, because the revision of logic was a fundamental part of the logicist programme. Frege did not try to examine whether arithmetic can be reduced to what Kant considered as logic, but to what he developed as logic. Thus showing that his system deserves to be called logic is a part of validating logicism. The second part, one which he states more explicitly, was of course to show that arithmetic is reducible to this system.

Frege was ultimately more successful in accomplishing the first part of the programme. Of course, what is now known as classical first-order logic is different from his system but still stems from this system essentially.

But before getting more into logic, which is our main issue, let us dwell on arithmetic and mathematics in general, as the strong tendencies to show these disciplines to be analytical is important for considerations about the nature of logic.

3.1.3.1 *Status of arithmetic*

According to Kant, arithmetic reflects our intuition of time; it analyses its structure. If Kant's doctrine about the status of geometry seemed to its critics to make the discipline more mysterious, then they must have had at least as much reason to consider his explanation of the status of arithmetic suspect.

Speaking somewhat vaguely, the connection of geometry and our intuition of space, though it can be legitimately criticized, definitely suggests itself. Yet it should be clear that Kant by no means wants to speak about the way we actually get to understand geometry or arithmetic. His approach strives to be strongly anti-psychologist – a tendency which Frege shared and defended extensively and with great clarity in his *Grundlagen der Arithmetik* (Frege 1884). Kant merely asserts that we cannot understand numbers and their relationships without having the concept of time and understanding the specific way in which it *moves*. He thus wants to make a conceptual, not a psychological, point.

Although there definitely is some plausibility to Kant's view regarding arithmetic, there is also a suspicion that it might after all fall into psychologism. Perhaps motivated by these worries, Frege presented a tentative hypothesis that arithmetic is an analytic discipline, the validity of its laws being based just on some rules guiding inferences of statements from statements. This meant that Frege challenged himself to present a logic which would be valid and at the same time would contain arithmetic. This containment should, of course, be understood in the sense that arithmetical laws should be derivable from the logical ones.

The attempt at the shift of the view of the epistemological status of arithmetic differs from the similar one in the case of geometry in (at least) one substantial respect. Frege did not attempt to legitimize any kind of pluralism; he did not want to create a new arithmetic but rather merely investigated what the old one is based on. Indeed hardly anybody would say that something like arithmetical pluralism makes sense. True, the development of modern logic brought non-standard models of Peano arithmetic, yet nobody would say that they represent alternative shapes arithmetic might actually take. Neither can we say that the plurality of axiomatizations of arithmetic, such as Robinson arithmetic, as opposed to Peano arithmetic, was devised as attempts at creating alternative arithmetic, in the sense in which the axioms of hyperbolic or elliptic geometry indeed established themselves as alternative geometries. A more extended discussion of this contrast can be found in my article Arazim (2017).

Now, talking about the status of arithmetic and whether Kant was right about it, we are, much more than in the case of geometry, led to connect this enquiry with the enquiry about the nature and status of logic. Let us now review the change of logic and a validation thereof which was a part of logicism.

3.1.4 Change of logic

In spite of the intricate interconnectedness, it can be said quite determinately that it was much rather the logic, not the arithmetic, which Frege changed. He, however, made no move towards the logical pluralism, wanting instead to improve the old logic. Or better, replace the old logic, which only appeared to be correct, by the really correct one. The move to some sort of pluralism was undertaken much later, notably by Carnap with his principle of tolerance. The failure, if it is one, to consider the option of pluralism could also be perceived in those who developed non-classical geometries. For some time they developed alternative geometries, but not only did they not countenance the possibility of pluralism in geometry, they were not even convinced that the new geometries will be better than the old one. They were just open to the possibility that this might prove to be the case. As we already mentioned, Helmholtz proposed that it could be up to the tribunal of empirical evidence to adjudicate between the rival systems.

It is not easy to determine what Frege might have considered as a criterion of logical validity, that is, how he purported to recognize some statements as distinctively logical truths. Nevertheless, he certainly did not want to think that logic has a fundamentally different epistemological status from the one Kant ascribed to it. We have mentioned that Helmholtz made moves towards regarding geometry as an empirical discipline, indeed he was occasionally expressing this view quite explicitly. Frege was very far from trying to do something similar to either logic or arithmetic. Indeed, in these respects he strongly adhered to Kant and in a way even wanted to strengthen his basic anti-psychological and anti-empiricist line.

According to Frege, Kant just made a hasty judgement regarding the nature of arithmetic. Frege thus saw the problem rather in the detail than in the whole of the Kantian epistemology. He did not undertake attempts to legitimize something like a change of logic. He did not think explicitly of the shift as of something we can choose to do and rationalize. His view is thus essentially still Kantian, as he merely thought that the true logic guiding our reasoning was not the one Kant inherited. Put simply, he considered his new logic as a discovery of what already is there, not as something we can opt to use instead of Aristotelian logic. His revolution in logic certainly is something which was necessary for the idea of logical pluralism to get off ground at all, yet it was up to later authors who could regard Frege with the luxury of hindsight to actually formulate logical pluralism.

Logic thus, according to both Kant and Frege, cannot be chosen. Here we can be reminded of Wittgenstein's (rather rhetorical) question as to whether we can choose what we believe:

> Liegt es denn in meiner Macht, was ich glaube? oder was ich unerschütterlich glaube? Ich glaube, daß dort ein Sessel steht. Kann ich mich nicht irren? Aber kann ich glauben, daß ich mich irre? Ja, kann ich es überhaupt in Betracht

ziehen? – Und könnte ich nicht auch an meinem Glauben festhalten, was immer ich später erfahre?! Aber ist nun mein Glaube begründet? (Wittgenstein 1984 [1969], paragraph 173[10])

Our beliefs concerning the validity of logical laws are thus, according to both Kant and Frege, a typical example of those we do not have the possibility to choose.

Frege of course was not the only important figure in this quest for the foundations of mathematics. Dummett even says that not only without the work of Frege but also without the work of Dedekind and Cantor 'mathematics would have remained only one step away from magic' (Dummett 1978, p. 283). Because he had this purpose of stating the rules of mathematical language games clearly, Frege had to see logic as something which should enable us to fulfil such a purpose, that is formulate the rules of inference in mathematics and perhaps in other disciplines, as well.

This project involved both the reconstruction of the mathematical practice and its rectification or even revision in order to get rid of paradoxes and unclarities which were hindering the discipline. On the other hand, what seemed to be the healthy part of the old mathematics had to be preserved. The Fregean change of logic can already in many ways be used to show why and how a new logic can be developed and how logical pluralism can arise by the development of more logics for these purposes and possibly also how it can be justified. The need for formulating a new logic arises when we have to find a language suitable for expressing inference rules which cannot be expressed adequately by the languages we have at hand. This already points towards logical expressivism, a view about the purpose of logic due to Robert Brandom. We will nevertheless need much more preparation to formulate an adequate statement of this thesis.

3.2 Summary of Kantian logic

We have only touched on all the intricacies of Kant's approach to logic. The analogy with geometry was brought into the picture in order to show that Kant had brought up the possibility of discussing logical monism as opposed to pluralism. By beginning to talk about the reasons why there can be only one logic he opened up the possibility of argument and opposition. We should not think of the cases of logic and geometry as completely analogous, though. Most importantly, logic is a discipline of even greater generality. A change of logic is therefore something even more shocking and seemingly impossible than a change of geometry.

Kant was clearly ready to use the term *logic* in many different contexts. What he called *formal logic* and Frege then overthrew was for him the very core of rationality. It is summarized in his table of judgements. Now, the table of judgements leads to the table of categories, which is central for Kant's transcendental logic. The task of transcendental logic is to explain the very constitution of the world we live in with regard to its most basic features, such as that we live in a world of objects which possess or lack properties. Logic is in Kant's view intimately connected with the very basic features of the world we live in, at least to the degree that we constitute this world through our epistemic apparatus. The idea of changing logic is thus preposterous, as this would completely tear down the boundaries of the conceivable.

At first sight it might seem that Kant did not care so much about formal logic. He just accepted what he inherited and used it for his much more elaborated transcendental logic. A mere comparison of the great amount of space he dedicates to transcendental logic in his *Critique of Pure Reason* and the scarce amount he gives to formal logic explains easily why such an impression comes to be. Much more than in the case of geometry time was needed to realize that Kant actually did say something about formal logic, namely that he asserted logical monism. Besides being a monist, that is, believing there to be only one true logic, Kant also believed that this one logic cannot be somehow improved or modified, at least in any significant way (recall the dictum about the impossibility of any substantial progress in formal logic since the time of Aristotle).

Frege and also Husserl condemned this extreme kind of Kantian conservatism about logic (in Frege 1884 and Husserl 1913). They do not display a belief in logical pluralism, though. In fact, the possibility of the dispute between pluralism and monism does not yet truly occur to them. Nevertheless, the question of the bounds of logic or of logicality arises thanks to Kant. John MacFarlane shows in his thought-provoking dissertation 'What Does It Mean to Say That Logic Is Formal' (MacFarlane 2000) that Kant has a view of what makes logic formal which is capable of three specifications. The formality and logicality are, MacFarlane claims, the same issues. Kant approved of the idea of special logics, that is logics which capture the rules of judgement in various specific areas and which are, exactly because of this specificity, not formal. The main thesis of MacFarlane is that by saying that logic is formal we can legitimately mean one of three distinct things (we will present and discuss this thesis later on) and this potential ambiguity is also among the factors enabling the plurality of logics to emerge.

The development of questioning and discussing what logic should consist in was implicitly initiated by Kant, who enabled us to look for the desiderata of something we want to call *logic*. Earlier, the Aristotelian logic was taken for granted and one could at most ask why this logic is the way it is and what its salient properties are. Kant went along this path and so consequently opened up the space for a debate over these salient properties and presented a more nuanced view of them. Thus it became possible to weigh out these properties and treat them as desiderata of what we want to have as logic.

After a long development, then, the possibility of actually choosing, rather than finding, logic with the desiderata emerged. Of course, it had to be shown that new systems which resemble what used to be considered as the only possible logic can be developed into a viable shape. Kant famously wanted to investigate the conditions of the possibility of our knowledge. He saw logic as one of the most important pillars on which our cognitive capacities stand.

3.2.1 Changing the pillars

If logic is rightly compared to one of the most important pillars of our cognition, it is legitimate to doubt whether we can change such a pillar without causing the collapse of the whole building. Wittgenstein brings in a remarkable claim that something is stable in our knowledge only if something else is moving around it.[11] One would perhaps more readily acknowledge the opposite, namely that for there to be something which can move, there must be something stable to create the space where it can move. This is exactly the Kantian way of looking at things, namely investigating the conditions of possibility of cognition. Yet the opposite and complementary direction of thought Wittgenstein confronts us with, namely to regard the stable areas of our conceptual frameworks as dependent on the less stable ones, is worthy of attention as well. It points to a holistic approach to cognition, emphasizing the interconnectedness of seemingly only remotely related fields of knowledge.

We can thus see that logic fits right into our overall cognitive frame when it holds tight, and we can observe the productive flux of the knowledge from other disciplines. Yet what if logic starts to move? Should this kind of a movement also be enabled by something else which remains (at least relatively) motionless? What could be more motionless than logic? Let us also remind ourselves that Wittgenstein (1984 [1969]) claims that the motionless part of our cognitive framework is something which cannot be observed, which is even brought into existence only thanks to the movement we observe around it (see the last footnote). We can choose either that this motionless part will be something that used to move around logic or that it is something deeper yet; something which was even more implicit than the logic which started changing. I suspect we have to choose a combination of both, namely of some deeper logic (as the deeper layer) and also of mathematics or at least some mathematical methods, which interplay with logic and used to be considered as less fundamental than logic itself. Both these opinions have been expressed by various authors already. The thesis that there must be some deeper logic underlying the pluralism we witness today is held by Robert Hanna in his *Rationality and Logic* (Hanna 2006). Mathematics and logic got much closer to each other during the nineteenth century and this relationship proved to be even more fruitful later in the twentieth century. Later on we will talk about the attempts to demarcate what is logic by the tools provided by model theory, a prominent branch of mathematics. Some proponents of this approach, such as Gila Sher, emphasize the closeness of mathematics and logic very much, some even assert their identity.

Indeed, this tendency to marry logic with mathematics is first and foremost a continuation of what Frege was already attempting with his project of logicism. And as we have noticed, this project made sense only thanks to Kant, as he enabled us to ask such questions to which programmes like logicism can be an answer. We will investigate the role of mathematics and of the *deeper* logic (if there is one), yet let us reflect on a more general point regarding the relationship between the more and the less stable regions of our knowledge. Besides Wittgenstein's metaphor, we are, of course describing something which is very close to the relationship between what Quine (1951) called the *periphery* and *the centre of the body* of our knowledge in 'The Two Dogmas of Empiricism'. But Wittgenstein's picture adds the fascinating element of movement and the relationship between what rotates and what functions as an axis.

We should not forget that when we describe a body as moving or otherwise, any such description is always to some degree relative to a particular point of view. We can regard one and the same object as stable relative to the movement of another one, yet at the same time as moving with regard to something else which is typically larger and functions as a background of this second movement.

As we have embarked on the search for the stable background of the changes of logic, we must make or rather remind ourselves of some important general epistemological points.

3.3 Holism and its problems

The general epistemological framework I work with here is holistic, inspired mainly by Quine and Wittgenstein and also by other important figures of modern analytical philosophy. The basic holistic thesis is that there is no specific area of knowledge which has any kind of absolute privilege in the sense of immunity to revision. The other side of the same coin is the thesis that any assertion can be upheld come what may, at least in principle. After the developments of philosophy and science in the twentieth century, holism is, I believe, more or less inevitable. Yet there are authors, such as Michael Dummett, who were very vocal against it and for good reasons.

Obviously enough, the general idea of holism sounds dangerous and threatens to confuse all our epistemological categories, indeed throw us in epistemological anarchy. The general idea and many of its formulations and illustrative examples, as put forward in Quine's 'The Two Dogmas', make us wonder what order there may remain in our cognitive scheme when any empirical knowledge has got a similar status as the most fundamental assertions of logic.

Dummett, as we will presently see from some citations, is one of the figures who expresses the concerns that holism might confuse everything and justify almost any assertion, as we can say that any assertion can be true only if we adjust other parts of our theories correspondingly. Yet a sound holism should not lead us to a picture of knowledge which is completely reliant on our deliberation so that we decide what is and what is not true. Let us remind ourselves of Wittgenstein's aphorism 173 from Wittgenstein (1984 [1969]).

Wittgenstein at least expresses a doubt about the degree to which we decide what we believe. He also says that 'Es ist immer von Gnaden der Natur, wenn man etwas weiß' (Wittgenstein 1984 [1969], aphorism 505).[12] When we thus emphasize that our belief and therewith knowledge does not depend exclusively on our decisions, we are on a good path to getting rid of the suspicion that holism makes the shape of our theories into a product of our whims.

Quine's assertions about the possibility of preserving even the most parochial empirical piece of knowledge in face of recalcitrant evidence and about the possibility of revision in the very deepest recesses of our cognitive scheme are actually quite in order but, of course, they have to be understood properly, in the context to which they belong. From the holistic point of view, a sentence can have its meaning only in the context of the rest of our theory (or theories). And the Quinean glosses might be confusing exactly because they are rather concentrated on individual sentences of which the truth value is being discussed.

We have to understand that the overall structure is exactly what makes some sentences more or less immune to revision when facing recalcitrant experience, while the others can be revised with a light heart. What can be correctly said is that any individual piece of knowledge, every sentence we consider as to its truth, can possibly play different roles in different theories, one time being rather a fundamental, another time rather a parochial, part of it. It is clear that various conceptual schemes are possible, yet it is very unclear to what degree we are free to change the scheme. The modern development of philosophy and science showed us that we are much more free than people could imagine before, yet the idea of us just arbitrarily choosing which theory to adopt is an overly simplifying and misleading one. Even the revision of a theory needs some theoretical background, though of course not all of it can be explicit. Perhaps some kinds of revisions cannot even be called rational, as they pertain to what enables rationality to come into existence in the first place.

This holism is naturally paired with inferentialism about meaning because any meaningful linguistic unit, be it a word or a sentence, has its meaning thanks to the role it plays in the overall structure. Jaroslav Peregrin shows in his *Meaning and Structure* (see Peregrin 2001) that the original holism of Quine can be naturally developed into inferentialism. I find it more apt to call the explicans of meaning *role* rather than *position* of the expression in the overall structure, as such a term suggests activity and propensity to move, as opposed to the static term *position*.

4

The holistic view of logic

Let us return to the problems of holism, this time with more attention to the attacks on it by Michael Dummett. This author expressed concerns about holism quite similar to those we already spoke about, but it still can be illuminative to use his antidote to excesses, without losing all the good we gain by adopting the holistic perspective. Quine and other authors suggest that we should abandon the notion of meaning completely, as it is ill-defined and thus pernicious. This amount of revolutionary zeal starts to sound somewhat troubling. How could we indeed make do without such a vital concept as that of meaning? Is it not obvious that appeals to it can be very useful to move debates in which the parties are talking past each other forward (and resolving philosophical disputes by pointing to misconceptions about the meaning of our expressions was, of course, one of the core aspirations of analytical philosophy into which Quine is typically included)? Does not sacrificing the notion of meaning imply doing the same with that of language and in some perhaps longer run even that of rationality?

In the last chapter of his *Elements of Intuitionism*, Dummett writes that holism precludes us from debating the legitimacy of any given logic at all, in particular the respective merits of the classical and intuitionist one. We cannot criticize a given logical law of inference because it cannot be understood except as a part of the whole of our science. Ultimately, Dummett believed, holism collapses into formalism (Dummett 1977, p. 254):

> The effective collapse of holism into formalism is not obviated by taking mathematical language as only a part of the wider language, as a holist will naturally do; for the mathematical theory ceases to have any independent significance, and becomes merely a complex of paths for deriving consequences within some empirical theory; and, since the empirical

theory stands and fails only as a whole, no question can arise over whether such derivations are justified in themselves. Such a view is in practice indistinguishable from that variety of formalism which lays stress on the applications of mathematical theories, such applications being seen as supplying empirical interpretations of previously uninterpreted calculi. A mathematical theory needs, on this view, no other justification than that it, 'works'.

Indeed Dummett seems to be onto something here. The most pressing problem of holism becomes that it makes meaning vague to a point when it becomes unintelligible as to why we should continue using the word *meaning* at all. What is it supposed to mean that a given theory *works*? A theory can obviously work and contribute to our lives in many different ways. Pragmatism can surely give us deep insights into the nature of meaning and perhaps ultimately even logic. Yet it is also dangerously simple to use it just to get rid of difficult theoretical problems of various disciplines, namely by saying that these need no rational explication, as they (in some mysterious way happen to) work. To illustrate the concerns, let us remind ourselves of the closing words of probably the most crucial programmatic text of holism, Quine's 'Two Dogmas of Empiricism':

> Each man is given a scientific heritage plus a continuing barrage of sensory stimulation; and the considerations which guide him in warping his scientific heritage to this continuing sensory promptings are, where rational, pragmatic. (Quine 1951, p. 43)

Despite all the insights of Quine's famous article, does this statement not sound evasive and unsatisfactory for someone who wants to understand the development of such disciplines as mathematics or logic?

Another major problem of holism is the very notion of the whole which is supposed to confer meaning on our linguistic expressions. This notion is plagued by as much vagueness as that of usefulness we just discussed. Indeed, how do we recognize what area of our linguistic practices constitutes a particular space of meaning? Clearly, to understand a meaning of a word or of a sentence, we have to understand that of (plausibly rather many) other words and sentences. But of how many? Potentially any two sentences can in some context be seen as somehow connected; one may for example become an evidence for the other one.

Yet it is absurd to suppose we can assess the inferential interconnections between all the expressions of our language or, given one individual sentence, that we can somehow overview all the inferential relationships it is capable, in appropriate contexts, of entering into. It is not just psychologically unrealistic because of the sheer number of such relationships. The problem rather is that such relationships cannot possibly all be known explicitly in the fashion that we could know all the (meta-)sentences expressing the inferential relationships, as this would engender an infinite regress of explaining the sentences we previously used for explanation or in some kind of vicious circle, as the explaining sentences will contain something we wanted to explain at the outset.

Furthermore, there is no end to the varieties of possible contexts, in which we are at loss as to how to adjudicate about problematic inferences. That is, there is some openness to the inference rules of our language and thus ultimately also to the meanings. This is a well-known lesson, given by Wittgenstein on many occasions in his *Philosophical Investigations*.

If we want to construe a reasonable version of holism which can be helpful in illuminating the plurality of logics, we have to accept that the whole we speak of must be somehow delimited and that meaning always has to be to some degree opaque. So the meaning of a given sentence cannot be constructed as dependent on the whole of our linguistic practices. It is not necessary to suppose that our linguistic practices form some coherent unity; we can indeed divide our language into various areas, each of which can be meaning constitutive. These are not to be thought of as isolated; they can clearly interact, but each of them has got some autonomy with regard to determining the meanings of its expressions. A meaning of an expression is also something which has to continuously develop and thus it is deceiving to see it as something given which we either do or do not know. To summarize the main points on our way towards a viable holism, we have so far concluded thus:

1. Holism is necessary for an explanation of change and plurality in strongly a priori disciplines such as logic or geometry.
2. Holism has its dangers, mainly that of vagueness and evasiveness when it comes to explicating meaning and truth conditions of linguistic units (mainly sentences).

3. Holism thus has to be reduced – the interrelations between linguistic units have to be to some degree local (they have to form specific domains).
4. Meaning has to be essentially dynamic, the interrelations have to constantly develop and therefore we do not have to adjudicate about all the inference relations between linguistic units.

4.1 Special speech acts

When we assert something about the meaning of a given expression, we are obviously describing something. Just as we describe colour, smell and various other sensual qualities of the things surrounding us, we also describe meanings of words, collocations, sentences and so on. Yet, important philosophers already taught us that describing is not such a simple affair as it might seem. From the idealist point of view the things we describe are not given to us independently of our practice of describing. What seems like an empirical description which can be refuted or vindicated by adequate data can turn out to be much more fundamental for our understanding of the very essence of a given thing. Quine of course points to at least the possibility of saving any prima facie empirical piece of knowledge by regarding it as a part of the definition of the observed type of object. For example, we do not have to accept that not all ravens are black when we find one which is white, as we are free to decree that it is not really a raven, ravens being by definition – among other things – black.

The inferentialists such as Sellars, Brandom and Peregrin[1] go even further, claiming that such inferences as the following one are correct:

$$\frac{\text{Lightning is seen now.}}{\text{Thunder will be heard soon.}}$$

Should we not be prepared to endorse such an inference (i.e. say that it is not done according to a valid rule of inference), the doubt would be not only whether we know enough about these natural phenomena but rather whether we understand the concepts of lightning and thunder at all. When we embrace such a rule of inference, we can at the same time admit that it is defeasible. Nevertheless, it is still a rule.

In this way we see a fundamental openness of even our empirical notions and therewith also an indeterminacy of ontology of physical entities such as thunder or lightning. This must hold even more of much more airy entities as meanings. Indeed, philosophers had questioned to what degree we can count meanings among the existent things at all, prominently Quine (1948). Having no certainty about their existence, it then seems quite hasty to try to describe meanings in a way we usually describe the things we unproblematically consider as existent. Thus, we are in need of differentiating meanings from different kinds of entities; on the other hand, we should beware of declaring them for illusory, as Quine liked to do. Quine indeed showed us that the concept of meaning is much more complicated and less isolated from other ones than we expected; yet why should this prove that it is faulty? As intricate as it is, the possibility of making do without it seems to be everything but real. Despite the intricacy of this theoretical notion, it is indisputable that we use the notion of meaning in our everyday life and are capable of making judgements and come to agreement about it.

These judgements about meaning have every right to be called objective. Their objectivity has to be explained, though, in a non-trivial manner. First of all, we have to remind ourselves that when speaking we can be performing various different speech acts, as we were taught by Austin in his *How to Do Things with Words* (Austin 1962). It is a different thing to assert a fact, ask a question, issue an order or proclaim an event inaugurated. Austin himself believed that there are indeed many things we can *do with words* and tried to classify the various kinds of speech acts. Now the act of describing a given thing and that of inaugurating an event differ mainly by the fact that while describing is related to a reality independent of us and the speech act, in the other case the speech act does as much as constitute the reality in question.

When we speak about the meaning of a given expression, we are performing a special kind of a speech act which is somewhere between the two just mentioned. We both describe and create a specific kind of reality. As Jaroslav Peregrin points out in his Peregrin (2014a) (see chapter 4, especially pages 84 and 85), when we assert that a given expression has this or that meaning we are partly describing the common practice but partly also endorsing the rule and exhorting the others to follow. By doing this we contribute to making the rule valid and the corresponding description of linguistic practice true. The descriptivist image is thus only partially true and can be misleading and perhaps led someone to the temptation of rejecting the notion of meaning altogether because of its alleged incoherence.

Our linguistic practices thus constitute meanings, and in fact make our utterances meaningful. Yet the meaning we speak about is always to a great degree unstable and full of ambiguity. Our language forms a complicated system which is also very flexible and can therefore promptly react to all kinds of impulses. In a way, the language is something which is constantly being formed and created.

4.2 What belongs to meaning

We are approaching an essentially inferentialist account of meaning. A meaning of a given expression consists, at least to a very substantial degree, in its inference relationships with other expressions, constituted by the rules of correct inference. As we will yet further explain, the meaning of every expression always remains to a degree implicit. Even if we express some of the inference rules which determine meanings of a given part of our vocabulary, we again have to understand the vocabulary which was operative in this expression. On the pain of falling into infinite regress, we have to acknowledge that a non-trivial portion of meaning constitutive inference rules has to remain implicit. The rules guiding the expressions which we define in the formal systems are no exception to this. In fact, recall that Quine in 'Two Dogmas of Empiricism' argued that meanings in formal languages are just as unclear as those of the natural languages. The meaning of a given expression can thus hardly get fully expressed. The inferentialist approach to meaning is thus not to be attacked by those who demand to be shown analyses of concrete expressions in terms of their inference relationships.

Now, the inferentialist thesis is basically that the meaning of an expression is constituted by nothing but its inference relationships to other expressions. Is such a view viable? Even though the theory of meaning is not a principal topic here, I think it will be illuminative for us to give it a serious consideration, as it is ultimately very closely connected to the issues of the philosophy of logic and specifically that of logical pluralism. Ultimately, we will opt for a version of logical pluralism which depends on inferentialist tenets.

One attack on inferentialism which suggests itself is that it is a doctrine which detaches language from the extra-linguistic reality. Take a word such as *dog*. It obviously has to be somehow connected to actual dogs; otherwise, it would simply not mean what it means. The interconnections with other linguistic expressions cannot of themselves be sufficient to explain its meaning. Similarly, when someone claims *I will open the window!*, her utterance obviously must be somehow connected to her actions. Or better expressed, the meaning thereof with a kind of action we all know how to perform. The concern is that inferentialism cannot account for this interconnection. Yet Peregrin (2014a) suggests that we can think of a broader variety of rules which connects not only linguistic expressions among themselves but the language with the outside reality as well. We can thus think of rules of the kind *When you see a human you are acquainted with, say hello* or the rules of the kind *When you borrow money from someone, you are obliged to return it*. Surely, without understanding that these rules (at least *ceteris paribus* but this proviso accompanies every rule) hold, one could hardly be said to understand the meanings of the words involved (mainly *hello* in the first case and *borrow* and *money* in the second case). These rules, as is obvious already from the two examples, are just as capable of linguistic expression as those intralinguistic ones. Indeed, though they link our language with the extra-linguistic reality, they could hardly count as rules were they not linked to inference relationships between sentences, for example between *You see a human you are acquainted with* and *Say hello*.

We see that in this manner the rules connecting our language with the outside world and our actions can in a certain way be reduced to those purely linguistic ones (as the extra-linguistic reality that enters into the rules has to be expressed by yet other sentences). But is this not a fallacy, leading us to the absurd conclusion that the whole systems of rules, even of those connecting our languages with the 'real world' depend merely on our decisions and are thus not constrained by this very world?[2] We have already observed that a vast number of the rules we follow remain only implicit (and necessarily so, not due to our inability or laziness to make them all explicit) and being implicit, those rules cannot be instituted by our arbitrary decision.

4.2.1 The implicit part

Wittgenstein taught us the important lesson that we always have to rely on some implicit rules. Indeed, when we, for example, read an arrow-shaped signpost pointing in the direction we have to go in order to reach, say, a mountain we want to climb, then to follow the explicit rule expressed by the arrow we also have to follow lots of implicit rules regulating the interpretation of signposts.

For our language to be truly meaningful it clearly has to involve some rules regulating the usage of its expressions. There have to be some distinctions between what is correct and what is not correct to assert, as well as rules governing the way we make our assertions (be they grammatical, concerning etiquette etc.). These two categories of rules, that is the rules of the content (actual meaning) and the rules of the form (mere grammar), probably cannot be sharply divided, but the nature of this boundary will not occupy us further here. When thinking of the rules which make our practices into genuinely linguistic and rational ones, we can name lots of examples. This very naming makes these rules explicit, if they were not such before. Yet we can always say that these rules are enabled thanks to various other ones, mainly rules of interpretation. Every rule is thus accompanied by at least one further rule, which we can call a metarule. This means that we cannot ever hope to somehow list all the rules which we have to follow in a given rule-guided set of practices. Each time we make some rules explicit, new implicit ones become operative and guide the expression and interpretation of the original rule.

What does the implicitness of a rule consist in? Obviously, the rule is not (yet) expressed. If we disentangle this, we realize that such a rule is not something we have chosen to institute by some sort of (maybe whimsical) agreement in our society. Clearly, some rules were instituted in this explicit fashion but many were not. The systems of rules constitutive of our language games are thus (mostly) not something arbitrary and detached from the world we live in. Putting the rules, in our case inference rules, at the heart of language thus does not lead to making the language *spin in the void*.

This is actually already a second way of defending ourselves from the McDowellian charges, the first one being that of countenancing the rules governing the interconnections of language with the extra-linguistic reality and our extra-linguistic actions. Every rule, though, has to be, at least in principle, capable of being made explicit and thus expressed in a language. I think that pointing to the necessary implicit ingredient in any system of rules provides a strong defence of inferentialism against the Dummettian (and McDowellian) worries.

4.3 Making the rules explicit

Yet the notion of an implicit rule is far from clear; in part it might seem like an unacceptable twist in our understanding of what a rule really is. When thinking of rules, we obviously primarily mean those which are explicitly stated. The worry might be whether the alleged implicit rules are actually not mere regularities in our conduct. I think we have to link the implicit rules to the explicit ones. Thus I claim that the implicit rules can be distinguished from mere regularities by the fact that they are capable of being expressed; they can be stated as rules. The mere regularities can clearly be stated as well, yet not as rules; they can just be described.

What do we need to make some rules explicit, which are the specific tools for such an undertaking? Robert Brandom presented in Brandom (1994) his bold thesis that this is exactly the role of logic. Logic provides us with tools such as the conditional or the negation which enable us to express the inference relationships in our language. For example, we typically treat the inference from *This is a dog* to *This is a mammal* as a correct one, yet equipped with logical tools (in this case the universal quantifier and the conditional) we can explicitly express the rule we follow, namely in the sentence *If something is a dog, then it is a mammal*. Thus Brandom calls logic *the organ of semantic self-consciousness*.

Making the rules explicit enables us to discuss them and eventually either accept or refuse or modify them. Why should we ever need to do this? Well, in many areas of our lives we know situations in which we realize that some systems of rules that are commonly accepted actually lead us astray and that it is no longer meaningful to pursue the given practices as we did previously. Some sort of a change is needed then, and this change can be undertaken in a rational manner only if we make the rules we have followed so far explicit because then we can discuss their meaningfulness and utility.

Besides the possibility to critically reflect on the rules we follow, we also have to appreciate that sometimes we happen to be unsure what the actual rules we follow are. Imagine someone, call him Peter, says, 'Fido obviously is a mammal because it is a dog' and another person, say Paul, retorts, 'Well, all dogs we encountered were mammals but perhaps Fido is not'. Then they have to clarify the rules that are accepted by both of them or at least acceptable for both of them, specifically the one that every dog is a mammal. Presumably in many cases the ruling will be clearly in favour of one of the people disputing; he or she will simply get the rules right. But in not a few other cases the resolution will not be found so easily, and ultimately the participants will have to settle on the shape of the relevant rules they could both accept. Thus they will not just express the rules they already follow or endorse their pursuit by other people but they will partly have to create the rules as well. The practice gives them leeway as to how they should formulate the rules explicitly, indeed the practice of making inference rules explicit is continuous with that of creating new rules and in many cases we cannot hope to tell them apart.

4.3.1 The width of the domain of implicit

A naive view might have it that there could be some implicit rules, yet the more we succeed in expressing them, the less numerous they become. Eventually we might even come to a point at which all the rules we follow are rendered fully explicit. Yet this view is based on a fundamental flaw. In fact every act of expression creates new space for the sphere of the implicit. Let us see why.

Let us return to Wittgenstein's example of a signpost that we must understand how to read.[3] In order to understand the rule which tells us, for example that going in the direction it points to means going to town A, we also must have a grasp of the rule for reading signposts, namely that we have to follow the pointed end of a given signpost. And when we make the rules for reading an arrow-shaped signpost explicit we can still ask ourselves what rule we follow when we interpret the signpost-reading one and so on infinitely.

I think we can make a general point here that every rule opens some space for interpretation and that by that token there has to be some implicit understanding thereof. By expressing some implicit rules we always bring a new sphere of the implicit in the form of the interpretational know-how which tells us how to understand this expression.

Despite the omnipresence of implicit rules, it makes sense to say that the implicitness is sometimes more and sometimes less present. Indeed, it makes a difference as to what kind of tools we use for the expression of the implicit rules. We should at least demand that they be clearer than what they explicate; they should bring the level of potential confusion down. When we use for example the conditional to express an inference rule because there was some unacceptable imprecision in our understanding of the rule, such that we either were not sure whether that rule holds at all or at least were unsure about its precise form, the final form of the rule should help us overcome these unclarities. For that we have to understand the conditional sufficiently, it must not be a source of even more unclarity, and we have to understand how to use it to make rules explicit and how to understand the rules formulated by the use of it.

4.4 The holistic approach to logic

Since at least Frege few things are as non-controversial about the development of modern logic as the fact that the movement was fuelled to a great degree by its fruitful mutual influence with mathematics. Frege was himself also a capable mathematician and brought about important results regarding his logical system which inspired many logicians and mathematicians who came after him. Even though he relied on works by many other authors who preceded him, I think that he is justly seen as a crucial figure in the history of logic due mainly to the fact that he showed how modern logic can help to make mathematics clearer. Indeed, he enabled mathematics to express the concepts which were needed to move forward and leave behind some paradoxes of mathematics as it stood in the nineteenth century. We should begin our discussion of the relationship between mathematics and logic by an important disambiguation.

4.4.1 How can logic be mathematical? – First sense

There are two important senses in which we can say that modern logic is mathematical. And though they are closely related and in many contexts coextensive, we should nevertheless generally keep the difference between them in mind. In the first sense, then, modern logic is mathematical because it uses mathematics and mathematical methods for its development and therewith also influences mathematics back. Indeed, modern logics can be seen, studied and developed as a part of mathematics proper. Having become mathematical in this sense does not have to prevent modern logic from retaining any goals logic traditionally used to have before its mathematization in the nineteenth century.

4.4.1.1 How can logic be mathematical? – Second sense

Modern logic can also be said to be mathematical because it seems to be best applied in the area of mathematics. When Frege was developing his system he was somewhat ambiguous between regarding it as a universal system of logic which is to be applied to any kind of reasoning and between regarding it as an instrument to be mainly used in mathematics. Indeed, in Begriffschrift he famously warned about the complications of applying his system:

> Das Verhältnis meiner Begriffschrift zu der Sprache des Lebens glaube ich am deutlichsten machen zu können, wenn ich es mit dem des Mikroskops zum Auge vergleiche. Das Letztere hat durch den Umfang seiner Anwendbarkeit, durch die Beweglichkeit, mit der es sich den verschiedensten Umständen anzuschmiegen weiß, eine große Überlegenheit vor dem Mikroskop. Als optischer Apparat betrachtet, zeigt es freilich viele Unvollkommenheiten, die nur in Folge seiner innigen Verbindung mit dem geistigen Leben gewöhnlich unbeachtet bleiben. Sobald aber wissenschaftliche Zwecke große Anforderungen an die Schärfe der Unterscheidung stellen, zeigt sich das Auge als ungenügend. Das Mikroskop hingegen ist gerade solchen Zwecken auf das vollkommenste angepasst, aber eben dadurch fur alle andern unbrauchbar. So ist diese Begriffschrift ein für bestimmte wissenschaftliche Zwecke ersonnenes Hilfsmittel, das man nicht deshalb verurtheilen darf, weil es für andere nichts taugt. (Frege 1879, p. v)[4]

Being mathematical in the sense of being the logic of specifically mathematical (or perhaps more generally, scientific) reasoning might narrow the scope of logic. But of course it still holds that mathematics is a very general discipline which can be fruitfully applied almost everywhere. We should therefore be rather cautious when speaking about narrowing the scope of logic by focusing it on mathematics.

The first sense in which modern logic is mathematical is perhaps less controversial, but even this second one can support itself rather well. And they both strongly support the suggestion that development in logic should be regarded in connection with development in mathematics. This would mean that there is a holistic connection between the two disciplines.

4.4.2 The interaction between logic and (the rest of?) mathematics

Let us now see what the recent attempts at interconnecting logic and mathematics look like and what they can tell us about logic. As we saw, it was particularly the discovery of interconnectedness with mechanics which helped to legitimize the alternative geometries. On the other hand, it also, at least implicitly, showed us some limits of the sphere of geometry. We got somewhat closer to understanding what geometry is and which systems can function as geometries by relativizing the boundary between geometry and mechanics. Now we examine whether a move towards holism with respect to logic can bring us comparable progress.

Thus we start considering the relationship with mathematics, as this is a promising attempt at arriving at a specific and thus viable form of holism. Mathematics is a good candidate for basically two reasons. On the one hand, mathematics is in many respects a solid discipline which is well established and undoubtedly of value. On the other hand, it seems to have quite a lot in common with logic. Both these disciplines are definitely very general and formal in the sense of being arrived at by a great degree of abstraction from our more specific and individual knowledge. This enables them to be applied in virtually any area of discourse. Anything can be counted and anything can be reasoned about.

Furthermore, it is obvious that applying mathematical methods to logic naturally brings about the plurality of logical systems we know today. When we study logic, for example by means of algebra and see the connectives as sorts of algebraic operators, it is only natural to consider also the operators which are different from but still analogous enough to the operators we know and still consider them, by exploiting the analogy, as connectives of a slightly different kind.

4.5 Logicism revived as the model-theoretic approach to the demarcation of logic

We have already spoken of Frege's programme of logicism. Frege presented it as a programme aiming at showing that arithmetic (and therewith a large body of other mathematical knowledge which can be reduced to it) is essentially a part of logic. In order to think such a programme viable, Frege had to consider logic as something clear and solid, something which can help us understand less clear disciplines, such as arithmetic and mathematical disciplines in general. There are clearly many points of view from which we can assess one discipline as more clearly understood than another one and Frege surely had good reasons for his views. Yet the abounding pluralism which we witness in logic today shows that logic is not so clear and unproblematic as many would guess. In mathematics, on the other hand, we can also discover a great variety of alternative disciplines and overall mathematics is far from being a single unified science with clear boundaries. Yet still the pluralism does not seem to be so problematic in it as in logic.

Maybe it is because pluralism in mathematics is seen as less problematic than in logic that some theoreticians renew logicism, yet in a reversed order. They think precisely that mathematics is in some ways more firm, so as to be able to help us with the problem of logical pluralism. Instead of the Fregean programme of reducing parts of mathematics to logic, they strive to reduce logic to mathematics and show that it is in essence its part. These authors present their versions of demarcation of the sphere of logic which are based on a model-theoretic approach. This is so both for historical and philosophical reasons.

The general idea of this approach is that logic should be a discipline which completely disregards the identity of the objects we talk about. In other words, logic is about no particular objects but shows us the necessary laws of discourse about any objects at all. This is also a sense in which logic can be said to be formal, one of the three senses identified in (MacFarlane 2000) (we will introduce and discuss the other two kinds of formality of logic presently). To illustrate the idea by concrete examples, let us think of a discipline which is not formal in the sense in which logic should be. Zoology surely cares about which entities it talks about. When it tells us something about the evolutionary origin of dogs, it surely cannot say the same about different animals such as cats, whales or rabbits, let alone about entities which are not animals at all, such as stones. Yet logic does not distinguish the entities it talks about.

We can put the problem in more linguistic terms. Zoology presumably has its specific vocabulary, including, among others, words such as *dog*, *sparrow* or *animal*. When zoology asserts some sentence which is true due to the zoological reasons, such as *Dogs are mammals*, it surely can affect the truth of the sentence if we exchange some of the zoological terms for others, for example if we put *sparrows* instead of *dogs* or instead of *mammals*. Now there are sentences which are obviously true for logical reasons, even if they contain zoological vocabulary, take *If something is a dog, then it is a dog* as an example. And this sentence is true independently of what we speak about. Therefore, we could as well interchange *cat* for *dog* and be in advance absolutely positive that the new sentence will be just as true.

4.5.1 Origins

This approach to demarcating logic could, as we already noted, hardly be possible without Frege's idea of logicism, even if it strives to realize the programme in a reversed order. It rather reduces logic to mathematics than the other way round. Let us now briefly review its history, at least insofar as it can help us understand its essence and the motivation and philosophical background which is behind this attempt at a demarcation of logic. Though this approach, at least in its most canonical form, involves a variation on Frege's logicism, its historical roots can be traced deeper.

MacFarlane traces this line of thought back to some passages from Kant. One of the central theses of MacFarlane's dissertation is that there are actually three related yet different ways of spelling out the intuitively plausible assertion that logic must be *formal*. When we say that logic is formal, we can mean it in one of the three following ways (described in MacFarlane 2000 on p. 62):

1. Logic is constitutive for our use of concepts as such.
2. It abstracts entirely from the identities of objects.
3. It abstracts entirely from specific semantic content.

These different ways of being formal are, according to MacFarlane, indistinguishable for Kant because of his overall philosophical background formed by transcendental idealism, yet this alleged impossibility to distinguish them in the Kantian framework will not concern us here. Let us see, though, a quote which demonstrates Kant's adherence to the second kind of formality of logic:

> Weil aber die blosse Form des Erkenntnisses, so sehr sie auch mit logischen Gesetzen übereinstimmen mag, noch lange nicht hinreicht, materielle (objektive) Wahrheit dem Erkentnisse darum auszumachen, so kann sich niemand bloss mit der Logik wagen, über Gegenstande zu urteilen. (Kant 1954 [1787], A60/B85)[5]

This quote suggests that Kant thought that logic should definitely be formal, at least in the second sense. Macfarlane adduces further quotes to illustrate that the three senses of formality are in fact equivalent for Kant.

Model-theoretic demarcations of logic are based on taking the second sense of formality, that is disregard for identities of objects, as essential for logic. A precursor who anticipated the model-theoretic approach to demarcating logic more directly and attempted at spelling it out was Bernard Bolzano. The modern proponents are more linguistically orientated and typically think of logic as of a science studying correct argumentation which of course takes place in language. Bolzano considered logic rather as science of thought or of an ideal language of thought. Overall, Bolzano contributed to the discussion that is focused on what is today often called *the problem of logical constants*. In the modern form, the problem is concerned with finding criteria for identifying an expression as specifically logical. Bolzano, due to his different philosophical background, spoke rather of *ideas* than of expressions.

4.5.2 Logical constants

The problem of logical constants has been formulated in various ways but basically it is about finding the expressions which are logical. It is a natural idea that a given discipline must have, probably among other things, its specific vocabulary in order to be the very discipline it is. We can hardly imagine mathematics to be what it is had it not used the expression *number* or something with the same meaning. Similarly zoology could hardly make do without the term *animal*. Now some words are apparently closely related to logic. Indeed, in the case of zoology and many other disciplines, it appears that the science could indeed have a different shape without ceasing to be zoology and in this shape forbear the usage of many of its terms, though only of those less central than *animal*. Logic, on the other hand, is indeed hardly imaginable without using words such as *not, and* etc. Logic can even be to a great degree understood as a study of these very words in the way in which zoology is a study of animals. Of course, when speaking of words, I do not mean so much the words in their concrete acoustic or graphic form we know from, for example English or Italian language, I mean rather the words together with their meaning, understood as the role they play in the overall structure of our language.

It thus makes sense to ask what should belong to the logical vocabulary, which expressions should belong to logic. Here a need for disambiguation may be felt. We can distinguish between the search for logical expressions of natural language, such as presumably *and*, *not*, *or* and so on and the search for logical expression of formal languages, such as the truth-functional connectives of classical propositional logic. The numerous differences in the behaviour of the former and the latter, most prominently the difference between the complicated and opaque character of natural language expressions and relative definiteness and clarity of those of formal systems leads to the suspicion that it is an entirely different thing to look for the demarcation of the logical expressions of a natural and those of a formal language. Nevertheless, this suspicion is not well founded.

4.5.3 Natural and formal logical constants

I definitely agree that we should not underrate the differences between the way natural and formal languages work, including their logical words. What are the principal differences between these and can we show that they force us to distinguish between the logical constants of natural and formal languages?

The meanings of natural language expressions are quite easily prone to change and vagueness; those of formal languages, on the other hand, are designed in such a way as to minimize both these properties, thus becoming stable and as clearly defined as possible. When speaking of a purported logical constant of natural language, such as *not*, it makes sense to ask how much its meaning has changed during the last fifty years. This question might be somewhat less natural than asking about the development of the word *cool*, yet it makes sense. On the other hand, asking whether $\neg$ has changed its meaning in classical logic makes practically no sense. One who asks it does not really understand how logical theories work. Indeed, should the negation sign be used differently, we would readily say that we are dealing with a different logic.

On the other hand, I do not see why we should not regard this important difference rather as one of degree, though of a considerable one. Any expressions, even those of the natural languages, must be at least somewhat stable and those which we might consider as logical perhaps more than the others. Using formal languages we are much more careful about the meanings we want to give our words and the clarity of the rules governing their use, yet it is not obvious that we are doing something fundamentally different from using natural languages. Besides that, in formal languages we are free to simply stipulate which expressions we want to count among the logical ones. Therefore, if we want our demarcation to tell us something interesting about them, we are well advised in considering their connection with their counterparts in natural languages. And after all, if we manage to arrive at an interesting account of what it means to be a logical constant of any given language, no matter whether natural or formal, we would have a more powerful theory.

4.5.4 Logical constants and logic as such

At least for the moment, we will try to see if we can identify some features an expression must have in order to be logical. What exactly should this bring us, though? We are trying to find some order in the chaos of all the logical systems by specifying a criterion for being a logic, thus making sure that we can still have a reasonable idea of what logic actually is even in face of the plurality of systems which apparently threatens our basic intuitions about logic, particularly its normativity. And getting at a reasonable demarcation of logical constants may help us very considerably. When speaking of various logics, we can distinguish the following relations two logical systems can stand in, as far as their respective strength is concerned. Let us have two logics, now determined in as general a way as possible, namely by their consequence or provability relation (for the moment, let us not distinguish between the semantic relation of consequence and the syntactic one of provability) – that is, by the set of pairs consisting of sets of formulae[6] and single formulae. A logic L thus has the following form (where S is the respective set of well-formed formulae and $\vdash$ the relation between sets of formulae and given formulae):

$$L = \langle S, \vdash \rangle.$$

It is crucial to be clear about what formulae could be featured as conclusions or among the set of premises, that is what formulae are members of the set S for a given logic. For every logic this has to be determined in some way, we will presuppose that in the typical recursive manner we know from classical propositional logic, where we have an infinite stock of atomic formulae and connectives (or quantifiers or modalities in other logics) which create new formulae out of some simpler ones. Now when we have two distinct logics L_1 and L_2, we can distinguish the two basic relations they can stand in with respect to each other:

1. They can share their language and thus the set of formulae, that is S_1 is equal to S_2 (the notation being obvious) and differ just in their relations of consequence. In this case we say that the one logic is an alternative to the other one.
2. They can also differ in their language, thus there is a formula A such that $A \in S_1$ and $A \notin S_2$ or the other way round. In this case we call the logic with the set of formulae containing A, an *expansion* of the other logic.

Note that the relation of being alternative logics is symmetric. Also note the logic L1's being an expansion of L2 does not prevent L2 from being an expansion of L1, even though typically logic L1 is an expansion of L2 when it simply contains it. Furthermore, L1 can be both an alternative to and an expansion of L2. Classical and intuitionistic propositional logics can be mentioned as well known examples of alternative systems, while standard modal logics, for example S5, are extensions of classical logic, as we can also use the necessity operator □ to create formulae. A modal logic based on intuitionistic propositional logic would be both an alternative to and an expansion of classical propositional logic. To be precise, the restriction of the modal intuitionistic logic to non-modal language is then an alternative to classical logic.

Now let us return to the question of logical constants. When we find a reasonable demarcation we will decide, for example, whether the necessity operator □ is a logical constant. It should be clear that the solution to the question of logical constants would narrow down the number of logical systems we have to consider as to whether they indeed deserve to be called *logics*. Should there remain logics among which to choose, they would all be merely alternative logics. This suggests that it should be a very good strategy to devote our attention to the question of logical constants. We cannot say in advance how much progress can be achieved by finding a solution to it, yet there has to be some. We are thus able to tackle the question of logical pluralism piecemeal, which is very good given how complicated it is and how grudgingly the answers offer themselves.

4.5.5 Criticism of demarcating logical constants

Yet, before we carry on with the problem of logical constants, we have to consider an objection against the division of labour between choosing among the logical systems which are expansions of one another (i.e. establishing the correct extension of logic by solving the problem of logical constants) and choosing among alternative logics thereafter. Indeed, when we narrow down the set of logical constants, how can we be sure that, when employed in, for example, intuitionistic and classical logic, they are the same constants? What does the identity of a logical constant consist in? Susan Haack in Haack (1974) opens the question whether the division of non-classical logics into what she calls *deviant logics* and *extensions* of classical logic (a distinction obviously similar to our distinction between alternative logics and expansions) really can be drawn (see her discussion of the translation between modal logic S4 and intuitionistic logic on pages 4–7 of Haack 1974). But it is fairly obvious that we are thus getting back to the Quinean objection we already encountered. In his *Philosophy of Logic* (Quine 1986, p. 80), Quine asserts:

> Here, evidently, is the deviant logician's predicament. When he tries to deny the doctrine, he only changes the subject.

By the *doctrine*, Quine means logic (in particular, classical logic). Thus, slightly paraphrased, Quine's thesis is that by trying to change logic, the deviant logician merely changes the subject. There are thus no alternative logics, according to Quine. When the classical and the intuitionistic logician dispute about the law of the excluded middle, they in fact do not both speak of the same disjunction and negation. Thus there cannot in fact be, Quine believed, any real dispute about which of the two given logics is better; when someone tries to convince us that our logic is somewhat flawed, we cannot really make any sense of what we are being told.

Now, it appears that Quine takes quite a heavy burden of proof upon himself. We normally seem to understand the dispute between, for example, the proponents of classical and intuitionistic logic as being a question as to whether the law of excluded middle is universally valid. They appear to be speaking both of disjunction and negation and assert different things about them. Historically, this dispute surely was perceived in some such manner by, for example, Brouwer and Hilbert at the time of their passionate debates about the legitimacy of non-constructive reasoning in mathematics. But Quine wants to convince us that both Brouwer and Hilbert as well as many contemporary logicians and philosophers of logic are at fault when they think their dispute actually has got this character. Yet he offers surprisingly little argument to change our usual perspective. He seems to think that logic should be a discipline of absolute certainty; there cannot be any higher tribunal to adjudicate its laws (on page 81 of Quine 1986, he asks, 'If sheer logic is not conclusive, what is?'). The sketchy attempt at argumentation (Quine apparently thought his point to be fairly obvious) involves, on the one hand, a version of his radical translation argument and, on the other hand, and less explicitly, also some sort of inferentialism about the meanings of logical constants.

The inferentialism can be read from Quine's words *changing the subject*. We indeed are going to embrace inferentialism about meaning in general, not just with respect to logical vocabulary, yet our inferentialism will not lead to the Quinean conclusion that it is impossible to change logic. To understand inferentialism, it is good to realize that an important part of the meaning of, for example, the word *dog* is that we can infer *Rex is a mammal* from *Rex is a dog*. Let us now consider the following form of inference (with A and B standing for any sentences and ∨ obviously for disjunction)

$$\frac{A}{A \vee B.}$$

The validity of this inference rule (together with the analogous one with B above the inference line) indisputably tells us a lot about the meaning of disjunction. Indeed, the idea of something being a disjunction without obeying this law is hardly intelligible. Should somebody convince us that the connective ∨ indeed does not always have to obey this law, we would rather think that the person is confused and is using the sign ∨ for something else than disjunction as we know it. But what about the *tertium non datur*? We would probably be bewildered if somebody told us that this law is complete nonsense and in fact never holds, that is, that all its instances are false. Yet many of those who oppose this law merely say that it is not valid in all its instances. The intuitionists historically asserted that it is not valid in mathematical reasoning, and some asserted that it fails also in other contexts.[7] Yet this is very well compatible with the excluded middle's being valid in many of its instances.

Coming back to the word *dog*, we obviously can use it and know its meaning even if we cannot determine whether the following inference is valid:

$$\frac{\text{Rex is a dog.}}{\text{Rex has got lungs}}$$

There is always some indeterminacy to the meanings of our expressions and the inference relationships they bear to other expressions. Upon encountering some animals which were in every respect like the dogs we know, yet lacked lungs, we would obviously be free to both declare them to be anomalous dogs and to say that, even despite the resemblances, they are not dogs as dogs should have lungs. There would be nothing strange about our decision to thus sharpen the meaning of the expression. Despite this indeterminacy we obviously understand the word *dog* and we know what we are talking about most of the time that we talk about dogs. Why should we thus have determinate answers about the validity of all inferences involving ∨, in order to be sure we are talking about disjunction? Oftentimes, it is indeterminate whether a given dispute concerns rather matters of fact or matters of meanings. Ironically, one of the authors who did the most to teach us this lesson was Quine himself, already in 'Two Dogmas'. It is therefore unsurprising that many other theoreticians find his view about deviant logics to be in conflict with his overall epistemology. For example, Dummett glosses it in the following way:

> In 'Two Dogmas of Empiricism', Quine maintained that no statement, not even a truth of logic, was immune to revision as a response to experience. His example for the application of this thesis to the laws of logic was the suggestion that the law of the excluded middle be abandoned in face of quantum mechanics. . . . In the meantime, Quine himself has totally revised his position, as may be seen from the chapter *Variant Logics* in his Philosophy of Logic. (Dummett 1976, quoted from the reprint in *Truth and other Enigmas*, pp. 269–70)

Summing up, we have not found decisive reasons to say that the proponents of classical and intuitionistic logic may not be described as discussing the same things, namely disjunction and negation, and disagree about their properties. It is true that these inferential properties appear to be linked to the meaning of logical expressions much more closely than in the case of more empirical ones. Quine's view thus might point in a good direction, yet there is no reason to accept it in its full radicality. But let us also examine Quine's translation argument for the impossibility of genuine disagreement in logic.

Quine famously uses his translation arguments to demonstrate the inscrutability of reference and, more importantly, the indeterminacy of translation. His field linguist is forced by the circumstances to try and understand a language completely alien to his own. He is thus left with nothing but guessing the meanings of the expressions of the indigenous language as he observes the behaviour of the people he tries to understand. When he then comes close to understanding an expression *gavagai* that is used typically when rabbits appear, he might realize that he cannot determine whether the word indeed means the same as *rabbit* in English or perhaps rather *undetached part of rabbit* or *rabbit stage*. Quine presents these theses in multiple places in his writings, such as in his relatively late work *Pursuit of Truth*:

> Considerations of the sort we have been surveying are all that the radical translator has to rely on. This is not because the meanings of sentences are elusive or inscrutable; it is because there is nothing to them, beyond what these fumbling procedures can come up with. . . . How much grotesqueness may we allow to the native's beliefs, for instance, in order to avoid how much grotesqueness in his grammar or semantics? These reflections leave us little reason to expect that two radical translators, working independently on Jungle,[8] would come out with interchangeable manuals. (Quine 1990, p. 47)

It may pose some difficulty to understand what exactly Quine had in mind in this passage. Apparently, there can be more non-equivalent translations, yet their difference also turns out to be much less important than might have seemed at first sight; indeed in many – maybe most – cases it proves to be practically irrelevant. Despite this, we can still speak of better and worse translations. Indeed, there are relevant guides which determine to a sufficient degree how we should translate the alien idiom. One of them is, as we already made clear, the overt behaviour of the users. The other one, then, is the *principle of charity*. When translating, we have to be charitable and thus render the utterances of the speakers as meaningful and as true as possible. This principle does not stem from some sort of optimism about the rationality of human race but from the very nature of the process of translation.[9] When the translation renders the aliens as saying seriously some obvious absurdities, it is natural to consider the translation as a wrong one. And should we renounce the principle, there would be no bounds on the range of admissible variant translations, anything would go.

In the case of logic, the principle of charity (which Quine also paraphrased by the maxim save the obvious), according to Quine, leads us to translate the speaker as being in complete agreement with us as far as logic is concerned.[10]

The principle of charity thus allegedly forces us to be extremely uncharitable when interpreting someone who adheres to a different logic than we do. This should already awake suspicion about Quine's argument as it stands. Note that in order to refute Quine, we do not have to assert that a good translation or interpretation of an interlocutor can never involve forcing (some parts of) our logic on the interlocutor. Rather, we just have to show that the forcing is not always necessary and does not have to be complete and therefore an interpretation which takes the interlocutor to be speaking, for example, about the same disjunction and negation when disputing about the law of the excluded middle can be reasonable and admissible in some contexts.

In fact the difference between interpreting the deviant logician as speaking about the same connectives and ascribing different properties to them or as arguing in favour of analogous, yet different connectives is typically of as little importance as that between interpreting the word *gavagai* as *rabbit* or as *undetached rabbit-part*. Thus if on the one construal the dispute is supposed to make sense, then so it has to make sense on the second one.

It should be stressed that when arguing against Quine here, we have attacked only a relatively marginal part of his overall philosophy of meaning and translation. Most importantly, nothing has been said against the principle of charity. It remains a great insight of Quine's; we are just criticizing the way Quine uses it in the particular case of logic. We have to obey it even in this case but it is by no means established that we can do so only by constantly forcing our logic on everyone. I even doubt the notion of some logic being *ours* in some strong sense. Thus, when person A speaks with person B, we do not have to presuppose that A has to have definite answers regarding the universal validity of the law of the excluded middle. A will probably have to interpret B as recognizing the law in most cases but still possibly refusing it in others. While saving the obvious, A typically would have to interpret B as not denying that two plus two equals four, just as not denying that it is raining when it is in fact visibly raining and also as not denying that something is the case or is not the case in most contexts (i.e. that the law of the excluded middle holds). Yet he does not have to interpret B as either adhering to the law of the excluded middle in full generality or as denying it in some cases. Thus no particular logic has to be imposed by the translation.

This is, again, not to say that nothing logical can be imposed by the translation. But matters are much more complicated than Quine envisaged.

I guess he wanted to safeguard us from too naive a view, one which would have it that logical meaning is always the same when we use the same signs. The question of whether, for instance, both a classical and an intuitionistic logician use connectives endowed with the same meaning does not have a simple, universal answer. Here I concur with Stewart Shapiro, who claimed that the very concept of having the same meaning has an open texture in the sense of Friedrich Waismann;[11] that is it is open-ended. In some contexts it may be more reasonable to claim that two logicians use the same terminology with the same meanings; in other contexts it might be more reasonable to say to the contrary that they use them with different meanings. Shapiro provides specific examples in chapter 5 of Shapiro (2014).[12]

We have thus shown that it is not nonsensical to have a disagreement about the validity of logical laws. The distinction between one logic being an extension of another and being its alternative makes sense (even though the boundary might occasionally be fuzzy). Thus it is possible to have a plurality of logics which share the logical vocabulary; having different opinions about the properties of a given set of logical constants does not by far have to involve changing the subject, as Quine had thought, and the problem of logical constants is a meaningful one and distinct from the general problem of deciding which logical systems are really logics.

5
Model-theoretic demarcations of logical constants

After this detour, which helped us to legitimize the search for logical constants, let us now get back to our original intention to reshape our notion of logic by adopting a more holistic perspective about it. In the case of geometry, in which the plurality of various systems also awoke uncertainty regarding the essence and bounds of the discipline, we found out that it was by considering its relationship with mechanics that we could make sense of the new systems and see that they all can in fact serve as geometries. In the case of logic, we want to examine if similar progress could be achieved by reconsidering the relationship with mathematics in general, particularly with set-theory. Such attempts have their ramified history, something which we will now revisit.

5.1 Tarski's idea

Alfred Tarski had the idea of demarcating what he called *logical notions*, which generalized the idea of Felix Klein who had come up with a means of characterizing various geometries. His approach is usually called the *Erlangen program*. Different geometries can be characterized by the kinds of permutations their notions are invariant under. Let us consider the space S as a set of points which can then form geometrical figures, such as triangles, squares and so on. We can thus consider a given triangle simply as a set of points. Then we can consider transformations of the space, that is one-one maps with the whole set of all points as their domain, as well as range, that is maps giving to each point another point (possibly itself), that is a map f such that f: S → S.

Then we can extrapolate the map f so as to make it applicable to the objects of higher order than the points, that is sets of points, sets of sets of points and so on. Thus not only every point has got its image under f, but also a given set of points T has got its image, defined naturally as $f(T) = \{x; x$ is a point such that there exists a point $y \in T$ with $f(y)=x\}$. Thus we can, for instance, speak of an image of a given triangle under the given transformation of the universe. We will now define what it means for a notion to be invariant with respect to a given class of transformations of the space.

Definition 5.1.1. *Take any property defined by a formula of our language with one free variable $\varphi(x)$. We say that the notion expressed by this formula is invariant with respect to a given class C of transformations of the space S if for any $f \in C$ it is true that φ holds of an object o of the appropriate type if and only if it holds also of f(o).*

Let us now see what sets C of transformations it can be useful to consider. One of them is the group of similarity transformations, that is those that to a given figure (regarded as a set of points) give as its image a similar figure: a figure, so to speak, of possibly different dimensions, yet with the same shape. Thus, no notions concerning the dimensions of a figure are invariant under these similarity transformations, yet the notions regarding the shape, such as being an isosceles triangle, are. These notions are exactly the notions Euclidean geometry can express. One can now compare the geometrical notions as to their generality. A given notion φ is more general than a notion ψ if it is invariant under a superset of the set of transformations under which ψ is invariant. We can now consider both the notions which are less general than those of the Euclidean geometry and those which are more. The less general notions are not of much interest for geometers but as an example we can mention the notions which are invariant only under the identity transformation which respect the identity of every specific figure and those which are invariant under transformations which preserve the dimensions of figures. Thus, when we have means to express the length of a figure, the notion of being a triangle with sides of given lengths would be an example of the notion invariant under this class of transformations. More general notions are those invariant under affine transformations which map a triangle always on a triangle, yet not necessarily a similar one and the notions invariant under bicontinuous transformations. That is those which map a continuous figure on another continuous one, so that they do not as if tear it apart. The former notions are studied by affine geometry, the latter ones by topology.

Now Tarski, inspired by Klein's approach, studied the notions which are invariant under the class of all the permutations of a given universe (which now can have anything as its elements, not merely points). He had already studied these notions with Lindenbaum in the 1930s (see Lindenbaum and Tarski 1936) and together they proved that every relation definable in the simple theory of types is invariant under permutations of the given domain. Yet it was only in 1966 in his lecture 'What Are Logical Notions?' that Tarski explicitly embraced the thesis that the logical notions are exactly those which are invariant under all permutations of the given universe of discourse (unbeknownst to him, he was preceded with this idea by Mautner 1946). In his famous article from the 1930s, 'On the Concept of Logical Consequence' (Tarski 1936), he, somewhat surprisingly given his work with Lindenbaum, as is noted by Feferman (Feferman 1999, p. 5), does not yet bring this idea up. In this important article he invokes ideas similar to those of Bolzano, namely that we should distinguish between the logical and extra-logical vocabulary and treat logical vocabulary as that which determines whether a given sentence is a logical truth. In this article he still remained somewhat sceptical about the possibility of systematically demarcating the logical expressions. Nevertheless, he already hinted at the possibility that classical logic might be too restrictive in its choice of logical constants.[1]

5.1.1 The role of logical constants

Logical vocabulary should be the one that is essential for logical truth and logical entailment. Let us now consider once again a sentence which is a good candidate for being regarded as a logical truth. We have to be cautious and I am merely saying that it can be regarded as such because our main problem is to determine which logics are real (or rather somehow legitimate) logics and therefore cannot be really sure in advance which sentences are really logical truths. So with this precaution in mind, take the purported logical truth *If Fido is a dog, then Fido is a dog*. Clearly the truth of this sentence is guaranteed by the behaviour of the words *If . . . then*, all the others are in this respect irrelevant. We can now highlight three similar facts about this sentence:

1. All the other expressions besides *If* and *then* can be substituted by different ones of the appropriate type (we substitute predicates for predicates, individual terms for individual terms, etc. – we will not discuss the notion of an adequate substitution more closely here, though this notion might be surprisingly evasive) without the sentence's ceasing to be true. All the other expressions besides *If* and *then* can thus be replaced by suitable variables.
2. All the other expressions can be reinterpreted so that they mean something different without the sentence's ceasing to be true.
3. No change in the world would cause the sentence's ceasing to be true.

The first two points make it obvious why the logical expressions are commonly called the *logical constants*. They are that which is not fluctuating in our propositions. While all the other expressions can be changed, the logical expressions have to be kept constant if we do not want to change the logical status of a given proposition (such as the status of a logical truth). By replacing the extra-logical parts of our propositions by suitable variables, we display what is normally called the *logical form* of our propositions. The fact that we have to look for a suitable demarcation of logical constants shows that we do not have a clear idea of the logical forms our propositions can have. Indeed, the problem of demarcating the logical constants is in fact the same as the problem of demarcating the possible logical forms of judgements.

MacFarlane (2005) tries to identify the root of our uncertainty regarding the possible logical forms. As in his dissertation (MacFarlane 2000), he approaches the problem from a historical perspective. He notes that while before Frege there was an agreement on what the logical structure of a judgement can be, as it was elaborated, for example, by Kant, the Fregean syntax based on regarding the relations as functions which take objects as arguments and yield a truth value gives us a great flexibility as to how we see the logical structure of a given proposition.

Traditionally, logicians distinguished between the so-called syncategorematic and categorematic signs, the first ones pertaining to the form, the others to the specific content of our propositions. The syncategorematic expressions serve, as MacFarlane nicely puts it, as a glue which binds the matter together to create a meaningful sentence. The matter can be inserted into the forms built of the syncategorematic signs, the forms which were perspicuously classified by Kant in his table of judgements. The syncategorematic terms have, according to the traditional perspective, no meaning of their own; they merely serve to provide the suitable forms of sentences.

The Fregean approach is based on identifying the forms of our sentences by abstraction. MacFarlane invites us to consider the following sentence:

Every boat is smaller than Moby Dick.

The logicians before Frege would have regarded this sentence unproblematically as a universal affirmative one, in which we say of the subject *boat* that the predicate *to be smaller than Moby Dick* holds of it. According to Frege, we can see it as a sentence of the form:

$$\forall x \big(\Phi(x) \to \Psi(x)\big)$$

On the other hand, the $\Psi(x)$ (*to be smaller than Moby Dick*) can be seen as obtained from a two place relational symbol $X(x, y)$ (i.e. *x is smaller than y*). But we can also see this whole original sentence, as a result of applying the function *Every boat is smaller than x* to the argument *Moby Dick*. Overall, it is not clear anymore what the logical form of a given sentence is; it is up to us and our need for analysis that we postulate the form of a given sentence.

Besides this, as MacFarlane also notes, the vocabulary of Fregean logic, such as the connectives and quantifiers, cannot be clearly seen as either syncategorematic or categorematic. The predicates are in many ways like the syncategorematic terms because they are, in Frege's sense, *unsaturated*. If we refuse to count them among the syncategorematic vocabulary, which we certainly should,[2] then we cannot count the quantifiers and connectives either, as they are functional unsaturated expressions, just as the predicates.

Thus the need to look for the demarcation of logical constants and with it for the logical forms of our propositions has become very real since at least Frege. Tarski's proposal was found very fruitful and was developed by many of his successors. Let us now examine the theoretical background it has.

5.1.2 Why Tarski's criterion

Tarski's criterion for being a logical constant, namely to be invariant with respect to the permutations of the domain of the universe, appears to be a very natural one. We already mentioned the three senses distinguished by MacFarlane in his dissertation (MacFarlane 2000) in which logic can be said to be formal. This approach thus highlights the second sense of formality of logic. Thus logic, according to this approach, should be the most general discipline and this is achieved by its indifference to the objects that are spoken of. Logic has no specific subject matter, which is also the reason for its universal applicability.

This criterion offers a mathematically clear demarcation of logicality. If we embrace it, we can demarcate logic while avoiding some potentially controversial issues of the epistemology and philosophy of logic. Besides this, the criterion it poses for logicality surely seems reasonable at its face value. Logic should definitely be a very general discipline and being indifferent to the identities of the objects spoken about seems to be a way of becoming this. Indeed, not many authors have opposed the idea that what Tarski found was indeed a necessary criterion for an expression to behave as a logical one. For example, Michael Dummett also proposes calling *logical* exactly those quantifiers which are invariant to permutations of the universe of discourse (see Dummett 1973, p. 22).

As intuitive as Tarski's approach is, it has its difficulties. Tarski really just brought up the idea in a semi-formal way; it was up to later authors to provide a more mathematically precise formulation. The problem that is especially pressing is that his criterion is defined by the behaviour of the logical constants on the one given domain (or universe of discourse, if you prefer the term). In this sense it is all too liberal, as it allows, for example, for such a connective as McGee's *wombat disjunction* (McGee 1996). Speaking about connectives in general, the standard conjunction, disjunction, conditional and negation are demarcated by the invariance criterion as logical, as we can understand them set-theoretically, for example conjunction as the intersection of extensions of two predicates, and so on.[3] Now, the mentioned wombat disjunction behaves as classical disjunction on the domains which contain wombats and as conjunction on all the others, which obviously makes it invariant under permutations of any given universe of discourse, that is logical according to Tarski's criterion. We will now review some of the proposals to technically amend Tarski's approach so as to escape this counterexample and similar ones.

5.1.3 Bijection invariance

The systematic development of the idea put forward by Tarski has already been pursued many years before his lecture was published and became widely known. We will understand the historical development better if we consider for a moment the extension of logic which results from adopting Tarski's criterion. What gets counted as logical constants by the invariance criterion? Tarski gives us only a few hints, just to get a taste of what his approach amounts to.

Obviously, no individual members of the universe of discourse are logical. We will have to go a step further and consider the sets of individuals. Yet in fact only two such sets are logical, namely the empty set and the whole universe of discourse. When we consider the binary relations, we find the identity, its complement, the universal relation (which holds between any pair of individuals) and the empty relation (which holds between none) as the only logical ones. Tarski notes, 'This is interesting because just these four relations were introduced and discussed in the theory of relations by Peirce, Schröder, and other logicians of the nineteenth century' (Tarski 1981, p. 150).

The situation becomes more interesting at the next level, namely of sets (or, more generally, relations) of sets. These can be called quantifiers. Consider the two quantifiers you know from classical logic, namely the universal and the existential one. On a given universe, each can be seen as a set of subsets of the universe of discourse or as a (second-order) predicate in the model-theoretic sense. The existential quantifier is a set of all the nonempty sets, while the universal quantifier has got only the whole set at question as its member. And obviously, both these quantifiers are thus invariant under the permutations of the universe and therefore get counted as logical. So far, the results speak for the extensional adequacy of the criterion.

Yet, this is not everything, not by far. Actually, any quantifiers which say anything about the cardinality of the sets are logical. Take just any cardinal κ and the corresponding quantifier Q (claiming that there are exactly κ entities satisfying the given formula) is logical. This is surely not hard to swallow in the case of finite cardinals, as these quantifiers can be defined in classical logic with equality in an obvious manner. Yet the quantifier expressing that there are, for example, exactly $\aleph_1$[4] many things with a certain property or the quantifiers expressing that there are at least or at most $\aleph_1$ many things already make one somewhat unsure about the extensional adequacy of the criterion. Tarski himself does not say much more about the extension his criterion gives to logic, yet he notes that all the notions from *Principia Mathematica* are logical notions in his sense (he proved, as we already noted, this result himself together with Lindenbaum a few decades earlier, see Lindenbaum and Tarski 1936). A more exact characterization of the extension of logic demarcated by the invariance criterion was offered later by Van McGee. But before we get to this characterization, it will be informative to get to know the extension more by individual examples of demarcated expressions which go beyond the unary cardinality quantifiers.

The criterion has to be, nevertheless, amended. As we noted, it is concentrated only on the given domain of the universe and so enables the obviously inadequate wombat disjunction to be counted as logical. The remedy is simple – instead of considering the notions which are invariant only under the permutations of the given universe of discourse, take rather those invariant under bijections f: $M_1 \to M_2$ between models, that is maps from one model to another which are both injective (they give different images to different values) and surjective (every member of the range model M_2 is an image of some member of the model M_1). The permutations of a given model are obviously special cases of these bijections for f: $M_1 \to M_2$, where M_1 is the same as M_2. There is no reason to suspect that the amended criterion loses any of the original appeal of making sense of the idea that logic should be the most general discipline, this idea is thus captured rather even better.

5.1.4 More examples of the extension

We already saw that the classical quantifiers, as well as many others, are in fact invariant under the bijections between models. All the quantifiers we saw so far were of the simplest possible type, namely sets of sets. We will say that they are of the type <1>. By this we mean exactly that given a universe M, the quantifier Q is of type <1> if it is a set of subsets of M. In a similar vein we can also speak of quantifiers of the type <1, 1> which will be relations between subsets; that is a quantifier Q is of the type <1, 1> if Q⊆P(M)×P(M). Furthermore, we can then say that Q is of the type <2> if Q⊆P(M×M). Thus, we can then obviously speak also of any other type such as <1, 3, 2>. Let us sum this up in a definition.

Definition 5.1.2. Let a quantifier Q be given. Then we say that it is of the type $<n_1, \ldots, n_k>$ if for any model M we have

$$Q \subseteq \Pi(P(M^{n_i}))$$

Where Π is a Cartesian product.

Study of these generalized quantifiers was pursued by Mostowski and later was further developed by Lindström (see Mostowski (1957) and Lindström 1966). In the course of his study of the generalized quantifiers, Lindström also proved his famous theorem regarding the classical logic with its two quantifiers. The theorem says that classical logic is the strongest one among those using quantifiers of the types just defined which has both the Löwenheim-Skolem theorem and is compact. Yet, as is noted by Gila Sher, there was a difference between the approach of Mostowski and Lindström, the first author having a philosophical agenda and claiming that logic really is a broader discipline than the classical system and has to include his generalized quantifiers, the other remaining silent on the import of his results:

> Lindström, unlike Mostowski, was silent regarding the philosophical significance of his generalization. One might say that his remarkable theorems solidify the distinguished status of standard first-oder logic, but here again, it is unclear whether Lindström himself considers compactness and the Löwenheim-Skolem property to be essential ingredients of logicality or mere mathematically interesting features of one among many genuinely logical systems. (Sher 1991, pp. 62–3)

The generalized quantifiers have lots of applications in linguistics, as many of them model the functioning of natural language expressions with relatively complex semantics. The history of the development of generalized quantifiers, as well as their relation to linguistics, is very nicely captured by Gila Sher in her book *Bounds of Logic* (Sher 1991). The definition we present here is the same as hers and we can see that it envisages only first-order quantifiers. This appears to limit the logic when compared with Tarski's original programme, which countenances *logical notions* of any order whatsoever. We will yet see that this limitation is actually not substantial.

For the moment let us see some more of the generalized quantifiers which are invariant under bijections between domains, together with their correlates from natural language. The examples are taken from Sher (1991), chapter 2.

Among the cardinality quantifiers of the type <1> we should mention also the quantifiers *there are finitely many* and *there are infinitely many*, which cannot be defined in the classical logic. Furthermore we have the quantifier *most x*, written as M^1, which is defined for a given model M in the following way (where evaluation e is a map assigning a member of the given universe to each variable):

Definition 5.1.3. $M^1x(\varphi)$ is satisfied by an evaluation e in model M iff $|\varphi| > |\backslash\varphi|$, where $|\varphi|$ is the cardinality of the set of individuals from M which satisfy φ and $\backslash\varphi$ is the complement of φ (and φ is itself understood as a set of the elements which satisfy the formula φ).

This quantifier already gives us significant additional power with respect to first-order logic, yet it is not very close to the use of the word *most* in the natural language. Take the sentence *Most dogs bark*. We do not have any means of expressing this sentence with the quantifier M^1. Here in fact we need a quantifier of a slightly more complex type, namely M^2 of the type <1; 1>. This quantifier is then defined in the following way:

Definition 5.1.4. $M^2x(\varphi, \psi)$ is satisfied by an evaluation e in model M iff $|\varphi \wedge \psi| > |\varphi \wedge \neg \psi|$.

Now the mentioned sentence can be formalized when we take D for the predicate *is a dog* and B for the predicate *barks*. The formalization is simply:

$$M^2x\big(D(x), B(x)\big)$$

We can use this quantifier in more sophisticated ways. We can for example express the sentence *Most dogs hate all cats*, where we use C(x) for *x is a cat* and H(x,y) for *x hates y*:

$$M^2x\big(D(x), \forall y\big(C(y) \rightarrow H(x; y)\big)\big).$$

Furthermore, we can also express the sentence *Most dogs hate most cats* in the following way:

$$M^2x\big(D(x), M^2y\big(C(y), H(x, y)\big)\big).$$

Sher provides many other interesting examples of quantifiers which can be used to formalize sentences such as the following:

- Sixty per cent of the female students in my class are A-students.
- Mostly women have been elected to Congress.

- Only human beings have brains.
- They are outnumbered by us.
- The same percentage of boys and girls who took the test received a perfect score.

The quantifiers used to express these sentences are all invariant under bijections between domains. Both the definition and verification of invariance of each one of them are fairly obvious and can be found in *Bounds of Logic*.

We can thus see that generalized quantifiers can indeed model a lot of important expressions from our natural languages. This expressive power can be seen as an argument in favour of this demarcation of logic (and so it was used particularly by Sher), and classical logic seems to be unnecessarily restrictive in comparison. It was already Mostowski who suggested that the classical logic is not all there is to logic and Tarski, as we saw earlier, suggested as much even before proposing the criterion of demarcation we are now discussing. Sher explicitly states the following:

> Given the breadth of the logical enterprise, we discovered that the standard terms alone do not provide an adequate superstructure. . . . Mostowski's claim that standard mathematical logic does not exhaust the scope of first-order logic has been vindicated. (Sher 1991, p. 65)

She then calls her first-order system *Unrestricted first-order logic*, in order to suggest that classical logic is a system which is unnecessarily restrictive and that the logical expressions thereof do not form an interesting class of logical expressions which deserves to be isolated and studied as a distinctive logic. She also argues that the term *Unrestricted first-order logic* is preferable to terms such as *extended logics*, *generalized logics* or *abstract logics*, as these would suggest that classical logic still is in some sense the real or at least basic one, the core that the other ones somehow extend, thereby leaving the sphere of logic proper. Because she developed the Tarskian criterion in a very systematic and meticulous way, and because she was among the most passionate advocates of it, this criterion for logicality came to be called *The Tarski-Sher thesis*.[5]

5.1.5 Another characterization and a demonstration of force

Before we proceed to some of the objections to this approach and our evaluation of it, one further characterization of it should be presented. We have already seen some of the results of this demarcation using the bijection invariance, namely examples of the quantifiers that are undefinable in classical logic and which model the way some inferentially important expressions of natural languages work. Sher herself admits that her approach is that of taking logic as a system which is open for us in the sense that we cannot simply list the logical constants of the unrestricted logic (together with their semantic specifications), but we can in course of our investigations discover that a given expression is in fact logical because it satisfies the invariance criterion (for an exact statement of the criterion, see pp. 54–5 of her *Bounds of Logic*). Later we will evaluate the bearing of this conception of logic on the verdict about Frege's logicist thesis, yet it should be noted that Sher presents an inspirational picture of the relationship between logic and mathematics, namely that although the mathematical notions belong to logic (indeed, she unsurprisingly embraces the logicism but more about this later), we can also treat the mathematical notions we want to study as extra-logical and examine them in the models of a logic which does not contain them. So for example we can study the properties of the quantifier *there are uncountably many* in the first-order set-theory (with the background of classical logic in which such a quantifier cannot be expressed). After we get a sufficient command of the properties of the given expression, we can adopt it in our logic and thus work thereafter with a richer logic containing the new expression. This conception of logic is, needless to say, quite unorthodox.

Indeed, whether we like it or not, this open character cannot be changed. But still a characterization of unrestricted logic can be provided. This characterization does not tell us much about which quantifiers are invariant under bijections between models, yet still gives us an alternative way of describing the very same system. The result is due to Vann McGee (see McGee 1996) and characterizes the logical notions demarcated by the *Tarski-Sher criterion* by means of the logic $L_{\omega,\omega}$, which is an extension of classical logic, enabling infinite disjunctions and concatenations of quantifiers. An inductive definition of the formulae of this logic is the following (taken from Feferman (2010), p. 8):

- For a given n-ary predicate symbol P, a sequence of variables $x_1, \ldots, x_n$ (abbreviated as $\underline{x}$), $P(\underline{x})$ is an atomic formula; also each equation between variables is an atomic formula;
- if φ is a formula then $\neg\varphi$ is a formula;

- if Φ is any non-empty set of formulas then $\bigvee \varphi[\varphi \in \Phi]$ is a formula;
- if φ is a formula and U is any non-empty set of variables then $(\exists U)\varphi$ is a formula.

The semantic interpretations of the formulae are given by the Tarskian satisfaction conditions for a given model, as known from the classical logic. Mcgee has proven that *unrestricted logic* is in fact the same as $L_{\omega,\omega}$. This can be read of the two theorems he has proven. The first one concerns the invariance criterion in the original Tarskian shape, namely as the invariance under permutations of a given domain:

Theorem 5.1.5. *Let Q_D be a set-theoretic object based on the domain D. Then Q_D is invariant under arbitrary permutations of the domain D of individuals if and only if Q_D is definable in $L_{\omega,\omega}$.*

McGee himself is sympathetic to the *Tarski-Sher thesis* and in this spirit claims of this result that it 'gives us good reason to believe that the logical operations on a particular domain are the operations invariant under permutations' (p. 575). Yet we have already seen that a logical constant cannot be specified only relative to a given domain, McGee himself provided the already mentioned counterexample of *wombat disjunction* (viz 'in order for an operation across domains to count as logical, it is not enough that its restriction to each particular domain be a logical operation' (McGee 1996, p. 576)). Therefore, it is rather the second of his theorems that is of interest for us.

Theorem 5.1.6. *An operation Q across domains is a logical operation according to the bijection invariance criterion iff for each cardinal κ≠0 there is a formula of $L_{\omega,\omega}$ which describes the behaviour of Q on domains of cardinality κ.*

This theorem shows what we could have guessed already, namely that in changing Tarski's original proposal into the Tarski-Sher thesis, the meanings of the logical constants do not depend on the one universe of discourse, yet they still are not truly independent of the models. Instead, they depend on the size of the universe of discourse, as we can still think of such problematic quantifiers as $\forall_3$, which behaves as a universal quantifier on infinite domains and as existential quantifier on finite ones. Obviously, many other analogical quantifiers can be thought of and one plausibly would not like to have them among logical constants. This is an issue we will have to consider soon. Just for the moment, let us remark that we can somewhat generalize this criterion as was remarked by Feferman. In order to get a characterization of the operations independent even of the cardinalities of domains, one has to take for each $\kappa \neq 0$ the formula $\varphi\kappa$ together with the formula stating that there are exactly κ elements in the domain to create the formula Ψ_κ and then make a disjunction of all the Ψ_κ for all the cardinals greater than zero. This, nevertheless, as Feferman remarks (Feferman 2010, p. 10) goes well beyond the system $L_{\omega,\omega}$, as standardly conceived.

5.2 External and internal attacks on the Tarski-Sher thesis

The criterion of demarcation we have just presented has stirred up many discussions. The authors have approached it from many different angles; some belonged to the *Tarski-Sher movement* and thus criticized it, as it were, from the inside. These authors include for example Solomon Feferman, Dennis Bonnay (see Bonnay 2008), Vann McGee and Timothy McCarthy (see McCarthy 1981). In fact, we already saw that the criticism advanced by McGee, namely that Tarski's original criterion makes the logicality of an expression depend merely on its behaviour on a given domain, has been accepted and the criterion correspondingly adjusted to invariance under bijections between domains. We will yet come to see more of the development of this movement and more alternative shapes of this demarcation. Yet before entering into these subtle points, let us consider briefly a criticism which is much more sweeping, as it comes from outside of the movement. This criticism comes from John Etchemendy and is formulated most prominently in his book *The Concept of Logical Consequence* (Etchemendy 1990).

5.2.1 The foundations of Tarski's idea

John Etchemendy does not speak so much about the actual *Tarski-Sher thesis*, he attacks the very idea of Tarskian semantics. As the criticism of this kind bears of course also on the demarcation of logic, we have to discuss it here, at least briefly. The interested reader may find my discussion thereof also in my article on this topic (Arazim 2015).

In section 5.1.1, we have listed three similar kinds of invariance to be found in logical truth and consequence. Logical consequence and logical truth should depend on the division of expressions into the logical and extra-logical ones and the logical ones are fixed in the sense of being invariant in all the three ways mentioned in section 5.1.1. Tarski definitely wanted logic to be independent of empirical findings. It should also be fairly general from the linguistic point of view and thus not depend either on what language we use or on how we use it. The logical constants should be something to be found in the foundations of every reasonable language. These requirements should be met by the construction hinging on the *logical form* of our statements. Tarski wrote:

> Since we are concerned with the concept of logical, i.e. formal consequence, and thus with a relation which is to be uniquely determined by the form of the sentences between which it holds, this relation cannot be influenced in any way by empirical knowledge, and in particular by knowledge of objects to which the sentence X or the sentences of the class K refer. The consequence relation cannot be affected by replacing the designations of the objects referred to in these sentences by designations of any other objects. (Tarski (1936), p. 414)

The logical consequence should for Tarski be necessary but not every consequence which is necessary is logical, as it does not have to be formal. It should also be noted that the Tarskian explanation of both the formal and the necessary consequence is based on the simple notion of material consequence, which means mere truth preservation. Thus, when we say that the formula φ is a (merely material) consequence of the set of formulae Γ and write $\Gamma \vDash \varphi$, we mean by that simply that either one of the elements of Γ is false or that φ is true. Now, the logical consequence is reduced to material consequence, being truth preserving and also robust in one of the three senses mentioned on page 61. Now there are, according to both Tarski and the established orthodoxy, consequences that are necessary, yet not formal. A potentially controversial example could be the following, synthetic inference:

> There is lightning now. $\vDash$ A thunder will be heard in a moment.

A more widely accepted example which was very much discussed in the literature (also by Etchemendy and Sher) is the following one:

This object is red all over its surface. ⊨ This object is not green all over its surface.

The mere logical form of these statements does not guarantee that the latter is a consequence of the former. In the first case, the consequence is apparently overly contaminated by the *world*, in the second rather by the specifics of the language, namely by the properties of colour predicates. The logical consequence should be truth preserving for deeper reasons, so to say. Etchemendy's criticism is based on his fundamentally different conception of logic and of consequence.

5.2.2 Representational versus interpretational semantics

According to Etchemendy, it is essential that we have to choose one of the three (in section 5.1.1) aforementioned kinds of robustness of truth preserving that distinguishes the logical consequence among the other types of consequence, namely the robustness against the changes in the world (which leads to representationalist semantics), against substitutions for non-logical expressions and against reinterpretations of these expressions (yielding substitutionalist and interpretationalist semantics). Now, there are proponents of all the three kinds of robustness and also those who doubt the soundness of the distinction between them. Tarski himself seemed to prefer the interpretational semantics, yet there are controversies about his actual intentions.

Both Etchemendy and Sher state repeatedly that their focus is not historic and does not concern the actual development of Tarski's thought, yet this does not prevent them from coming back time and again to small nuances in Tarsi's expressions in his writings. Indeed, there is a lot which can suggest that Tarski's approach was interpretational. First of all, he had his reasons to prefer it to the substitutional (the second of the three) one because it does not depend on the specific makeup of the language we are using, more concretely on the richness of its vocabulary. This differentiates Tarski's approach from that of Bolzano, even though we should remember that Bolzano did not countenance substitutions of expressions in some actual language but rather in what he conceived as an ideal language of thought (for a very good overview of the historical development, see the trilogy of articles Koreň (2014a, 2014b, 2014c)). As is pointed out by Sher (p. 137 of Sher 1991), we could imagine a language with *Sartre* and *Camus* as its only individual terms and *was active in French resistance* and *was a novelist* as its only predicates. Then the sentence *Sartre was active in the French resistance* would turn out to be a logical truth merely due to the scarceness of our vocabulary, which is surely an undesirable result (insofar as we can consider this fragment a language and speak of logical truth or even simple truth in it). The substitutional approach still has got its adherents, most notably Quine (1986). Recent defences of this approach include Dogramaci (2017) and McKeon (2004). It clearly has its merits in that it enables us to work with merely syntactic notions. But we will not discuss the respective merits and drawbacks of the interpretational and substitutional approach; we will more or less (for our purposes harmlessly) conflate them, though often we will slightly prefer the interpretational approach when contrasting it with the third, namely the representationalist, one.

We will focus on the distinction between what Etchemendy calls the *representational* and *interpretational* semantics. Tarski does seem to be an adherent of the merely interpretational approach. This would effectively involve reckoning with only one model, the one representing the whole world. A consequence is then logical when it does not depend on what is denoted in the actual world by the expressions involved in the statements. Tarski's exposition proceeding by the generalization of Klein's programme surely suggests that we speak of transformations of all the points in the world.[6] The article Tarski (1936) is also in this spirit. Yet both of these were actually lectures for a broader audience. It was therefore suggested that Tarski merely formulated his thoughts in a simpler manner and omitted some technical details, such as the plurality of models (this is suggested in Sher 1996).

Putting the historical question aside, it should be noted that the merely interpretational approach would surely be beneficial, as it would have reduced the concept of logical consequence to an overall much simpler concept. Tarski himself wanted his approach to clarify the concept of logical consequence without the need to get involved in difficult philosophical controversies regarding such notions as that of a possible state of affairs. When we start varying models in order to simulate the possible states the world could be in, we can hardly escape the mentioned controversies.

Etchemendy points out repeatedly that the merely interpretational approach cannot give an acceptable extension either of the concept of logical consequence or of logical truth. Indeed, if we have but one universe of discourse, namely the actual world, and if we have the standard logical constants of classical logic with equality, then the statement *There are at least two things* (formalized as

∃x∃y(x≠y)) will simply turn out to be logically true by this criterion, according to Etchemendy. He compiles many more interesting examples of the purported inadequacy of the Tarskian analysis.

But it is hard to comprehend why Etchemendy does not allow for the possibility of the Tarskian semantics as we know it, with the multiple models, and keeps reiterating that semantics must be either representational or interpretational. Etchemendy does not allow for the possibility of models containing non-existing entities, even though it is fairly obvious that we are free to reason about the model with a domain inhabited by nothing but unicorns, as was pointed out by Sher (1996) and Priest (1995). More importantly, though, it should be obvious enough that we cannot in every case judge whether a given model models rather the way the world might be or the way our language could work. To come back to Etchemendy's example of the sentence *There are at least two things*, we cannot say that its being true is simply an accident concerning what the world is like. We also make the sentence true by the way our language works, namely that we distinguish and name at least two things in the world. Yet we are perfectly free not to do so and thus think of a model with just one element of the domain.

Sher (1996) says, quite unsurprisingly, that it is clear to anyone who is acquainted with the model-theoretic semantics of classical logic that the models model the changes both of the world and of the language (MacFarlane (2000) prefers to say, very reasonably, that the various models model various *contexts*). This is entailed also by the impossibility to draw a clear distinction between the synthetic and analytic judgements, which we learned about not only from Quine (1951) but also from Sellars (1974) and others.[7] Yet Etchemendy came to favour what he sees as the representationalist approach later, namely in (Etchemendy 2008). In *The Concept of Logical Consequence*, he certainly seemed to prefer it to the interpretational one, yet still did not want to embrace it, as it suffered, according to him, from what he called *Tarski's fallacy*.

5.2.3 Whose fallacy?

All three approaches to logical consequence and truth – the representationalist, the substitutionalist and the interpretationalist – have their respective merits, yet the placing of them into three separate categories is rather doubtful (we have illustrated briefly how difficult it is to divide the representationalist and the interpretationalist ones, yet I think the same could be said also about the remaining two distinctions). There is nevertheless one thing they have in common which makes Etchemendy call them all *quantificational*. They all reduce logical truth and consequence to material truth and consequence together with some sort of a quantification over something, in the case of interpretational semantics over all the admissible reinterpretations of the non-logical vocabulary. A given sentence is a logical truth if it is true and all the admissible interpretational variants thereof are also true. Logical truth is thus in a way reduced to simple truth and in the same vein the logical consequence is reduced to material consequence.

Tarski thus implies that the truth of a universally quantified sentence guarantees the necessary (and, indeed, logical) truth of its instance, which is what Etchemendy calls *Tarski's fallacy*. Let us review the alleged fallacy for the case of consequence. We will mark the fact that a sentence φ is a consequence of the set of sentences Γ by the standard

$$\Gamma \vDash \varphi.$$

Now Tarski allegedly commits a fallacy concerning the modality (which we will now mark by $\Box$, yet this time we will rather use it just as a shortcut for the operator *necessarily* from English rather than for the operator of any of the modal logics). When Tarski attempts to prove that his analysis of logical consequence is correct, he has to prove the following:

If $\Gamma \vDash \varphi$, then $\Box$ (at least one of the statements from Γ is false or φ is true.).

Instead he merely succeeds at showing the following:

$\Box$ (If $\Gamma \vDash \varphi$, then at least one of the statements from Γ is false or φ is true.)

Put more concisely, he commits the simple mistake of interchanging $\Box(\varphi \to \phi)$ for the desired $\varphi \to \Box(\phi)$. What are we to make of this? Is Etchemendy justified in this strong criticism? Concerning Tarski himself, it is clearly difficult to resolve the controversy about what Tarski had in mind at which point. Yet it seems indeed very odd that a logician of his importance would fall prey to such a banal mistake. Here we can be quite in accordance with Sher (1996, p. 655).

The important question for us is whether the model theory can be accused of such a mistake and thus a misconception of the notion of logical consequence that it is trying to explicate. Etchemendy is worried that the Tarskian definition does not guarantee us the necessity of the consequence in question. It can be, he believes, just a mere chance that something is true in all the models, even if we use all the models we have, not just the one actual model Tarski possibly countenanced and which Etchemendy keeps insisting is the only admissible one for the Tarskian (i.e. according to Etchemendy's view of Tarski, an interpretationalist) conception.

Of course, we can speak of the various degrees of adequacy of a given model of some phenomenon. But it definitely seems that the Tarskian analysis does capture, by means of models, the various contexts we can get into rather well. As Tarski himself was aware, an analysis of a concept cannot match the concept completely; the explanation typically involves some adjustment by the definitions we adopt. Yet the models obviously enable us to speak of the various ways the world might be, of the various things it may contain and the properties we can ascribe them. Etchemendy's point is that logicality cannot be simply equated with generality. This is certainly in general true but Tarski was obviously after a specific kind of generality such that it enables us to do two things:

1. Identify the logical form of our propositions.
2. Make the logical consequence depend merely on this form.

The first condition is to be met when we get the right demarcation of logical constants, the second one can be realized afterwards, if we show that the logical truths do not depend on anything but the logical form. And this is exactly what the Tarskian analysis attempts to do by varying the models, that is changing both the domains and the realization of the extra-logical symbols. Sher herself expresses a slight reservation:

> The foundations of Tarskian semantics reach deep into metaphysics, but the link between models and reality may have some weak points. In particular, Tarski has never shown that the set-theoretic structures that make up models constitute adequate representations of all (formally) possible states of affairs. (Sher 1991, p. 139)

I myself doubt whether we can demand from an analysis that it represent all the possible states of affairs. Sher does attempt to prove so much both in Sher (1996) and in Sher (2008). Yet, besides the adequacy we have to consider also the simplicity of the explaining theory and in this respect the Tarskian analysis fares rather well. It thus cannot be refuted on the general grounds provided by Etchemendy, rather we have to judge it as to its ability to demarcate the logical constants in a reasonable way. Etchemendy does not pay much attention to the possibility of getting a demarcation which would justify the overall quantificational account; indeed he calls the very problem of logical constants a red herring in chapter 9 of *The Concept of Logical Consequence*. He remained faithful to this conviction even later:

> No selection of logical constants rules out the possibility discussed four paragraphs back: arguments that satisfy the reductive definition due to the *brute fact* that their instances preserve truth, but which do not display the guarantee of truth preservation that makes an argument genuinely valid. (Etchemendy 2008, p. 270)

He believes that all the expressions of a given language – not merely those from the set of purported logical constants – should be studied as to their inferential properties by logic. Actually, not only expressions of a language but also pictures such as a map of a city can have consequences (i.e. that town A is to the south of town B), according to Etchemendy (see p. 286 of Etchemendy 2008). This is in a way undisputable, but then we will, as we already noted, run the logical entailment together with other kinds of necessary entailment, at least with the analytical one. This would rob logic of its purported generality and formality. Surely one is free to reconsider the fundamental properties of *logic* and what one wants it to deliver but I believe we should try to find such a usage of the word *logic* which would retain as much as possible of the traditional intuitions regarding the discipline, in particular those suggesting that it is a discipline very central for our rationality.[8] Etchemendy's proposal seems to depart from the traditional line of thought about logic (surely much more than Tarski). Thus we have seen that the most prominent external attack on the Tarskian approach does not succeed, and it will be rather the internal critique of the *Tarski-Sher thesis* that we should consider in order to see how good a criterion for delimiting logic it actually provides.

5.3 Internal objections

The objections coming from inside the *Tarski-Sher* movement are mostly concerned with how exactly the relationship between logic and mathematics should be conceived. One of the problems concerns the extent of logic and the desideratum that it be even above mathematics as to its formality and generality. The other concerns are in regard to the problem of the foundations of logic and its potential dependency on set-theory and, what is particularly pressing, on its undecided problems. Logic as demarcated by the Tarski-Sher criterion thus, according to some, fails to be the discipline which it should be, namely the one which is constitutive of rationality as such (recall the relevant kind of formality of logic invoked by MacFarlane which we mentioned in section 4.5.1.).

5.3.1 Once more about the relationship between logic and mathematics

We have already noted that lots of the authors interested in demarcating logical constants and logic as such are very much concerned with the question whether Frege's logicism is a correct view of the relationship between logic and mathematics. Tarski remains somewhat reserved about this issue, but Sher claims that her approach to demarcating logic actually vindicates logicism, though she comes to that conclusion from a rather different direction than Frege. Instead of showing that mathematics is a part of logic, she attempts to show rather that logic is a part of mathematics. We should just cautiously remind ourselves that for Frege it was just arithmetic, not the whole of mathematics (he was particularly eager to highlight that he thought differently of geometry in his letters to Hilbert), that he wanted to look into the question as to whether it is not a part of logic and he saw the discovery of a contradiction in his system as a sign that his logicist thesis was false.

The newer authors rather think that after the development of logic and mathematics, which made them safer from paradoxes, the time has come to merge the disciplines as they doubt there are any principled reasons to distinguish them. Yet given that Frege's own project failed, we should be wary about these tendencies. Both Frege and his heirs are blowing logic up; they are making it broader than the orthodoxy of the time considers it to be. We have already noted that the Tarski-Sher thesis has some solid philosophical motivation; it captures our intuition that logic should be general and formal. Indeed, the *Tarski-Sher thesis* says that formality and generality are in essence one and the same thing, although Dennis Bonnay thinks otherwise and considers Tarski as a proponent of the generality of logic, while Sher, according to Bonnay, is convinced rather of its formality. Nevertheless, their approaches are co-extensional which, according to Bonnay, serves as a witness for the philosophical well-foundedness of the approach:

> Both arguments[9] converge towards permutation invariance, and the convergence is non-trivial. As a matter of fact, the intuitive starting points are different, but both arguments conclude on the basis of the formalization of these intuitions that invariance under permutation is the right criterion to characterize logicality. This agreement suggests that Tarski's thesis is conceptually well-motivated. (Bonnay 2008, p. 36)

Yet both Bonnay and Feferman take issue with the *Tarski-Sher thesis* and more generally with logicism, both for similar reasons. Feferman brings three principal objections (see Feferman 2010, p. 10):

1. The thesis assimilates logic to mathematics, more specifically to set-theory.
2. The set-theoretic notions involved in explaining the semantics of unrestricted logic are not robust.
3. No natural explanation is given of what constitutes the same logical operation over arbitrary basic domains.

Feferman in fact had already brought about in Feferman (1999) one very interesting result, namely that the *unrestricted logic* (UL) demarcated by the criterion of Tarski and Sher in fact contains the full second-order logic. He proves, using McGee's results about UL, that the quantifier $\forall X$, quantifying over all the subsets of the given domain can be expressed in UL. This result helps us to see more clearly what the relationship between logic and mathematics looks like if we accept UL as the true logic. A great survey of the mathematical properties of second-order logic can be found in Shapiro (1991). I do not intend to repeat these results to any large extent, let me mention just one which became particularly popular. Cantor's continuum hypothesis claiming that there is no set cardinality between $\aleph_0$ and $2^{\aleph_0}$, that is that $\aleph_1 = 2^{\aleph_0}$, is decided by second-order logic, either the hypothesis or its negation is a logical truth of second-order logic, though we do not know which one.

This suggests that the second-order logic and then of course also UL are deciding about something they should keep open and let more specific disciplines decide about. Already Etchemendy complained about the overgeneration due to the Tarskian analysis of logical truth and consequence and here we see the problem re-emerge, though in a more concrete shape. UL, according to some authors, overgenerates because it takes over too much from mathematics and particularly set-theory.

5.3.1.1 Further objections

Why is it an issue that logic swallows a lot of mathematics in this way? Feferman admits that various views are possible on whether and how logic and mathematics should be divided:

> It will evidently depend on one's gut feelings about the nature of logic as to whether this is considered objectionable or not. For Sher, to take one example, that is no problem. (Feferman 2010, p. 10)

Sher (2008) criticizes Feferman for relying merely on his *gut feeling* when he expresses his disapproval of the idea of making logic so vast as to include the set-theory. Bonnay, on the other hand, sees the UL as obviously plagued by the problem of overgeneration. Is there anything else besides our personal taste which could tell us whether and how logic and mathematics should be distinguished? Before proceeding to the discussion of the issue, let us explain more the other two objections Feferman presented against UL.

The second of Feferman's objections concerns the fact that UL incorporates also the set-theoretic notions which are not robust. This means in our case that besides swallowing the set-theory, UL also has to answer some of the questions that standard set-theory (with the Zermelo-Frankel axiomatization) cannot decide, such as the continuum hypothesis. Thus, logic not only overtakes some of the work of mathematics but makes both stronger at the same time by uniting the two.

The third objection Feferman comes up with is that UL actually includes – that is counts them as logical constants – operators which behave differently on universes of different sizes. In fact, by moving from the invariance under the permutation of a given domain to invariance under bijections between domains, we have safeguarded ourselves from such unwelcome logical constants as McGee's *wombat disjunction*, yet there are others lurking. The logical notions are now, as to their logicality, not dependent on the one universe but on the size of a universe in general.

We can thus still have, as we mentioned earlier in this chapter, a logical constant $\forall_\exists$ which behaves just as the universal quantifier on the domains of our preferred cardinality, say on all the finite ones, and as the existential one on the others. As the bijection compares the behaviour only between the universes of the same size, this quantifier will clearly be counted as logical by the *Tarski-Sher* demarcation criterion. Typically, this is seen as a problem for UL, as such a quantifier appears to be quite irrelevant and useless for logic. The existential and the universal quantifier certainly appear to be fulfilling an important role, for example, in mathematics. But can we really imagine such a mixed quantifier to be of any use? Besides this pragmatic point, as perhaps there could be some rare use to be made of such a quantifier, there is a strong intuition that logic should contain just those laws of reasoning which are fundamental for our rationality in general. Both Feferman and Bonnay surely see the presence of the operators the behaviour of which changes with the cardinality of the domain to which it is applied as a big problem, indeed as a refutation of UL, yet Sher herself remains unmoved. She bites the bullet and embraces these operators, claiming that there is nothing wrong with them:

> My point is not that there is no value in a specific concept of natural operator (or natural connection between an operator's behaviour in different universes), but such a concept has nothing much to do with our idea of logicality. . . . All and only formal operators are logical and each logical operator describes one way in which an operator takes into account some formal features of a given situation. Thus all logical operators are unified in being formal, and a logical operator is the same in different universes. . . . Since the size of the universe is a basic formal feature of objectual situations, it is – and should be – a central parameter of some objectual formal operators. (Sher 2008, pp. 333–4)

To complete our picture of the controversies and enable us to make a qualified judgement about the opinions of the rivalling parties, we yet have to mention that Bonnay and Feferman come with their demarcation criteria which are similar in spirit with the *Tarski-Sher thesis*, yet differ from it both as to their philosophical motivation and even more by their results.

5.3.2 Other invariance(s)

Both Feferman and Bonnay came up with different invariance criteria that in different ways satisfy the bulk of the desiderata Feferman spelled out in the three objections to the *Tarski-Sher thesis*. We will mention only the criterion due to Feferman, as it is representative enough and Bonnay's criterion would force us to digress too much. Remember that he wanted to get a demarcation which would not make logic swallow too much of mathematics, use only absolute set-theoretic notions and also connect the behaviour of the connectives on different universes. He achieves that by considering rather homomorphisms as the maps under which the logical notions should be invariant.

Definition 5.3.1. An operation Q is logical-F^{10} iff it is invariant under any surjective homomorphism between universes.

This criterion makes logic ignore not only the identity but also the number of objects. The homomorphism is required to be surjective, yet not one to one. More objects can be mapped on a single object. This demarcation criterion has got very different results from the one we were discussing so far. What gets counted as logical by this criterion is the existential quantifier, the universal one, the standard connectives. So far so good, yet also for example the operator WF on relations which holds of the well-founded ones. On the other hand, all the non-standard quantifiers are out, as well as the relation of identity. Feferman himself has got mixed feelings about this result. He surely believes it to be better than that of the other demarcation, yet still the system thus demarcated is not a standard one. Not fully embracing his own criterion, Feferman admits:

> I have been moving more and more to the position that the classical first-order predicate logic has a privileged role in our thought, and so I have been looking at various arguments which justify or challenge that position. (Feferman 1999, p. 32)

He then envisages ways of adapting his criterion so as to get to the demarcation he desires; the moves he proposes are limiting ourselves to the unary quantifiers, that is those of type <1>. This would have the effect of getting rid of the quantifier WF. Furthermore, there is also the possibility of going a little bit ad hoc and simply postulating the identity relation as a further logical constant. Of course, the opinion on the logicality of equality differed historically; there were authors who did not consider it as logical (for example, Quine), yet the first-order logic with equality has the advantage of being able to define the quantifiers speaking of finite cardinalities. With these devices, we can draw an interesting line between logic and mathematics by saying that logic contains what can be said about arithmetic finitistically, while speaking about such things as in the sets of natural numbers already transcends the realm of mere logic (and possibly requires us to use some specifically mathematical epistemic capacities, such as Kantian pure intuition). Nevertheless, Feferman's approach obviously makes one suspicious of some circularity. Sher accuses Feferman of being partial and in advance decided to twist the criteria so as to get the classical first-order logic. Van Benthem says as much:

> The choice of the homomorphisms as the relevant equivalence relation invests precisely the amount of indifference needed to engineer the landing in monadic first-order logic. I conclude that Sol's account has its merits, but changes nothing in the general limitations of invariance approaches. But to me, this is not a bug, but a feature! (van Benthem 2002, p. 434)

There are many other authors who bring different variants of the invariance criterion and deserve serious discussion, such as Bonnay's approach using potential isomorphisms as the mappings under which the logical notions should be invariant.[11] We nevertheless will not go deeper into the variety of proposals which emerged since Tarski presented his thesis. Let us rather ponder on the respective merits of the two basic approaches presented so far and on how we can decide between them and potentially other invariance criteria.

5.3.3 Comparing the criteria

Have the demarcations that we saw helped us somehow to understand what is and what is not logic? Can we make better sense of the plurality of logics thanks to them? And can we compare them as regards their merits?

The first thing which is bound to strike us is that many of the logics that have been developed have not really been taken into consideration by any of the proposed criteria for demarcation. How about the modal logics? Or even more simply, what about the intuitionistic logic? Neither of the criteria gives us a real answer as to their adequacy as logics. It is true that these demarcations should probably be seen as purported solutions merely to the problem of logical constants, yet it is clear that as they stand they block, for instance, the intuitionistic interpretation of the connectives. To be fair, we must repeat that there are really lots of demarcations based on invariance criteria and some of them (which we omit in order not to divert us too much) can give us a reasonable answer also regarding these logics. Moreover, more proposals can still come in the future, the study is continuing. These results can undoubtedly tell us many interesting things about logical systems. But can we really expect them to give a good sense to the plurality of logics and give a good meaning to the word *logic* in face of the plurality?

Let us assess the debate between Feferman and Sher. Which of the criteria is really better? By the way, Sher seems to be much more convinced about her demarcation than Feferman, who admits:

> Despite the various appealing results above, and despite my personal feeling that the logical operations do not go beyond those represented in FOL,[12] I do not find the various arguments for logicality based on any of the invariance notions considered here convincing in their own right. (Feferman 2010, p. 18)

What then is the verdict about the formality of logic that all these criteria are supposed to capture? Sher claims that her approach is the more principled one, being well founded on the idea of logic being a science of the formal. The character of logic appears to her to be something very objective and strongly independent of us and of how logic could be important specifically for us. As we already saw, the naturalness of the expressions demarcated has, according to her, nothing to do with their logicality, so that we do not have to worry about the expressions which behave differently on universes of different cardinalities. Feferman, on the other hand, is more open to the idea that we can have various demarcations and the notions of formality and generality can be interpreted in different and equally justified ways.

When we look at the original Kantian ideas about the one sense in which logic should be formal, as highlighted by MacFarlane, we can hardly use them to decide whether one of the two approaches is somehow more appropriate. Perhaps Sher's approach can boast somewhat more simplicity and being a bit more directly linked to the Kantian idea of ignoring the individual identities. Yet numbers can be still seen as specific objects of a higher order and cardinality should also be something logic should abstract from.

When Sher claims that Tarski's and her approach are, unlike the alternatives of Feferman and others, philosophically well founded, she makes no small leap to arrive at such a conclusion. When concentrating specifically on Feferman, she tries to engender the impression that while she constructs her logic from the idea of logic as the most general and formal science, Feferman merely relies on some arbitrary *gut feelings* (exploiting the passage from Feferman we already quoted), which leads him to be partial in favour of classical logic. Yet she takes for granted that logic should be formal and general and both these properties should be understood in the sense spelled out by the *Tarski-Sher thesis*. Given that there are more possibilities of how to understand both these notions, she appears to be also heavily relying on something not much more reliable than the infamous *gut feelings*.

5.3.4 Topic neutrality? The debate's impasse

As we mentioned, the logic of Tarski and Sher contains also the full second-order logic, and thus also a lot of set-theory. We tend to think that logic should be topic-neutral in that it contains nothing specific for any given area of discourse but merely the most general rules which are binding for any discourse whatsoever. Can we then say of set-theory that it is no specific discourse? Here we come again to the question of logicism; that is, the question whether and how logic and mathematics should be divided. Yet this discussion does not seem to be a very well-founded one. For Frege, the discussion about logicism may well have seemed to be meaningful because during his lifetime (and to a significant degree due to him) logic was merely beginning to become an unstable notion. Yet since his time, because of the plurality of logics, it is not clear anymore about which logic we are asking if it contains mathematics or is contained by it. Similarly, it is far from given that mathematics forms a unified body of science with clear boundaries, though we can perhaps afford to regard as mathematics everything which can be reconstructed in set-theory (though we would also have to specify which set-theory we really mean, as there are more non-equivalent axiomatizations of set-theory besides the most standard ZFC). Overall, I cannot see why one of the answers to the problem of logicism should be preferable independently of our demarcation of logic and how the one or another stance to the question should motivate us to demarcate logic in some specific way. Thus, neither Feferman nor Sher helps their positions very much by invoking their preferred stances on logicism.

It was thanks to Frege's way of looking at logic and mathematics and his study of their relationship that both the disciplines developed. In fact, as the various different logics developed, such as first-order and second-order logic, we should rather say that there is hardly a universal answer to the question of logicism that is available. When asking how much mathematics should be contained in logic, and thus whether we should rather prefer first- or second-order logic, Sher's UL or some other logic as the most correct one, we should ask ourselves what specific role logic should play in our overall discourse. I do not see that question being posed either by Sher or by Feferman; in the case of Sher it appears as if any such pragmatic question is irrelevant for her, as logicality is something completely independent of us and our epistemic or other pursuits.

Clearly when we make logic and mathematics coincide, asking about the importance of logic would be the same as asking about the importance of mathematics. And perhaps it is not as difficult to say what mathematics is good for, as it is applied by the natural sciences which obviously have a bearing on how we cope with the world we live in. Yet such an answer does not tell us very much, as it is guilty of appealing to the flat holism that Dummett warned against. The question thus has to be asked if we can say something more specific about the role of logic.

5.3.5 Foundationalism

So as not to be accused of leaving the demarcations based on invariance criteria too hastily, we should also mention a further set of arguments for and against the second-order logic and with it also UL. These arguments have again to do with the relationship between logic and mathematics. Some of the logics are said to correspond to the mathematical practice better than the others.

There are authors who have argued that first-order logic is not suitable for capturing mathematical reasoning and we should in fact adopt second-order logic (see Boolos (1975), Shapiro (1991 and 1996)). They base their argument mainly on the expressive weakness of first-order logic, as it cannot describe the structures which mathematicians study. Thus, for example, the structure of natural numbers cannot be described in a first-order language, as is witnessed by the fact that no theory can have only the structure of natural numbers as its model up to isomorphism. This is a consequence of the compactness theorem already but the undescribability of the structure is rendered even stronger by the celebrated Gödel's incompleteness theorem. Mathematicians, nevertheless, according to Shapiro, have a definite idea of the structure of natural numbers and they certainly know what they are talking about when they discuss its properties. The non-standard models are thus a phenomenon which is uncalled for and we should prefer the stronger logic which enables us to dispense with them:

> The purpose of formal axiomatization is to codify mathematical practice, one of whose purposes is the description and communication of structures. I conclude that a language and semantics of formalization should be sufficient to insure this communication. That is, the language of formalization should allow categorical characterizations.[13] It follows that first-order axiomatizations are inadequate. (Shapiro 1996, p. 720)

Interesting though Shapiro's argument is insofar as it contains valuable insights about mathematical practice, I do not see why we should be convinced that the aim of logic is to describe just those structures which mathematicians talk about. Furthermore, when mathematicians and logicians want to talk about the standard model of arithmetic, they are certainly free to do so simply by omitting the non-standard ones from their discussion. Shapiro is right that the debates about the size of the power set of the set of natural numbers (which is not robust in the sense required by Feferman, that is claims about the size are independent of standard set-theory) and thus the continuum hypothesis can be ignored in many of the debates concerned purely with number theory. So far so good, but why should it entail that it is preferable to adopt second-order logic rather than the first-order one?

Those who oppose second-order logic like to point out that as such it contains not only a lot of mathematics but also a lot of problematic mathematics. The continuum hypothesis is a nice example. It is something which is normally unsettled by set-theory, and it speaks against the second-order logic that it contains either the positive or negative answer to this hypothesis as a logical truth. Shapiro labels such views as *foundationalism*, claiming that their proponents are beholden to the mistaken idea of making logic an infallible and perfectly clear foundation of all of our knowledge. He invokes Wittgenstein's reflections on the groundlessness of our language games to show that there is nothing strange about logic containing problematic assertions. Gila Sher similarly denies, almost already in the title of her article (Sher 1999), that logic should be the science of the obvious, because when we make a theory of the logical then we already explicate it and make it dependent on the explication provided, that is in an important sense not obvious or founding every other kind of knowledge. So much appears to be undisputable and both Sher and Shapiro make a good point, yet only very theoretically. They in fact act, as if there could be no degree of the solidness of the foundations of a given science and as if Wittgenstein's reflections led to the conclusion that all the foundations of our language games and particularly of logic are equally good.

Actually every science should be solidly founded, though the solidness of its foundations can be assessed in various ways and could be always improved. Yet, in order for the science to be able to emerge at all, this securing of its foundations has to stop somewhere. It is up to the judgement of those who create a given science to get the right foundation. Possibly multiple foundations can be right, yet not all are equal. And if logic should in any way serve mathematics, I doubt it does it very well by discarding the non-standard models of prominent mathematical theories at the cost of containing mathematically substantial claims such as the continuum hypothesis. Yet let us not forget that we have not clarified what the role of logic should be and specifically how it should serve mathematics. Still, I do not see why the non-standard models should be a problem. Besides the fact that the study of these could be itself interesting, their existence tells us something about the standard one as well. It tells us how it is related to our reasoning and gives us at least the negative information of how we do not epistemologically access it.

5.3.6 Prejudiced demarcation?

While reviewing the exchanges between authors such as Gila Sher and Solomon Feferman, we saw that Feferman had the tendency, so much criticized by Sher, to prefer a demarcation which demarcates classical logic rather than any other system. It is clear that such an approach can be criticized for being prejudiced. If we are trying to figure out which of the systems really deserve to have the status of logic, it appears that we should be neutral at the beginning, merely examine what the criteria for being a logic are and after settling on that say which logics actually fulfil these very criteria. This is the way Sher wants to proceed and wants us to perceive her demarcation as such an unprejudiced one.

Classical logic, on the other hand, certainly has a special status in the community of logicians. It is the logic we standardly learn as first one and we can hardly ignore the impression that starting with any other logic would be much more difficult, though possible. The other logics appear to be a variation on the classical propositional logic and the classical first-order logic. First-order logic developed relatively late, we can read a very good summary of this important part of the history of logic in Shapiro (1991). This development, as Shapiro emphasizes, was by no means a straightforward one. Shapiro takes this as a sign of the contingency of classical logic, yet we can also take it as a sign that the shape of classical logic was arrived at by a lot of consideration and work in logic and mathematics.

These historical developments and the common practice of seeing classical logic as central in the community of logicians are certainly not great reasons to somehow prefer it over all the other logics. The major part of the community may very well be engaging in a misguided practice, yet without further argument we should rather suppose this not to be the case. Rather, we reckon with the collective rationality of the logicians and with the cogency of the development of logic. Of course, if this were all, we could simply say that which particular logic is a real logic is decided by the popularity of the logics. Instead of this absurd assertion I merely want to say that when we are discussing the respective merits of various demarcations, the standardness of the logics thus demarcated is, *ceteris paribus*, an asset.

On the one hand, it can hardly be denied that we have some, if vague, ideas of what logic should be independent of the various systems. Thus, we can point to the systems which fulfil these criteria or create new ones that are better suited; on the other hand, we want the demarcation in part just to bring some order into the spontaneous development of logics. We claim that the uncontrolled plurality of logics threatens us with confusion and unclarity as to what logic is and should be. Thus a demarcation should overall improve our conceptual scheme by bringing more order to it. Yet, as Quine always kept emphasizing, minimal mutilation of our standing theoretical framework is, again *ceteris paribus*, also something we should seek. Therefore, even though Sher's criterion might be somewhat more systematic than Feferman's (and even that is disputable), it is by no means clear whether this outweighs the exotic character of what we would get as logic by her criterion. And furthermore, her system also has significant faults of its own. Consider that UL has got an infinite number of quantifiers, actually containing, among other quantifiers, all the cardinality quantifiers corresponding to every cardinal. This appears to be very strange if we expect logic to be in some way relatively fundamental. Again, the extreme foundationalism Shapiro denounces is probably misguided, and, as Sher emphasizes, logic does not have to be the science of the obvious (much less a trivial science), yet inflating it in this way can hardly be warranted and beneficiary.

Yet any such expectations have to come from some source and we have to examine what it is that logic should achieve. Both Sher's and Feferman's demarcation are very interesting and can be potentially very useful for our reasoning, be it purely mathematical or also philosophical, about logic and its relationship with mathematics. But still they cannot philosophically support themselves, being built upon excessively vague intuitions about logic which have to be critically examined.

Even if we accept that one of the criteria really demarcates logic as the most general science, it still remains an open question why we need such a discipline. Would such a science not be a mere residuum of the other useful ones, which are useful precisely because they speak about something specific, while logic does not speak about anything (in accordance with the *Tarski-Sher thesis*)? It becomes clear that we cannot rest content with the framework of invariance demarcations and must move the discussion in a different direction. We have to investigate the role of logic more independently of the specifically mathematical presuppositions of these demarcations.

6

The role of logic

We have already generally examined the possibilities of changing our overall theoretical framework. We had to undertake this in order to counter the charges against logical pluralism which claim that we actually cannot change our logic. We have helped ourselves by using the Wittgensteinian metaphor of the pillars of a building and asked whether these could be changed. Inspired by the example of geometry and its pluralism, we have ventured to consider logic from a more holistic perspective, linking it thus to mathematics and asking what their relationship should be like. We faced a dilemma in that we did not know how to decide between the rival logics; we did not know what the criteria for the validity of logical laws were. In the case of geometry the situation was a little bit different. Euclidean geometry was strongly preferred over its rivals; it was obviously a good geometry and we rather wanted to see if the other systems could be called geometries, as well. When we changed our perspective on geometry and realized its interconnectedness with mechanics, we could appreciate that the alternative systems could reasonably work with corresponding adjustments in mechanics. The overall theories which contained both one of the non-Euclidean geometries and adjusted mechanics could equally well explain the world we see.

In logic we did not have a comparably strong and obvious preference for one of the systems. Clearly, the more familiar ones feel more natural but this slight hunch does not seem to prevent us from giving serious consideration to alternative ones as well. We noticed that there was an obvious candidate for doing for us the service that mechanics did for geometry, namely mathematics, especially set-theory. It is clear that the development of modern mathematics and logic are intimately intertwined and logic has become mathematical since the nineteenth century both in the sense that it uses more mathematical methods than before and also because it becomes unclear what the difference between logic and mathematics is. Frege was the one who clearly saw this and therefore formulated his proposal of logicism.

More recent authors who approached the problem of the plurality of logics in a way similar to ours tried to demarcate logic using specifically set theoretical invariance criteria. We saw that such demarcations can be quite succinctly formulated and yield interesting results. Yet we could not really rest content with them. Here is the summary of the issues we had with these demarcations:

1. The logicality of many of the prominent systems in fact remained fully undecided. Even intuitionistic logic was automatically put aside.
2. Despite the apparently clear general idea behind the invariance approach, it could have been spelled out in more ways, such as Sher's as opposed to Feferman's. We could not see how to adjudicate between these rival demarcations.

This showed us that these demarcations need a deeper philosophical foundation, without which they cannot really help us to get a clearer idea of logic in face of the plurality. This led us to our ultimate criticism and, for the time being, abandonment of the approach based on the final objection:

3. The approaches do not specify what the role of logic should be.

This final objection in fact explains the reason for the second one. As we have so far little idea about what we want logic to achieve, we cannot expect the invariance criterion to give us a satisfactory demarcation of logic. This does not mean that we have to reject the criterion; it is still too early to do that. We rather just state that, as of itself, the criterion is insufficient and needs a deeper philosophical foundation.

It is because of this need for a deeper philosophical foundation that we will not yet consider further attempts at demarcation of logical constants and logic which have been pursued since Gentzen in the framework of proof-theory. These proposals will be examined after we delve into the question of the role of logic and try to find a reasonable account of it.

The issue of utility of logic is a real one. It is by no means clear what logic should be good for, despite any initial intuitions. We have a tendency to say that logic is concerned with correct thinking or rather reasoning. Yet one could pile up examples of logical inferences par excellence validated by the most common systems of logic which can hardly be said to help us in our reasoning. Let us merely consider the rules which are typically used for the connectives in the sequent calculus of classical logic. Let us see, for example, the right rule for conjunction:[1]

$$\frac{\Gamma \Rightarrow A \quad \Delta \Rightarrow B}{\Gamma, \Delta \Rightarrow A \wedge B} \Rightarrow \wedge$$

The left rule, then, is:

$$\frac{\Gamma, A, \Sigma \Rightarrow \Delta}{\Gamma, A \wedge B, \Sigma \Rightarrow \Delta} \Leftarrow \wedge \qquad \frac{\Gamma, B, \Sigma \Rightarrow \Delta}{\Gamma, A \wedge B, \Sigma \Rightarrow \Delta} \Leftarrow \wedge$$

Obviously, the bottom sequents do not tell us anything new, all was already present in the sequents we started with. If we accept the standard structural rules of weakening, then both the rules for conjunction on the left are fairly obvious. The same holds for the rule for conjunction on the right. In fact, the conjunction just says what the comma already said, but on the level of the object language, as it were, not on the level of meta-language. All the other rules share this feature of conjunction. Indeed, the logical constants were famously called *punctuation marks* by Wittgenstein in Tractatus[2] (and this idea was then used for the conception of sequent calculus rules by Kosta Došen (1989)). The form of these rules should again make us wonder about the utility of logic, if this be logic.

In fact, there have indeed been sceptics about the utility of logic. A famous and classical example is Descartes, who wrote:

> I found that, as for logic, its syllogisms and the majority of its other precepts are of avail rather in the communication of what we already know. (Descartes 1999, part 2, paragraph 6)

As is noted by Vojtěch Kolman, Descartes did not merely show scepticism towards logic in its historical shape, but also towards the very idea of logic (see page 9 of Kolman (2002)).

All these rules appear to bring nothing new. We already know what the conclusion tells us before we apply the rule. Similarly, if you consider the standard model-theoretic definitions of the validity of a formula in a given model, they all appear to be mere platitudes, or even circular definitions.

Indeed, there are reasons to suspect that logic tells us only what is obvious and is thus, pace Sher, indeed the science of the obvious.

Similarly, the invariance criteria, if we were to accept them, can make one wonder what such a discipline as logic thus demarcated could be good for, as it tells us what holds no matter what we talk about. Does logic tell us something new? Wittgenstein suggested in *Tractatus* that the truths of logic are mere by-products of our language. It would of itself be an interesting fact that our languages have these by-products or, even more, that perhaps any language is bound to have such a by-product. But it behoves us to ask if we can find a better understanding of the role of logic, one which would show how it can actually be useful.

6.1 One more attempt at logicism

There is an option regarding the explanation of the role of logic which would lead us back to the *Tarski-Sher thesis*. We could say that, being a part of mathematics, the question about the utility of logic is then the same as the question about the utility of mathematics. Should we be perplexed about the utility of mathematics in the same way we are about that of logic? Hardly. Even though no clear-cut answer presents itself, it is rather because of how much – and not how little – we obviously use mathematics in multifarious branches and spheres of our lives. Logic, then, simply is a part of mathematics.

This line of thought practically makes logic disappear as a self-standing discipline. The very idea of logic is thus declared as flawed. This line of thought is ultimately possible; it basically uses the holistic move of subsuming logic under a broader discipline and then declares its role to be a part of the broader role of the larger discipline. Yet logic still appears to be a self-standing discipline which can be distinguished from other branches of mathematics such as geometry, arithmetic or algebra by its specific subject, namely correct reasoning. This is witnessed also by the institutional divisions of scientific departments in the academia. Furthermore, logic has got a venerable tradition as a self-standing discipline. Surely its development has changed it over the centuries in many ways. The tradition of seeing the development as continuous might be criticized, yet the burden of proof is rather on the side of the critics of the idea of logic as a self-standing discipline than otherwise. And even if we make logic into a part of mathematics, we should have an idea of how it differs from the other mathematical disciplines.

The option of saying that the role of logic cannot be specified can be suspected of using holism too excessively. It should be rather our last recourse, only after we investigate the possibilities to say something more concrete about the utility of logic itself and find all of them illusory. Let us now consider what the other possibilities are.

6.2 Logic as the bounds of reason

The proposal we are going to discuss now is different from the *Tarski-Sher thesis*, yet it is also based on regarding logic as fundamental for our very rationality. This time the thesis is that logic is the discipline which studies the most general traits of our reasoning, in fact those which we have to obey in order to reason rationally at all.

6.2.1 Various rules for reasoning

Obviously there are many ways in which our reasoning can be said to fail to follow some important rules and thus cease to be rational. We can imagine someone who says something absurd, for example, that the earth is flat. If the utterer of such a proposition grew up in our society, we would obviously have a hard time understanding how he or she could say something like that, yet we could still try to explain to the person concerned that she is actually wrong.

People could violate much more fundamental laws of reasonable thought, though. If someone says that eight is divisible by two, yet it is no even number, we would have to explain to the person the meanings of the words he used and some basic facts about arithmetics. The problem with the person would be more serious than the previous one, yet not incurable. And most importantly, in both of these cases we could say that the person was indeed still reasoning, though in a flawed and very confused manner.

Now if a person says something which contradicts the laws of logic, there apparently ceases to be anything intelligible in her words. The violation of the rules of reasoning is so crude that we cannot really count the reasoning with logical failures as real reasoning at all. Overall, there appear to be degrees of errors in reasoning, some of them thus being more grave than the other ones.

Caution is needed here, as what we are hinting at might create the impression that logic always has got to be obvious, even banal. Yet clearly we can imagine complicated and recondite logical consequences of a logical theory which looks simple. And surely, the best of the best logicians can be mistaken about such consequences. The very fact that people can differ in their expertise in logic shows us that logic cannot be understood as the science of the most banal truisms. Yet these remarks still do not anyhow falsify the hypothesis that logic is the science of the most fundamental traits of our reasoning.

Thus there is a hopeful conjecture that logic might be the science of the rules which are necessary for any reasoning at all, for rationality in general. Indeed, this is one of the senses given to the formality of logic by MacFarlane.[3] Let us now sum up the conception in the following way:

> (BL) Logic is the science which examines the rules that we must obey in order to be reasoning at all.

6.2.2 What about the plurality?

So far the thesis BL which we have just formulated appears to be excluding logical pluralism and suggesting that we have to examine the bounds of reason (or acceptable silliness) in order to determine the real logical rules. During our whole investigation we in general prefer not to jettison logical pluralism but rather to make sense of it. And, contrary to the first impression, this can be done, while also sticking with BL.

There is nothing shocking about the idea of a discipline having unsharp boundaries. It may well be unclear what the boundary between sociology and political science is, as well as between geometry and mechanics or, as we have already discussed, between mathematics and logic. By the same token there is nothing mysterious about the idea that our rationality as such might have an unclear boundary. The unclarity of the boundary does not mean its non-existence. Nor should we reject the talk of rationality as such, because the region thereof is extremely complicated and varied.

When we accept the possibility that our idea of rationality as such can be unsharp, then it is only natural to suppose that the theoretical explication thereof can be achieved in more than one way. This can then lead to a plurality of logics. But we should stress that our case is somewhat more complicated than that of the boundaries of the specific disciplines we talked about.

When we spoke about the unclarity of the boundaries between geometry and mechanics, the situation was similar to that of having a map of some area, on which we want to draw a borderline between two countries. We are not disputing about anything else on the map, we are happy with the way it depicts the territory in question. For our purposes it is just fine.

In the case of the boundaries of reason, it is rather the case that besides arguing about the borderline between logic and other disciplines on the map, we are discussing which of the various maps is the one on which the borderline is supposed to be drawn. Logic is in a way both on the map and the map itself on which it is. The maps among which we are choosing all purport to depict the various kinds of knowledge, which include our knowledge of the facts of biology, mathematics and the like. Furthermore, they also surely include some logical laws and truths, as well. Yet we are not sure which ones exactly. Therefore, it appears that we cannot find our way just by trying to understand logic as the science of the bounds of reason as such because we do not have a clear picture of the reason the bounds of which should be drawn by logic. Because of the double role of logic in demarcating rationality, that is its being both on every map of the territory of our reason and being this very map itself, the idea of demarcating it in this way appears to be fundamentally confused.

Yet, the general idea still must have something to it; logic seems to be something at the very bottom of our argumentation practices. Nevertheless, we saw right now that the quest for the bounds of reason cannot be pursued any more easily than that for the demarcation of logic. Some of the disputes about the demarcation of logic in fact do resemble those about drawing a reasonable borderline between some disciplines. The debates between model-theoretic demarcators have the form of looking for the right distinction between logic and mathematics.

But at least when logics, which differ in the sense in which classical logic differs from intuitionistic logic (that is, logics which share logical constants), are discussed, we see that matters get more complicated and we are in a situation when we have to look not only for a borderline but also for a map on which to draw. These considerations will nevertheless be useful for us later. For the moment, though, let us note that we have at least started casting doubts on the seemingly obvious thesis that BL is incompatible with logical pluralism.

But more work will be needed to actually show that logical pluralism can be maintained together with BL. Now let us consider another objection to the approach we are pursuing now.

6.2.3 Certainty

Lots of logical truths and laws indeed have the status of something which we cannot reasonably dispute about because they are so extremely certain. We thus tentatively formulated the thesis BL, claiming that logic should be the science of that which we cannot doubt. An important disclaimer is needed here. Of course, the thesis is meant in the normative sense that logic should examine that which we cannot doubt if we are to reason at all. If we violate the logical laws, our discourse loses the status of a reasonable one and it is to be refuted. Yet, of course, we can commit and in fact we commonly commit logical errors. Being normative and not descriptive, the thesis BL does not force us to embrace the patently false conclusion that we cannot commit a logical error, it explains that committing it means jeopardizing one's own status as a reasoner (at least for the present debate).

But there is a different problem we have to face, namely that BL might be too liberal and would also admit that which we do not want to include into logic. Throughout his *Über Gewissheit* (Wittgenstein 1984 [1969]), Wittgenstein speaks about various kinds of knowledge that we can hardly lack as reasonable human beings. Yet he chooses such knowledge which many would traditionally say can be doubted, such as the knowledge of one's own name, the fact that the Earth is more than a hundred years old or that this is my hand (at the moment I am looking at it). Wittgenstein is inspired by Moore's attempt to defend our common-sensical assertions against sceptical philosophy (see the articles Moore 1925 and 1939); for example, against systematic doubt of Descartes, as presented in his *Meditations* (Descartes (1641)). Wittgenstein wants to elaborate on Moore and in fact come up with a better defence of our common sense. He does this by systematically showing that each of these doubts would ultimately end up being non-sensical. These doubts ultimately cannot even be formulated, at pains of raising doubts about the very doubts themselves.[4]

Thus, if someone were to doubt whether he or she has indeed got exactly two hands, it would be adequate to doubt whether that person speaks meaningfully and is not, for example, confused as to the meaning of the word *hand*. According to Wittgenstein, then, these mundane truths occupy in our overall cognitive framework a place quite similar to that accorded to logic by BL. Yet nobody would like to count them as truths of logic. It would lead us somewhat astray to examine the cogency of Wittgenstein's argument, yet let us suppose that it is indeed conclusive (a view I myself adopt, by the way). Then we have to somehow adapt BL in order to save it.

One way to go would be to say that all these extra-logical certainties, unlike the logical ones, have their status merely due to contingent matters of fact, such as our physical makeup and the ways we have learned to communicate over the long course of our evolution. Such a rebuttal brings its difficulties, though. On the one hand it seems to show that these extra-logical certainties are not so certain after all or at least not as certain as the logical ones. And it is problematic to claim something like that, as was shown by Wittgenstein. Furthermore, this line of thought obliges us to embark on a discussion of what is and what is not contingent in our cognitive framework and use it to explain the status of logical knowledge, which is probably not a very good strategy as we would thus use an explanation hardly any clearer than what it is supposed to explain.

We will therefore have to take a different route, namely to claim that logical knowledge is necessary for our rationality in a different sense than other kinds of knowledge that might be necessary for it. We will get to this issue later and see that this specific sense of epistemic necessity can indeed be given. For the moment we lack the tools to formulate this proposal.

6.2.4 Choosing the map

We have noted that when taking logic as the science of necessary conditions of rationality and trying to demarcate it as such, we were in a situation of someone who wanted to draw a borderline on a map, yet without knowing on which map. We may seem to be disputing what is in the actual region depicted on the various maps and thus also which of the maps is true. Speaking about the region of rationality, we discuss what still belongs there, what is still rational.

Thus, we ask if it is rational to accept the law of the excluded middle and some say that it indeed is, while others claim that there are cases, particularly when we speak about infinitistic mathematics, where the law does not hold in full generality. How can we decide this question and similar ones? There is obviously a long tradition of disagreement and logico-philosophical schools which adhered to different answers in the controversy. The question can therefore either be a very difficult or a defective one.

I find it to be rather defective but with some reservations and provisos. It would be preposterously dismissive of all the discussions and the intellectual energy invested in them by brilliant minds to say just that. It can be very fruitful to investigate the consequences of adopting intuitionist rather than classical reasoning or vice versa for mathematics. Such investigations have led to valuable insights and were fuelled oftentimes by the desire to validate one or the other of the two logics in some way. And there can certainly be ways in which one or the other can be found better suited to mathematical reasoning and lead to more interesting results or to a better systematization thereof. Nevertheless, the quest for validating one or the other logic does not have good prospects to be successfully finished. What criteria could be declared as decisive in this case? And who would decide, as there has been such a long tradition of dissent among logicians and philosophers?

Here it will be useful to go back to the map metaphor. When we draw a map of some territory, we do this in order to have a sufficiently faithful picture thereof but for some specific purpose. And for different purposes, different maps can be useful for us. Each map thus gives prominence to some specific features of the region, while neglecting others. And it is also important that every map can become outdated, as it does not change its depiction in accordance with the changes of the very region it depicts. We can retain the idea that logic is here to give us an idea of the bounds of our rationality, yet we also have to ask for what reasons do we want to have a representation of these bounds? We entered this chapter with the goal of finding the *purpose* of logic, and the criterion BL is silent on this.

This means that we have to look for a reasonable purpose for drawing a map of our rationality as such. Perhaps there can be more reasonable purposes and therefore no uniqueness can be claimed by any proposal we may come up with. Let us now examine a first possible proposal and see how it fares.

6.3 Logic as a tool for gaining knowledge

A very natural expectation one can have of logic is that it will help us to gain knowledge. Inconclusively but suggestively put, logic is concerned with the laws of reasoning, and reasoning is a tool for gaining knowledge. Therefore logic is here to help us use this tool appropriately to obtain as much knowledge as possible. Let us remind ourselves of Aristotle's definition of deduction:

> A deduction is a speech (logos) in which, certain things having been supposed, something different from those supposed results of necessity because of their being so. (Aristotle 1997 I.2, 24b18–20)

This quote makes one think that the business of logic consists of broadening our knowledge by adding to it that which is entailed by what we already know. This is something lots of people tend to think about logic; indeed we can find such opinions voiced in many textbooks. Furthermore, some people who try just as we to demarcate logic adhere to this view, as is testified to by this quote from Gila Sher:

> Being finite and relatively short living creatures, we cannot hope to establish all our knowledge directly but have to resort to such indirect means as *inference* to obtain a considerable portion of our knowledge. (Sher 2008, p. 313)

Sher goes on to say that the truly formal inference which is studied by logic is particularly important because of its general applicability:

> Given that formal features of objects are constantly referred to in all discourse – one cannot talk about anything without saying that certain objects are in the *complement* or *intersection* or have objects falling under them, etc. – we can use our knowledge of these features to develop a wholesale method of expanding our knowledge.... Knowledge of some formal laws may be more useful for expanding our knowledge than knowledge of others, so it might be useful to build limited logical systems geared to those features. But in principle logic can provide us with rules for expanding our knowledge based on any laws governing the formal behavior of objects. (Sher 2008, p. 313)

The utility of logic is therefore supposed to consist in its ability to expand our knowledge and also in the way it can provide such an expansion. On the one hand, logic is universally applicable, as Sher emphasizes. On the other hand, the expansion guaranteed by logic should be particularly reliable, so that we can be absolutely (or at least to a very high, maybe the highest degree possible) sure that the conclusions added to our premises by means of logical inferences are true, provided those premises are. These two supposed virtues of logical inference are worthy of being examined more closely, each in its turn.

6.3.1 Broad application

If we accept Sher's thesis that logical laws are universally applicable (a thesis which many authors share, to be sure), it is understandable to see it as an asset of logic. But one can doubt both whether logic indeed is universally applicable and, even if it were such, whether this would be really such a great asset.

First, though, let us clarify what universal applicability means. By saying that logic can be applied to infer something from what we know in any context whatsoever, we do not purport to claim that we do not have to check that our premises are, for example, a conditional of the form A→B and A, that is the first subformula of the conditional, in order to be able to use *modus ponens* for inferring B. Obviously, we have to check the form of our premises and verify that a given logical law of inference enables us to draw conclusions from them. But this is everything that we have to check in order to learn new, true statement purely by means of logic. For any other kind of inference, that is extra-logical inference, we, in addition to the logical form of our statements, also have to check many other things in order to be able to use rules for the expansion of our, say, zoological knowledge. The rules for zoology thus allow only for a limited application and we cannot use them outside zoology. The same can be said for any other discipline, except for logic, as those who claim that it is universally applicable would advocate.

Is logic, then, universally applicable? I think we have to distinguish between asking this question in a descriptive and in a normative mode. In a descriptive mode we are asking whether the logical laws are used by us in any context. First of all, we obviously commit logical mistakes in our reasoning, so in this straightforward sense logical laws are not followed universally. A little bit more interestingly, if we take any logical system, that is a system of logical rules such as classical or intuitionistic propositional logic, then obviously none of these systems of rules is universally applied. If it were so, logical pluralism would be obviously wrong and debates about it would be futile. Instead there are, for instance, mathematicians who build their proofs according to classical logic, others according to intuitionistic logic and others according to other logics yet.

But this straightforwardly descriptivist thesis seemed to be much less promising than the normative one. Such a thesis would be that logic should be generally applicable or, to express myself more exactly, that logic spells out those principles of our knowledge which we should generally apply. In such a form, this thesis has had many adherents. Indeed, MacFarlane sees precisely this as one of the three senses in which one can demand logic to be formal. He then attributes this view to authors rather quite different from Sher, such as Ian Hacking (1979) and Kosta Došen (1989). This shows just how widespread this view is, given that Sher explicitly embraces it, as well, despite the fact that MacFarlane classifies her as one of the authors who subscribe rather to the conception of the formality of logic as indifference to individual identities of objects.[5]

In the last section we postponed the question whether it is wise to embrace this thesis that logic should be generally applicable, even if we tended to view it rather positively. But now let us see what the pragmatic consequence of accepting it would be. Otherwise put, would it help us understand the utility of logic? For one thing, logic would be easy to use in the sense that we would not have to think so much about its application. This is probably what Sher has in mind when she speaks of logic as of a *wholesale method for expanding our knowledge* in the previous quote. Unlike with the laws of chemistry, we do not need to consider first whether the premises we have are, as far as their content and not mere form is concerned, the ones on which the logical laws can be used to expand our knowledge. We can always use them at once. And also we can use them on more occasions and therefore can hope to expand our knowledge perhaps much more than with the less general rules.

This fact speaks for the utility of logic as an instrument for expanding our knowledge but in itself it would certainly not suffice. We have to also be sure that the knowledge by which it can expand that which is already present in our premises is typically of value for us. And here the universal applicability should rather awake our doubts, because the more general the rules are, the less specifically they can have importance for the areas of knowledge we want to expand, such as mathematics, chemistry, biology, sociology and so on. The more general the rules of inference, the more expected and thereby uninteresting are typically the consequence we draw by their means.

We see that the general applicability is closely related to the second of its purported useful properties, namely that of perfect certainty. Given that logical laws can be applied in any context (yet only in the sense we clarified, i.e. we, of course, always have to check the logical form of our statements in order to apply logical laws of inference), we do not have to check if the conclusions we draw by using them from our premises will be true, given the truth of the premises. Yet again, the certainty has the drawback of potentially leading to not very useful new conclusions. Very often it is by taking risks and guessing that we arrive at interesting conclusions from what we already know. The risk can be compensated afterwards by looking for supporting evidence and checking. Had we proceeded only by the most secure steps, we would have hardly arrived at the bold conclusions which, after getting the supplementary verification, can help us to make real progress in our cognition of the world or in other ways of coping with it.

The relationship between the generality and certainty of inference laws on the one hand and the utility of the conclusions we can obtain using them on the other hand thus seems to be getting close to that of inverse proportionality. The more you have of the former, the less you have of the latter and vice versa. When you then get to the maximum of the certainty and generality, perhaps you also get to the very minimum of utility.

The same question of the utility of logical inference is asked also in Dogramaci (2017). The author wonders why the robustness of logical inference with respect to changes of the matters of fact and details of the structure of our languages should be an asset to a reasoner. In this he continues the tradition of Kripke, who, criticizing the counterpart theory[6] in his *Naming and Necessity* remarks that Humphrey 'could not care less whether someone else (his counterpart), no matter how much resembling him, would have been victorious in another possible world' (Kripke 1972, p. 45) and thus in general asks why a reasoner should be interested whether what he claims holds also in different possible worlds if he in fact knows that they are not actual. Dogramaci ends up, somewhat surprisingly, claiming that logical inferences are so much promoted in our linguistic communities because their robustness (concerning shifts between possible worlds) is a guarantee of their extraordinary reliability. But as we have seen, reliability or certainty is by itself a dubious virtue.

What we have said so far about certainty and universal applicability was very general and cannot function as a decisive argument against the thesis that logic enables us to expand our knowledge. But we have at least opened the issue whether the conclusions of logical inferences can be useful for us and indicated that there are reasons to be sceptical about this utility. But let us now once again have a look at what kinds of conclusions logic typically allows us to arrive at.

Many of the prominent logics can be presented in multiple semantic and syntactic ways. It is legitimate to worry that the kind of presentation we choose may affect our judgement about the utility of logical conclusions. On the other hand, if all the syntactic calculi and all the semantics are in fact equivalent, then the worry can be dropped and if we reach some conclusion about the utility of logical inference, then it does not matter from which of the possible perspectives we were considering the logic we speak about. Yet in the case of many logics, for example the second-order logic as presented in Shapiro (1991), this is not the case, as its semantics is not axiomatizable. We will have to deal with such logics separately, yet first we will also have to decide as to their logicality, as it is possible that something which does not have a syntax corresponding to a semantic cannot be properly considered as a logic.

But for the systems where we do not have to worry about completeness and soundness, we can choose which presentation of the kind of conclusions logic arrives at we exploit. I will use a system of sequent calculi (which we already encountered earlier in this chapter) of the kind introduced by Gentzen (1935). We will, nevertheless, not fully honour Gentzen's exposition and rather choose Kosta Došen's (see his article Došen 1989 and his dissertation Došen 1980). He presents the rules for the logical constants in an invertible form. Typically they do not have to be such as, for example, they are not in the presentation in Švejdar (2002).

We have already seen the sequent rules for conjunction in the standard form. If we read, as is common, the sequent as saying that the left side of the sequent implies the right one in the way that the joint truth of all the formulae on the left guarantees the truth of at least one of those on the right, then clearly all instances of these inference rules are surely correct. On the other hand, if we tried to use them in the opposite direction, deducing from the bottom sequent the upper one, then their correctness is not anymore guaranteed. But Došen uses double line rules, such as the following one:

$$\frac{\Gamma \Rightarrow \Delta, A \quad \Gamma \Rightarrow \Delta, B}{\Gamma \Rightarrow \Delta, A \wedge B} \wedge$$

The double line indicates that the rule is applicable both ways: downwards and upwards. From this we can see nicely that the rule does not really say anything new. In fact, it only says that we can infer both A and B, which we already know if we are in possession of the upper sequents. In fact, the new expression $\wedge$ does not seem to be of much interest. When we are trying to expand our knowledge, we contrive methods how to prove substantial statements like A or B. When this job is done, then determining the truth value of $A \wedge B$ is quite easy and uninteresting. In fact, if we think of the standard semantic presentation of $\wedge$ via a truth table, then we see with the same immediacy that adding the conjunction of two statements to the stock of our beliefs cannot be particularly useful, as we already have to be equipped with both the statements. Neither can the syntactic or semantic rules really explain to us what conjunction is if we did not know it beforehand. In order to use these rules to deduce $A \wedge B$, we already have to know that both A *and* B are true, that is what the conjunction says. The situation is the same for all the other logical constants, as well.

It might be argued that we have found logical rules of so little use for the expansion of our knowledge because we considered just those of logics which are too weak to be really useful. Indeed, among those who affirmed that logic can be useful for such goals was Gila Sher, who also claimed that logic must be much stronger than classical logic. It is unclear whether the argument we used for the irrelevance of standard logical constants for our reasoning can also be extended to the generalized quantifiers of UL, also because it is difficult to have a concept of the totality of them. Furthermore, due to the lack of completeness theorem and therewith axiomatization for second-order logic and UL, it is not clear how to make exact sense of them as of sets of rules for the expansion of our knowledge. Yet it appears that by the way of analogy, a similar reasoning could be applied to argue that even the non-standard quantifiers of UL cannot expand our knowledge by anything really useful. At any rate, their relevance for reasoning is not clear and even if they were indeed relevant, it would still remain mysterious why UL must contain the more orthodox constants, which, as we have argued, can hardly be useful for the expansion of our knowledge. Besides this, the generalized quantifiers are in many cases not linked to expressions of our natural language in the way $\wedge$ is linked to *and*. This artificiality, far greater than that of $\top$ and $\bot$, makes their import even more mysterious. Yet it must be admitted that many quite artificial concepts of, say, physics do help advance our reasoning about the world quite considerably. Nevertheless, at this point we cannot in any sense really claim that logic is useful for gaining knowledge, and the investigation suggests that we should rather try looking for a different explication of the role of logic in our conceptual schemes.

6.4 Logic and the management of our beliefs

We saw that lots of arguments speak against the natural supposition that logic is a discipline which helps us to expand our knowledge. In order to be effective, our reasoning should maybe even abstain from following logical rules. We came close to the strongly sceptical judgement of Gilbert Harman:

> Even if they agree that logic is not itself a theory of reasoning, many people will be inclined to suppose that logic has some sort of special relevance to the theory of reasoning. . . . It turns out that logic is not of any special relevance. (Harman 1986, p. 11)

In fact, Harman also suggests that adjusting our beliefs according to laws of logic may not only fail to be particularly productive and useful, it can even be damaging for us. He points out that logic cannot be relevant for our reasoning in the straightforward way that our beliefs should be closed under logical implication (a principle which he calls the *Logical closure principle* on p. 12) because this would mean cluttering our mind with a host of irrelevant consequences of our beliefs. Consider any statement A. Then this statement obviously implies, among many other statements, also $A \wedge A$, $A \wedge A \wedge A$, $A \wedge A \wedge A \wedge A$ and so forth. If we believe that A then we cannot be required to believe such consequences because even if it were in some sense possible (which depends on how exactly we understand the notion of believing a statement) it would certainly be useless and divert us from much more important statements that we should consider instead.

Harman furthermore considers the *Logical inconsistency principle* which would require us to avoid logical inconsistency in our reasoning. This, according to him, cannot be a binding norm of reasoning either, because we see that it is oftentimes better to keep the set of beliefs even if we know that it is inconsistent because it can still be too precious in the situations when we have no accessible path to revise it and render it consistent and still keep the properties that make it precious for us. This nevertheless does not seem to be a particularly strong reason for refusing the principle. Defeasibility of a principle does not mean that the principle does not hold at all; it is on the contrary usual that we have to decide which of the conflicting principles we are going to obey, knowing that we will have to break some. Still, their being taken into consideration shows that even the norms that we decided not to comply with are relevant for us.

Of course, avoiding a contradiction can be very difficult and it is not only in our everyday life but also in science that we typically work with inconsistent theories and rightly so because abandoning them would be more problematic for us than the contradiction involved. This is often pointed out in the development of calculus, which originally involved the contradictory concept of the infinitesimal. Had Newton and Leibniz not pursued their research because of this, the development of mathematics would have suffered greatly. And ultimately the concept was replaced by one which is consistent.[7] The impression that contradiction is after all not so pernicious for our theories and that we can handle the contradictory theories without much harm also led to the development of paraconsistent logics.[8]

In addition to this, it can even be argued that contradiction is not only difficult to avoid but even, in a way, inevitable. Harman speaks of the liar paradox as of something which is inherently a part of our natural language. Similarly, it is natural to suppose that not all of one's beliefs are true and still stick with them. Summing up, in natural language we are constantly accompanied by contradictions. I do not think this means that we therefore should adopt a tolerant position towards them, only that they are not the only concern we have when forming beliefs. In fact, if we discover a contradiction, we should sooner or later see to it that it be resolved.

Nevertheless, putting the question of how to cope with contradictions aside, our considerations obviously concur with Harman that logic does not have much relevance to the theory of reasoning.

6.5 Can we say more about the role of logic?

Can we now say what logic is good for? I think that even if we did not arrive at direct answers to our original question, we have still arrived at some valuable insights which we should exploit more. In fact, we have seen that logic in principle does not help us extend our knowledge. This might seem disappointing but perhaps there is a completely different answer to the question of the utility of logic. It would be particularly satisfactory if we could find one which would connect the role of logic with its idleness for the expansion of our knowledge.

The doctrine which offers exactly this is that of logical expressivism, which originated with Robert Brandom.[9] Let us now present what this doctrine consists of. Afterwards, we will show how it resolves our problems about the role of logic and the emergence of logical pluralism.

6.5.1 Logical expressivism

Logical expressivism is closely linked to inferentialism, a semantic theory which identifies the semantic value of an expression with its inferential properties. Primarily, then, the semantic value belongs to sentences.[10] The meaning of a sentence is given by what sentences it can be inferred from and what other sentences can be inferred from it (possibly with further joint premises). Jaroslav Peregrin sums this up by defining the *inferential potential* of a given sentence (see p. 50 of Peregrin (2014a)).

Definition 6.5.1. *Let A be a sentence of a language L which has got an inferential relation between sequences of sentences and sentences $\vdash$. Let the sequences of sentences from which A is inferable be denoted as $A^{\leftarrow}$:*

$$A^{\leftarrow} = \{<A_1, \ldots, A_n> \mid <A_1, \ldots, A_n> \vdash A\}$$

Furthermore, let us denote the sentences that are inferable from A together with other premises as $A^{\rightarrow}$:

$$A^{\rightarrow} = \{<A_1, \ldots, A_{i-1}>, <A_{i+1}, \ldots, A_n>, A_{n+1} \mid <A_1, \ldots, A_{i-1}, A, A_{i+1}, \ldots, A_n> \vdash A_{n+1}\}$$

An inferential potential of A, denoted as IP(A), is then defined as the following ordered pair:

$$IP(A) = \langle A^{\leftarrow}, A^{\rightarrow} \rangle$$

IP(A) thus formally represents what the meaning of a sentence A is for an inferentialist. A sentence such as *Rex is a dog* has its meaning given by such facts as its implying *Rex is a mammal* and its inferrability from *Rex is of the species which is best friends with humans* and similar ones. It is just as well defined by its incompatibility with sentences such as *Rex is human* or *Rex has wings*. Note that it is indeed inference rules, not the actual inferences we make, that constitute the meaning of a given sentence, according to the inferentialism I want to propose here. Of course, a rule is constituted by some of our activities, most importantly by our corrective activities which we exercise all the time when we encourage someone to follow the rule and discourage the violation of it and, very importantly, by setting example by following the rule ourselves (because *exempla trahunt*).

As we can see, the meanings are primarily conferred to sentences, as only they constitute a move in a language game; only a sentence expresses something. Sub-sentential expressions, such as words, thus have their meanings only derivatively, as they contribute to the meanings of the sentences they occur in. This corresponds to the maxim Frege expressed already in the introduction to his *Grundlagen der Artihmetik* (see Frege (1884)). This by no means impairs the compositionality and therewith our capability to understand a potentially infinite number of sentences (Quine sums this point up in Quine 1990 and presents a detailed analysis of our mastery of language including an explanation of this ability to understand an unlimited number of sentences in Quine 1960).

Now some readers may already have been a little bit surprised by the examples I just used. It might seem that we can infer *Rex is a mammal* from *Rex is a dog* and the further premise that all dogs are mammals. By the same token, we need to know also that *Dogs have no wings* to be able to infer that Rex has got no wings. This much is, in a way, true but we still do not have to suppose that we need to see these statements as additional premises of the inferences, as we can also see them rather as formulations of rules of inference. Our corrective practices can as well establish those rules without explicitly stating them. What appears to be missing general premises are in fact formulations of rules which we use to infer; for example *Rex is a mammal* from *Rex is a dog*. Ultimately, according to the inferentialist view, without endorsing rules of this kind we would not really understand what such words as *mammal* or *dog* mean.

Principally, then, there is nothing absurd about the possibility of the implicit rules in our language. Yet logical expressivism needs to show that the implicit rules are not only possible but actually present and also fairly common in our languages. And indeed it can be argued that the natural languages not only actually are but by necessity have to be replete with implicit rules. A sentence can be compared to a chess figure, as it is constituted by the rules which guide its usage. In the case of the chess figure we can explicitly formulate the rules which guide it, as we can always use our language to do so. Yet in the case of language itself we cannot formulate all the rules explicitly as this would lead us to an infinite regress. This line of thought goes back to paragraph 85 of Wittgenstein (1953), which concerns the signpost.

This signpost can be interpreted in various different ways. A new explication of the rule has to be understood, as well as the original rule for the signpost which creates the need for new rules. Thus the codifications of the rules have to stop somewhere and we just simply have to follow some of the rules. Nevertheless, we still speak of rules, that is of something which has got a normative force, not about mere regularities in our behaviour.[11]

We can thus see that in our language we cannot forbear relying on implicit rules. Despite this fact, the implicit rules can be made explicit; we can actually say what the rules are, yet knowing that we thus rely again on other rules, those guiding our use of the language we used for the expression. Every time we make some new rule explicit, we in fact bring some implicit rules into play. Thus it can hardly be our goal to somehow reduce the implicitness as much as possible (its complete elimination being, as we already saw, impossible). Nevertheless, it may very well happen that some rules are better rendered explicit.

6.5.2 Why make the rules explicit

It can be argued that some things, not only rules, are better left implicit; their expression might in a way even be impossible. Vojtěch Kolman (2009) offers many examples of that which cannot be expressed appropriately. For example, he offers an example of a politician who speaks about how ethical he is. This makes us wonder whether he might not be an ethically problematic person precisely because of the way he speaks so nicely about himself.

Excellent examples of this phenomenon of the impossibility of making something explicit are due to Frege and Wittgenstein. Frege speaks in his *Gedanke* (see Frege 2017 [1918]) about the undefinability of truth and the impossibility to say explicitly that what we say we really mean seriously, as an actor could utter the same words in a theatre and thus not really mean them (thus not be interested in the *Bedeutung* but just in the *Sinn*, as Frege makes the famous distinction in Frege (1892)). The rules for interpreting whether one is speaking seriously or not have to be present only implicitly in many situations.

Wittengenstein then gives us a host of examples where we cannot really express our doubts about some very basic things, such as that we have never travelled very far from the surface of Earth (though, of course, since

Wittgenstein's time this has changed, as it became possible for humans to fly to space), that I have two hands and am watching them as I am writing right now, and so on. All these obviously true facts (and according to Wittgenstein, acknowledging them belongs to the fundamental rules of our language games) cannot really be expressed because when we utter them we do not manage to convey the information to the people we speak with but rather puzzle or amuse them. Perhaps Wittgenstein (1921) had something similar in mind when he claimed that solipsism is right, though it can only be shown and not expressed (statement 5.62 of Tractatus).

Having pointed to the limits of making something explicit, we should now proceed to show that in many contexts it can be very useful and even vital to make the rules we obey explicit. The most typical situation of ours is that we understand the language games we are playing; we know enough about what the others expect of us and we know what to expect of them, just as in chess. At least as far as the constitutive rules of chess are considered, that is. We know what the allowed moves are and which are illegitimate. It is a different thing, though, when it comes to the strategic rules which tell us how we should play the game in order to be successful at it, in the case of chess to win the match. Peregrin thus makes an important distinction between what he calls the *constitutive* and the *strategic* rules of the game.[12]

Most of the time, then, we are sufficiently acquainted with the rules which constitute our language games. Yet sometimes, the implicitness of the rules which are the foundations of our rule-guided practices may turn out to cause unclarities and render us unable to go on engaging in the practices which are important for us, as we become unsure about the rules which hold for those practices.

Let us come back to the problem that we already discussed on one occasion – imagine that we find at a relatively recondite place on our planet (or on another one) an animal which looks exactly like a dog, say a dachshund, yet we discover later by anatomical research that these animals in fact do not possess any lungs. What are we to say? We can very well imagine that two scientists would come to argue whether all dogs have lungs or not. The one supporting the thesis that there are dogs without lungs would argue on the basis of the discovery of the dachshund-like animals without lungs. Obviously our practices do not determine sufficiently which one of them would be right, which is exactly what would make their dispute futile and somewhat comical. In fact, it is not clear whether it holds that all dogs have lungs or not. Yet when scientists are able to say the sentence *All dogs have lungs*, they get into a position to decide whether this sentence should be accepted or not. Arguments can be given both for and against this sentence which can be seen as a formulation of rule, namely of a permission to say of anything which is a dog that it has got lungs. After they settle this argument, they can continue investigating the animals sans the dispute which was unsolvable before they had made the discussed rule explicit.

This example might be a little banal but still should be sufficiently illustrative. Robert Brandom remarked how important making the rules of inference (and also other kinds of rules, to be sure) explicit can be for us. He presented his ideas originally in his monumental *Making It Explicit* and then summed them up in *Articulating Reasons* (see Brandom 1994 and Brandom 2000). In the latter work he even distinguishes what he calls *expressive* rationality as one of the fundamental kinds of rationality, namely that which makes the implicit explicit. And indeed besides the example I just gave we could give better examples from the history of science of how important it is to clarify sufficiently what rules are guiding the notions we are using and settle on the rules if there is disagreement. For example, the development of non-Euclidean geometries was a development in the specification of notions such as plane, straight line and others which were not sufficiently determined by the implicit rules of the mathematics of 200 years ago. The development consisted in showing that these notions can be specified in more than one legitimate way. Thanks to making this explicit (ultimately by Hilbert 1899 in his *Grundlagen der Geometrie*) we could see that there are more geometries which can describe space and thus be used also in physics.

6.5.3 How to make the rules explicit

What is it that enables us to make these rules explicit? According to Brandom, it is logic. But by logic we do not yet mean the discipline we study in college, rather our logical capacity consisting in our ability to use the specifically logical vocabulary of our languages such as *not* or *if – then*, to make the implicit rules explicit. The logical expressions are the tools logic uses to make inference rules explicit. The two basic relations sentences can have between each other and which can be made explicit are those of implication and incompatibility. Thus one sentence's being inferable from another one and one sentence's not being assertible together with another one.

These rules are typically not guiding us in what we say or do. Most of the time, they rather just delimit what we can do, they are rather restrictive than prescriptive. When someone says that Rex is a dog, he is thereby not obliged to say that Rex is a mammal, despite the fact that the latter assertion is inferable from the previous one. Instead, he ought not say something which would contradict that Rex is a mammal. These restrictions of course prevent us from doing many things; on the other hand, they create the very language games we play and thus also broaden the range of things we can do, as Peregrin (2014a) emphasizes.

Now, as we said, it is logic with its vocabulary which is the instrument of making the inference rules explicit. In natural language we have many expressions which can serve these purposes, though it is not easy to delimit them in a particularly convincing and cogent manner. Despite all the fuzziness and peculiarity of those logical expressions of natural language, we can say that the expressions of logical systems correspond to them. They do not work in the same way, yet they bear some of the properties of the original expression which are particularly important for us.

We in fact have to realize that when we do what Brandom calls *making it explicit*, we not only just describe or restate the implicit rules of our practice. Besides the fact that such speech acts as description or pure statement are by far not the only important speech acts we perform and have a more complex structure than might be suspected, which was pointed to already by Austin (1962), the same author, as we already noted previously, pointed out that making something explicit is typically a different speech act than describing. He spoke, it is true, rather of making the force of our utterance explicit, that is specifying which illocutionary act we intend to perform, but his idea can also be applied in general to our situation when we make an inference rule explicit.

In fact the terms *logical expressivism* and *making it explicit* surely suggest that we just bring something which lie beneath the surface to the fore. Thus no change of rule is involved. Yet this suggestion and impression must be false. Or, at least, it cannot be the whole truth. Just reconsider the fluent nature of meaning we already spoke about in section 4.1 of this book, that is that meanings not only can but actually have to develop by every use of an expression and especially by an explicit description of its meaning, as it entails endorsement of the very meaning. Meaning of any given expression is being modified potentially by any use we make of it, though of course most of the uses hardly change anything and the meanings typically remain very stable. To be a use of the expression at all, the use has to be somewhat continuous with the uses that were already made of it and which constitute the identity of the expression as the speaker employs it in her speech; otherwise the speaker would simply not be recognizable as using the given expression at all. But then the speaker can use the expression in various different ways which will help to develop the meaning of the given expression.

I should like to say in figurative way that an expression we encounter points in various directions as to the manners in which it could be developed. Just think of the word *dog* that we have already mentioned. We are free to develop it both in the way that requires the dogs to have lungs and in the one which does not. Now when we state one of the rules guiding this expression, we typically sharpen the meaning, we not only render something implicit explicit, we also render something vague more specific, as when we state the rule that *All dogs have lungs* – we in fact also promote a modification of meaning of the word *dog*. When stating the rule, we also exercise our creativity; we not only express but to some degree also create the rule. Our practice thus changes.

Here I think I am, despite my respect for him, in conflict with Brandom a little bit. I think his model of language has it that our language could basically work without logic, since logic only makes its workings explicit. What I am saying obviously does not amount to denying this view in its totality; I rather propose a modification thereof based on appreciation of the creative element in making it explicit. Indeed, I still think that the expression *making it explicit* is basically a fortunate one, as it conveys Brandom's basic insight about the nature of logic, yet we should not take it all too literally.[13] The underdetermination of the correct formulation of rules which gives us some limited freedom to choose among the acceptable formulations will be important for us as a factor which enables us to explain the logical pluralism which we are at pains to understand, yet despite its importance in this context, the extent of this creativity should not be overrated, as this creativity is strongly limited (probably, however, as any kind of creativity). Indeed, the past usage and the rules instituted thereby determine a lot how we can develop the given meaning of an expression. As the concept of dog can be developed in a way which would necessitate that all dogs have lungs, one could not recognize the word *dog* as expressing the concept of dog should someone add the rule that all dogs can fly.

Brandom speaks of *expressive rationality* as one of the most fundamental forms of our rationality, which suggests that basically the more of the rules guiding our practices we make explicit, the more rational and indeed civilized we are. There appears even to be a sort of necessity in the exercise of our expressive rationality. One gets very close to a Hegelian picture from *Phenomenologie des Geistes* (Hegel (1807)) of the rationality which makes progress by the means of expressing the implicit. Besides this, the Brandomian picture enables us to give a good sense to the Hegelian idea of *moving concepts*. Because the inference relations between the concepts keep developing, we can say that the concepts are moving. Furthermore, we have the freedom in making the rules explicit, yet we also have to respect the established usage. Therefore, the concepts have great autonomy and independence from us and our individual decisions. When using the word *dog*, a user of the language is always potentially developing the concept, yet when his usage is too much at odds with the rules established in the community of those sharing their language with him, his use will not be accepted and will certainly fail to modify the concept. On the other hand, great minds can enrich and improve our conceptual schemes by developing the concepts they inherited in unprecedented ways, yet still in such ways that organically grow from the previous usage of these concepts, as when Kant developed the notion of morality or Einstein that of simultaneousness.

6.5.4 Two kinds of freedom in making the rules explicit

So far we have encountered one basic kind of freedom in making the inference rules in our language explicit, namely the freedom to decide which statements will be exactly put into logical relations we are making explicit. Typically a situation occurs when we are considering the sentences S_1, S_2 and S_3 which obviously are somehow linked by the relation of consequence and are free to decide whether it is rather S_2 or S_3 which is a consequence of S_1. Thus, we are free to formulate either the rule that all dogs have lungs, or that all dogs have lungs unless they are the strange dachshunds we spoke about. Both these options can obviously be formalized by the means of classical logic in the following manner:

1. $\forall x(Dog(x) \rightarrow HaveLungs(x))$
2. $\forall x(Dog(x) \rightarrow (HaveLungs(x) \vee StrangeDachshund(x)))$

This freedom is very significant, but it will be another freedom which will be of particular interest for us, namely the freedom to understand and correspondingly spell out the nature of logical relations themselves. So far we were thematizing mainly the issue as to which propositions bear certain logical relations to one another, such as that of logical consequence. This served to explain what their meaning consisted in, or at least a substantial part thereof. The logical relations thus played the role of the explainer in the riddle of meaning, which we took for granted that we understand what these relations are. And we must have a very firm command on these relations and be able to work with them in order to be rational at all.

Nevertheless, I claim that we still have some freedom in spelling out the rules governing the logical vocabulary and that this is the very source of logical pluralism we have been looking for and which other authors found elsewhere (notably Beall and Restall (2006), who made the term *logical pluralism* popular). We spoke about the implicit rules governing the essentially non-logical vocabulary. An essential feature of these rules, at least until we granted them an expression, was that they were to some degree indeterminate. The same holds for the rules which govern the behaviour of logical vocabulary. As the notion of dog is not fully determinate, neither is that of, say, conjunction or negation. As it can be reasonable to hold that all dogs have lungs, just as it is to hold that some do not have to and still speak about dogs irrespectively of which option regarding the lungs we choose, so it is possible to embrace the explosivity of contradiction as well as to reject it in some cases and still be legitimately talking about and employing negation and conjunction, irrespective of our stance on the explosivity of contradiction.

The freedom to modify the rules guiding logical expressions such as the conditional and therewith the nature of logical relations such as consequence is from one point of view the same as the first freedom to modify just any rules of any expressions at all. Yet from another and equally legitimate perspective it is different, as the logical relations it concerns are fundamental for the meaningfulness of any expressions of our languages whatsoever. We can say that the second freedom is different because it is a freedom on a higher level, yet in order to exercise this freedom we have to use the same means which enable the first kind of freedom. The logical expressions have a special status among all the others, yet we can partly and temporarily make them descend among the rest of the language and treat and modify, for example, the conditional just as we do with the word *dog*.

Every notion we use is governed by some rules which determine its contribution to the inferential properties of sentences containing it. It is possible that every single one of these rules can be individually made explicit, yet we can never hope to achieve the same for all the rules at the same time. Thus also the rules guiding logical vocabulary, that is the logical rules, can be rendered more explicit and thus also more specific. The situation is quite similar to that of geometry where we can say that a concept such as a line or a triangle can be specified and developed into the notion of Euclidean, as well as Riemannian or hyperbolic line or triangle, as already Sellars noted:

> Thus it is important to note that the use of the illustrating device to form functional sortals involves an important flexibility. Not all aspects of the functioning of the illustrating expression need be mobilized to serve as criteria for its application.... It is clear that the functioning of the illustrating word 'triangular' which is relevant to something being ·triangular·[14] is a generic functioning which abstracts from the specific differences between Euclidean and Riemannian geometries. (Sellars 1974, p. 435)

He then invites us to compare the situation of geometry with that of logic, as the classical and intuitionist negation are specifications of the general concept of negation, just as the Euclidean and Riemannian triangles are specification of the more general and implicit notion of triangle. Perhaps the Euclidean specification suggests itself more readily, yet alternatives are possible. The same situation is present in logic. We are thus free to choose how we want to spell out the notion at question, including that of, say, negation.

6.5.4.1 Yet how can we change logic without using it?

When speaking about the plurality of logics and our capacity to choose among various logics, a natural objection comes to mind, namely how can we make the decision without in fact using logic? It is obviously a kind of reasoning, and reasoning happening outside logic cannot be real reasoning, so no change of logic seems possible. This argument, nevertheless, is illusory and does not really work. The premise that every cogent reasoning has to be logical is ambiguous and when clarified in an appropriate way it fails to lead to the conclusion that logic cannot be changed.

We have already seen that the kind of inferentialism which we endorse includes logical expressivism, according to which reasoning can be correct without its being explicitly guided by the rules of logic. Every argument involves logic in the sense that it is possible only because of the logical relations between sentences. Yet the rules relevant for the workings of these logical relations are present only implicitly in our capacity to engage in reasoned discussion; we do not depend on the specific laws of either classical or intuitionistic or any other logic when playing the everyday game of giving and asking for reasons. In the same manner, we can speak of triangles, lines and space without relying on any of the specific geometries. Thus the general argument against the possibility of modifying logic is not so hard to debunk, yet we will now present its rephrasing along the inferentialist lines, which will require somewhat more work of us.

According to the thesis of logical expressivism, changing one's logic means changing one's practice of making rules explicit and modifying them. We thus have to make the rules of the new logic explicit and this has to be made, as always, by the means of logic. It thus appears that any endeavour to change logic is doomed to fail, even in the expressivist setting. If this argument is sound, we are faced with a painful dilemma from which logical pluralism can recover only with great difficulty. Let us list the answers we would be forced to choose from if the argument just mentioned were sound as it stands.

1. We could either say that there must be only one logic which serves the purpose of making the inference rules explicit, or so it seems. This logic would nevertheless be inaccessible for us; that is we would not be able to express it, as an expression of any rule, including the logical rules, means that the rules can be discussed.
2. The other possibility would be that no logic we use for expression really exists, as the rules we use for the expression change without our notice.
3. Finally, we could say that when changing logic we are in fact violating fundamental and precisely the logical, laws of reasoning and thus failing to be fully rational.

Now we should see whether any of these three options is viable.

6.5.4.2 Logic is unchangeable and/or unknowable

We are by now familiar with the idea of implicit rules guiding our practices and it is useful and sound, yet we have to use it cautiously in order not to fall prey to mysticism. We have already encountered examples of implicit rules, such as that of Wittgenstein's rules for the interpretation of a signpost. But in order for that rule to make sense it has to be capable of expression; we have to be able to make it explicit if it is not to become too mysterious. Thus we cannot say that something is a rule with true normative force unless there is some possibility to subject it to discussion by making it explicit. Note that when we listed a few examples of rules which seemingly cannot be rendered explicit, we always described only specific contexts in which the rules could not be rendered explicit. This does not mean that they cannot be rendered explicit with appropriate efforts in different contexts.

I am afraid that if you deny logical rules the possibility to be made explicit, you end up making them into either some metaphysical necessities or psychological ones because if unable to be rendered explicit, logic would not be under our control, it would be completely beyond us. I am not interested in debunking the metaphysical and psychologist views, as it would be too great a digression and I think we know about the dangers of psychologism from Frege (1884) and Husserl (1913), while the idea that logic is the doctrine of some metaphysically necessary features of the world seems so imbued with mystery that it is at any rate preferable to come up with a view which would avoid such a conclusion.

The psychologist option, unlike the metaphysical one, can theoretically be upheld together with the possibility that logic can change, unbeknownst to us, as our minds change, for example, due to their evolution. I do not think that the idea of logic not being fully under our control is absurd, yet in this form it is not acceptable, as it would mean that we can never be sure about anything in logic. Our logic, that is the ways we make inference rules in our language explicit, can change without us noticing the change, yet there always has to be the possibility for us to discover the change subsequently and be able to discuss it and possibly even reverse or deepen it.

Logic overall does not have to be fully explicit, yet every one of its rules has to be always capable of being rendered explicit. Thus, both the options which claim that logic has to remain completely implicit are not really viable. Furthermore, we have seen that logic can itself develop, though such a development is typically very difficult and slow. Besides that, we can actively contribute to this change; it does not have to be completely out of our reach and control, yet our active command of the change is even more difficult than the change itself.

6.5.4.3 Changing logic is irrational?

Let us now assume that it is in our power to change the logic we use. Then we can still face another objection to the possibility of logical pluralism in the framework of logical expressivism, namely that the change in logic can happen, yet it cannot ever be rational. To a degree it might be true that while revising logic we need to use it for this very revision; we indeed cannot just discard a logic we have employed to a certain point and build a new one out of the blue, yet a gradual change is very well possible. Indeed, we have a situation of the Neurathian ship which we have to change and repair while on the sea, as is captured in this famous passage:

> Wie Schiffer sind wir, die ihr Schiff auf offeener See umbauen müssen, ohne es jemals in einem Dock zerlegen und aus besten Bestandteilen neu errichten zu können. (Neurath 1932, p. 206)[15]

Even though every rule has to be capable of being rendered explicit, there is no denying that not all rules are rendered explicit with equal ease. In some cases we hardly have any doubt about the rules we follow and describe them without much effort, yet in the case of other rules this can be extremely difficult. And the rules of logic are among those that are most difficult to both formulate exactly and even more difficult to change. It is therefore no wonder that logical pluralism has emerged only very recently. Special intellectual effort was needed to create a *leverage* capable of making logic sufficiently explicit and thus amenable to rationally controlled change. If logic is something we typically lean on as we would on a firm certainty, we had to make something else similarly firm to enable us to make logic moving. As we already remarked, it was mathematics which played this role. But still, what was made moving in this manner, that is logic, had to be used itself for the expression of itself. We had to use some logic in order to render logic explicit. To escape paradoxical consequences, we have to conclude that a change in logic, besides happening on the relatively stable background of some mathematical laws, can always be only partial and gradual, yet this holds for any science. When we develop a concept from biology, such as *life*, or one from mathematics, such as *set*, we have to make the change only gradually, as otherwise there would be no point in calling the radically different concepts still *life* or *set*. The case of logic, though, is extreme, the change is very laborious. The various logical systems which have been developed and keep being developed serve to show us what this change could look like, that is how we could modify the tools logic uses for expressing inference rules.

As difficult as it is, we can also facilitate a change in logic by restriction of applicability of logical systems. Any logical system we contrive is a child of our general logical capacity – we would not be able to construct these systems if we lacked the expressive rationality and if we could not reflect on it. On the other hand, each of these systems can modify this capacity, as well, yet always only partially and typically needs a specification of its applicability. It would be comical if someone attempted to rectify all of our reasoning by declaring that from now on we should use only classical logic for formulating inference rules. Such a decree (order?) would not be obeyed not because of the inconsequence of the human race but because it would be meaningless. Our logical competence needs to keep a considerable degree of flexibility; its rules cannot be rendered as strict as in the system of classical or any other logic. Yet when we say that a specific discipline has to formulate its inference rules by means of some logical system, we propose something feasible.

To avoid misunderstanding, I am not saying that our practices of making inference rules explicit are guided by a system of logic which we have to obey but cannot discover. It may be wise to reserve the term *logic* merely to the mathematical systems we are used to calling so and not speak of some implicit logic but rather of our implicit logical competence. This competence does communicate with the systems we create but the systems obviously stem from our original capacity and are thus dependent on it. On the other hand, our practices can be influenced by the theories we develop and work with. Even though, for example, Frege introduced his logic mainly to serve science and particularly mathematics and it was necessary to delimit its primary sphere of applicability, it is still possible that by its presence in classrooms this logic inadvertently and slowly started to change the way we generally make rules explicit even in our everyday discourse.

What thus underlies all the different logics we have is not a great superlogic, as Robert Hanna claims it must be.[16] Rather it is our general logical competence. As with everything about our language, this competence can change and develop, also thanks to the theories we create. This instability is not a drawback but much rather a great asset, as progress may well require the modification also of such a basic practice as that of making our rules explicit. This change is not fully in our hands, yet we are always able to trace it and actively influence it.

Having identified the purpose of logic, we have also explained how it enables development of logic and therewith the plurality of logical systems. We thus embrace a specific form of logical pluralism. Now we should also consider an objection that our pluralism is trivial.

6.5.5 Dangers of a utilitarist view of logic

After making it more precise what variety of logical pluralism we are defending, we should consider one more objection to it which may come to the reader's mind, namely that it is a variety of a trivial form of utilitarism to which a cheap kind of pluralism all too unproblematically can be attached. Our approach is based on identifying a specific use we make of logic, rather than on seeking what is true in logic independently of us and what purposes we may find logic instrumental for. And it is then only natural that there can be more logics which can fulfil the purpose. But is this really so?

First of all, we do not claim only that different logics can be useful; this indeed is a trivial claim. Besides the fact that they can give their inventors and students the pleasant feelings that can accompany intellectual enterprise, one can find more persuasive examples of ways in which logics can be useful, as is summed up by Roy Cook:

> After all, logics have been central to the study of a number of phenomena, including many that have, at best, an indirect connection to human reasoning such as electronic circuit design, database management, and internet security. (Cook 2010, p. 494)

And even if for some logics we have not yet found such uses to put them to, we should not hasten to conclude that no such uses will be contrived in the future. So far so good, yet we do not just claim that more logics can be somehow useful but rather that more logics can fulfil the same purpose which we claim to be central for logic, indeed to belong to the very notion of logic, namely the purpose of making inference rules explicit. This is already a controversial claim.

The fact that various logics can serve this expressive purpose stems from our generally inferentialist understanding of meaning and, intimately connected with it, the dynamic nature of our concepts, including the very concept of expressive rationality and of making inference rules explicit.

6.5.5.1 Development of the notion of expressive rationality

How does the concept of expressive rationality develop? As in the case of any other concept, the development consists in an interplay of our theoretical conception thereof and our application thereof in individual cases. From the outset we implicitly understand what it means to make rules explicit, yet this concept is developed gradually by the concrete exercise of this expressive rationality.

Thus when we render various rules of inference explicit, we, in the very long run, come to see the fruits of this expressive work. When we are then somehow dissatisfied with our overall conceptual schemes, we can blame either the rules we are guided by and which we render explicit or, much more rarely, though possibly as well, the instruments we use for making the rules explicit. As with anything in our conceptual scheme, logic is subject to constant development, though its development is typically not very swift. The various logical systems can be seen as elaborations of possibilities of how our logical capacity could be changed. And as it can be changed and developed in multifarious ways (some of which, though, are particularly difficult) according to our decision, so there are many systems of logic. It is quite possible that some of such modifications would be seen as too extreme by most and the result of them would be something preferably not considered as logic at all, yet it is doubtful that we can make a definite delimitation.

There is some artificiality in the developed systems when we compare them with our everyday use of logic; indeed none of them really is the logic we in general use for expressive rationality because that logic is in essence dynamic and developing. The possible modifications (e.g. let us accept that the law of the excluded middle holds in all cases) of it encapsulated in the systems do not of themselves become truly used and thus do not really bind us merely by decree. They always have to prove themselves useful in the practice of expressive rationality and even if they succeed and become a part thereof, they still remain eligible to revision, as does anything in our conceptual schemes.

The logical systems in this way enable us to artificially speed up the development of our concept of expressive rationality, but this artificiality makes it difficult for them to prevail. But rather than decreeing that we should use this or that specific logic for rendering inference rules explicit in general, we can instead decide to subject ourselves to a particular system of logic in some well-delimited area of reasoning. A typical example that we mentioned already is that of using classical or intuitionist logic in mathematics, as per our decision. Another comparably convincing example of subjecting a discipline to a specific logic is nevertheless difficult to find.[17] And hardly any other logics can claim to have done a similarly important service to any area of discourse.

6.5.6 How about the necessity of logic?

When I emphasize logic's ability to develop, the question might naturally arise as to whether logic is still in some sense necessary. Given that any logical law can eventually be relativized and perhaps revisited, does this not entail that logic is a purely contingent matter of the conventions that we happen to adopt at a given point?

Strange as such a position might appear, something very close to it was already espoused by respected authors. Payette and Wyatt (2018) denounce what they call *logical generalism*, that is the thesis that logical laws are universally valid in all contexts and argue in favour of *logical particularism*, that is the thesis that any purported logical law holds only in some specific contexts. Even more radical is Gillian Russell (2018a), who advocates, perhaps with a little grain of salt to it, *logical nihilism*. As the title suggests, she claims that no logical laws really hold, as there are exceptions to all of them. Though I find something to sympathize with in both of these approaches, I see the matter differently.

My whole approach to logic is based on doctrines pertaining not only to logic but also to meaning in general. From among those, I espouse Quine's holism, including his attack on the distinction between synthetic and analytic statements. For many authors, including perhaps Quine himself in his later works, the most important lesson to take from 'Two Dogmas' is that there are no truly necessary statements. But we should not forget the second half of Quine's message – that none is in a strong sense simply contingent, neither.

This means that the distinction between what is necessary and what is contingent has to be rethought. The most straightforward way to do this is to consider them as a matter of degree. Perhaps this approach has its limitations, but it should suffice for us here. From this perspective we can say that there is indeed nothing such as complete necessity, just as there is nothing such as complete contingency. Sellars captured this perhaps more clearly than Quine when he noticed that every statement has nomological force to it. When we say that after lightning there is thunder, it is both an observation and a law which gives the concepts of *lightning* and *thunder* their content. In this way, every statement is to some degree necessary. Quine might have been aiming at the same point when he noted that every statement can be upheld in face of recalcitrant experience.

Statements pertaining to logic are typically considered more central and more immune to revision than those about lightning or thunder. On the other hand, reasoning does not have to be based on a fixed logic and the logical rules which shape the logical space can develop, just as all the other rules. But as the notion of absolute necessity proves to be ill-conceived, so is that of complete contingency. So, I am not claiming that the logical laws are contingent in the standard sense because I refuse to accept this standard sense in my conceptual repertoire.

6.5.6.1 *How to recognize the revision?*

If logic can undergo revision, how can we recognize that such a change in fact took place? The answer might be a little disappointing because the distinction between a change in meaning and its continuation cannot be taken literally. It is rather a metaphoric expression of the dynamics inherent in any rules and meanings, including the logical ones.

A rule and its applications in reality are closely related, in fact almost identical. On the one hand, the Wittgensteinian slogan that *meaning is use* holds. To say that there is a well-established practice in a given society of driving on the right side with people both in general abiding to it and also penalizing those who drive on the left, and so on, yet still one should really drive on the left side of the road, is clearly nonsense. But any established practice has to transcend all its past realizations and will tend to point to the future ones. Now, these will happen in new contexts and will by necessity bring a new development of the rules. Whether these applications in novel contexts were just continuous with the past ones or whether they meant a break with the tradition cannot be universally decided and judged. This is not because the real shape of the rule before entering the new context is particularly recondite. The very notion of the definite shape of a rule is misleading.

In some sense, then, the debates about a change of logic are meaningless. That logic has changed can be said only from a certain limited perspective, not in an absolute sense. The same holds also for claiming the opposite, namely that logic has not really changed. We thus see that the standard categories of change and stability do not apply so quite unproblematically to meaning and to logic. Some dynamics and movements are so inherent to rules and meanings that they can be said to be themselves kinds of movements rather than entities which sometimes happen to move. Yet, just as a physical movement, the movement which pertains to rules and meanings is always relative and there could often be equally legitimate accounts of a certain systems of rules which regard the same rule as stable and others which regard it as moving.

Logic can still be said to be necessary, yet the notion of necessity is understood in a strongly relativized sense. Furthermore, it does not exclude a specific kind of dynamism even for what is necessary. Rather than asserting or denying that logic is necessary in the sense in which it is understood by analytical and logical mainstream, I propose rethinking necessity, at least in respect to rules and meanings.

Although we have already explained why we should be sceptical about any attempts at demarcating what can be still considered as logic, we should now turn our attention to an important movement which seeks to provide a demarcation of logics by the means of proof-theory. Despite the fact that we will not be able to literally espouse these approaches, it will be instructive to see what they can still be useful for and compare them with the demarcations we already discussed, namely those which demarcate logic by the means of model theory.

7

Proof-theoretic demarcations of logic

Despite our overall rather negative attitude towards the demarcation of logic and a pluralist view which emphasizes logic's capacity to develop (our view is therefore much more rightly called *logical dynamism* than logical pluralism, yet more about this in the following chapter), we should still consider the significance of proof-theoretic demarcation proposals. It will be interesting to compare them with the model-theoretic ones, as on the one hand they form the main two demarcational movements and because they, unlike the model-theoretic ones, are closely related to the general philosophical stances which enabled us to arrive at our view on logic.

The fact that the proof-theoretic approaches are closely related to inferentialism and logical expressivism is obvious, as Brandom, as well as Peregrin, make it themselves fully clear that their inferentialist theses were inspired by proof-theory. Gerhard Gentzen (1935) came up with the idea of defining logical constants, that is in his case the standard connectives and quantifiers, by means of the inference rules, either in the calculus of natural deduction or in sequent calculus. As for us the difference between these two kinds of calculi will not be so important, we will for simplicity's sake focus only on sequent calculi. Thus, a particularly simple example to begin with is that of conjunction, as defined by the left and right rules we already mentioned. These rules state just that when you have both A and B, you have their conjunction and, vice versa, having the conjunction, you also have both these conjuncts. We already mentioned the rules guiding logical constants, as they pose a challenge to explain how logic can be useful, to which purpose we found logical expressivism to be a particularly useful doctrine. But now the rules are important for us because one can see them as jointly capturing what conjunction is. It is given by the rule which tells us from what it can be derived and from the rules telling us what can be derived from it. Gentzen himself claimed that the rules serve as *sozusagen Definitionen* of the logical constants in Gentzen (1935), section 5.13. Now such an approach seems very natural for conjunction, inferentialists try to generalize it and countenance something like Gentzen's rules for any meaningful expression in our languages. As we saw, meaning is thus explicated as an inferential role.

Since inferentialism came into existence as a generalization of Gentzen's ideas, it seems natural that inferentialists would prefer the proof-theoretic approach to logic over the model-theoretic one, which appears to stem rather from a generally referentialist approach to meaning, that is the view that the meaning of an expression is given foremostly by what it designates (or would designate in some specific situations). And the choice of the proof-theoretic approach has got consequences on the result of our demarcation, for example, the second-order logic has clearly a problematic status from this perspective, as it is not complete.

Let us first review some of the demarcation proposals, particularly two of them which were truly seminal, namely those of Ian Hacking and Kosta Došen.

7.1 Demarcation proposals

The attempts at a proof-theoretic demarcation of logic have their long and complex history,[1] beginning, as we have mentioned, with Gentzen, and then including for example Karl Popper or William Kneale.[2] These authors have attempted at demarcating what is and what is not logic, that is to determine the extent of logic, while possibly leaving the question about what is correct in the demarcated extent open, just in the sense of demarcation we already spoke about when discussing the model-theoretic approaches to demarcation. In other words, they were striving to demarcate logical constants while leaving their correct interpretation open (e.g. whether rather intuitionistic or classical logic gets negation and disjunction right). The shared goal of the two opposed schools is reflected also in the title of Gila Sher's book *The Bounds of Logic* and Kneale's article 'The Province of Logic'. As we are nevertheless not concerned with the history of these attempts but merely the relevance of their results for our philosophy of logic, let us proceed to a very important article by Ian Hacking (1979) with, once again, a suggestive title: 'What Is Logic?'

7.1.1 Hacking's proposal

When introducing his demarcation, Hacking approvingly quotes Dummett to the effect that logic should be concerned rather with inference than with truth,[3] thus showing his inferentialist preferences in logic. His overall project is very ambitious, as he wants (as Gila Sher) to reopen the question of logicism and give an answer to it by his demarcation. He sums up his criteria for an expression to be a logical constant in the following passage:

> A logical constant is a constant that can be introduced, characterized, or defined in a certain way. What way? My answer is about the same as Kneale's: a logical constant is a constant that can be introduced by operational rules like those of Gentzen. The question becomes, 'like' in which respects? Different answers will mark off different conceptions of logic. My answer is that the operational rules introducing a constant should (i) have the subformula property, and (ii) be conservative with respect to the basic facts of deducibility. The second clause means (finitistic) provability of the elimination theorems. (Hacking 1979, p. 303)

As was pointed out by Göran Sundholm (1981), alongside other imprecise statements he makes in this article, Hacking seems to use the term *conservativity* in two distinct, though related, senses, without distinguishing them sufficiently. On the one hand, he wants the system of logical constants to be conservative in the standard sense over the rest of the language (a criterion he shares with Brandom and logical expressivists in general); on the other hand, he wants such a system which enables us to proof (finitistically) some structural properties about the language with the logical constants based on their validity in the language lacking those constants. There are three structural rules which are of particular importance to Hacking: reflexivity, dilution and cut-elimination. Besides this he also wants the subformula property. Let us review these rules and properties and consider their importance.

The subformula property states that every formula occurring in the course of the proof is a subformula of a formula in the sequent proved. It is clearly a very neat property, yet Hacking does not really substantiate why it should be essential to the very idea of logic. Somewhat vaguely we can say that this property guarantees perspicuity of the proof, and indeed every step in the deduction obviously belongs to the proof; we are thus better safeguarded from allowing anything dubious to creep in.

Reflexivity of course is the property that every formula is a consequence of itself, that is the sequent A $\Longrightarrow$ A is always valid. Dilution, more commonly called weakening, is the fact that given any sequent, you can deduce a sequent with extra formulas both on the left and right side. Rule of cut is a generalization of the transitivity of consequence relation and says that from the sequents $\Gamma \Longrightarrow$ A, Δ and Σ, A$\Longrightarrow \Pi$, you deduce Γ, $\Sigma \Longrightarrow \Delta$, Π (thus you cut the formula A away). Gentzen proved that for the calculus of classical and intuitionistic logic, this rule is eliminable and Hacking requires such elimination to be provable for any system he wants to consider as genuinely logical.

In fact Hacking claims that all of the rules of reflexivity, dilution and cut will be 'readily assented to' (Hacking 1979, p. 293) as jointly sufficient conditions for any relation between logically simple (or atomic, i.e. not containing any logical vocabulary) formulae to count as a deducibility relation. On the same page, he claims that he is not trying to find necessary conditions. Nevertheless, once we have some deducibility relation for the atomic language, he requires of its logical expansion that all these properties hold also for the logically complex formulae and this be provable on the basis merely of their holding for the atomic formulae. This is his somewhat unorthodox use of the term *conservative*, namely that the system of deduction rules including the logically complex formulae preserves the structural rules just mentioned. But since he wants this kind of conservativeness, it then appears, in spite of his explicit disavowal, that he considered the structural rules just mentioned as also necessary for a consequence relation.

A question is in order here, namely, why should we consider exactly the properties mentioned by Hacking as either necessary or sufficient? Yet Hacking gives no substantiation of these conditions. Nevertheless, we can admit that most of the systems of logic we know have them and that they therefore certainly are not completely arbitrary. Especially in mathematical reasoning these rules appear as quite natural. Nevertheless, from a broader perspective, such as the one of logical expressivism that we adopt, these conditions seem difficult to justify. Maybe we can say that the transitivity of the consequence relation is necessary to create something we can really call a system of inference rules from which we can then abstract the inferential role of a given sentence or expression and consider it as its meaning. As far as reflexivity is concerned, we can at least say that it does not do any real harm.

There may be no great reasons for it but also hardly any against it. And as the proofs in sequent calculi have to begin with reflexive sequents, we can use this technical fact as a rationale for this property of the consequence relation.

The issue of weakening is more pressing, though, and Hacking's failure to substantiate this condition causes more trouble. There is an established tradition of non-monotonic logics and our everyday practice provides a great amount of counterexamples which confute the universal validity of this principle. There are of course also possibilities of defending monotonicity by reinterpreting the sentences which figure in the putative counterexamples. Nevertheless, little reason can be attached to closing the option of embracing non-monotonic logics.

But perhaps the correct reading of Hacking would be that given the material inference relations among logically atomic sentences, the structural rules have to be preserved by the extended system if they are present in the one lacking the logical vocabulary. Given this interpretation, Hacking tells us about his motivation for it when he is replying to criticism of an earlier version of his paper, criticism coming from Christopher Peacocke (see Peacocke 1976, p. 231), who asked why should we not just stipulate the rules for the complex formulae as well as for the atomic ones? Hacking counters that only with these elimination theorems can we say that the rules really introduce the constants in question, as otherwise we would introduce them not only by means of their left and right rules but also by the introduction of the structural rules for the whole system. The rules would then not be sufficiently local, Hacking claiming that 'one is not then defining logical constants in connection with some previous language fragment. Rather one is creating, as a totality, a new system of logistic' (Hacking 1979, p. 298).

It is surely only laudable to oppose an excessive holism and thus get a solid grasp of the specific properties of each individual logical constant. Yet it is not clear to what degree the holism should be tamed in such a way. Obviously, Hacking wants to prevent dangerous expressions such as the infamous Prior's *tonk* (presented in the article Prior (1960)) to be allowed into the system. The classical proposal (presented in Belnap 1962) of how this can be done is to demand the rules for the logical constants to be conservative. Hacking sympathizes with this proposal, yet furthermore wants to ensure conservativity in the unorthodox sense of provability of his favourite structural rules for the complex formulae. While his motivation remains somewhat vague, he can be credited with showing quite nicely another respect in which the meaning of a logical constant is necessarily holistic, namely when he points to the fact that the tonk connective does not have to cause the trivialization of the consequence relation; in Hacking's setting the problem of this connective is that it does not enable us to prove cut-elimination and therewith the consequence relation ceases to be transitive, as we can derive A$\Longrightarrow$AtonkB and AtonkB$\Longrightarrow$B, but not A$\Longrightarrow$B until we stipulate (because we cannot prove it) that the transitivity holds also for the formulae containing tonk.

Hacking's criterion ultimately leads to what he considers as the ideal logic, which is in its power somewhere between standard first-order and second-order logic (see p. 303 of Hacking's article). On the other hand, he also proposes ways of modifying his proposal, so as to get different, yet related, results. He says of demarcating criteria in general:

> A good criterion is one which is sharp but which can also be relaxed in various ways. (Hacking 1979, p. 308)

He then allows for relaxations of his criteria by, on the one hand, being less strict about the proofs we accept as proofs of the validity of the structural rules. In his core system, Hacking wants these proofs to be finitistic (a notion which he leaves somewhat underspecified), yet we can allow also for proofs using transfinite induction, thus creating a stronger system and marching towards second-order logic. Another relaxation would allow modal logics, as well, namely allowing the rules to put more restrictions on side formulae or even previous steps in the proof; otherwise weakening would not be provable. Hacking thus comes up with a very appealing idea that the logicality of an expression could be seen as a matter of degree. In fact, he also mentions that already the first-order quantifiers are not such pristine logical constants as the connectives because their rules put restrictions regarding the variables in the side formulae. I find this idea of logicality being a matter of degree particularly appealing and we shall in fact return to it later on.

7.1.2 Logical constants as punctuation marks

Kosta Došen's proposal (presented in Došen 1989) derives from ideas very similar to those of Hacking, yet also goes further. The fundamental idea is that logical constants should be independent of any specifics of the language into which we introduce them. This corresponds to MacFarlane's third sense of formality of logic, namely that it is topic-neutral. Various expressions can be applied only in certain areas of discourse, such as zoology or mathematics, but logical ones should be applicable everywhere without distinction because of their topic-neutrality. We already encountered Došen's presentation of rules for logical constants in sequent calculus – he uses the rules with double lines, indicating that the derivation can go in both directions. He remarks that the rules for logical constants are schematic, for example the rule for conditional:

$$\frac{\Gamma, A \Rightarrow \Delta, B}{\Gamma \Rightarrow \Delta, A \to B}$$

The conditional is the only specific linguistic object appearing in the formulation of the rule; everything else are mere placeholders. Therefore, we can say that the conditional can be applied in any area of discourse and is thus topic-neutral because its constitutive rules are schematic in the sense just explained. It belongs to the very nature of any language that it is open to the introduction of logical constants, no special provisions need to be made in advance.

What are the results of this demarcation; that is what systems does it grant the status of logic? Došen emphasizes that his criterion is open in two important senses. First of all, unlike Hacking, Došen is silent about the structural rules. He does not contend there to be any connection between his idea of logicality as schematicity and the structural rules, such as weakening, contraction and the like. The same rule for conditional can thus give us both the classical conditional, the intuitionistic one (if we prohibit weakening on the right) or the relevant one (this time by prohibiting weakening on the left). In this sense Došen allows multiple systems as logic by remaining impartial about the structural rules.

Another sense in which his criterion is fundamentally open is that it only tells us which expressions are logical constants, not which ones are not. It is namely by no means a given that when we do not know of any schematic rules which would inferentially characterize a given expression that there cannot be any. Using terms from computability theory, we can say that the set of logical constants is (rather) not recursive but just recursively enumerable.

Furthermore, it should be noted that Došen's criterion does not guarantee conservativity of the constants, since the introduction of the conditional into a system with weakening only on the right side will make the weakening on the left side derivable, as well.

Both Hacking and Došen agree that the rules for the logical constants they give cannot be really seen as definitions of them and we can read both better and worse arguments for this thesis in their articles. Hacking provides what he calls a *do-it-yourself semantics*, thus suggesting that, besides the inference rules, some further work must be done in order to really catch the meanings of logical constants. He notes that the Gentzenian rules are *peculiar definitions* (p. 296) which of course reminds one of Gentzen's own dictum of *sozusagen Definitionen*. Furthermore, he admits:

> First, it is clear that these rules could not define the constants for a being that lacked all logical concepts. One must understand something like conjunction to apply the conjunction rule, and one must have some surrogate for some sort of quantifier to apply the rule for universal quantification. (Hacking 1979, p. 299)

A few sentences later, Hacking claims that the Gentzenian rules cannot be said to define but merely to *characterize* the logical constants. Hacking thus seems to be far away from the inferentialist picture of what meaning is and how it works. In fact he sounds very much like a typical critic of inferentialism; see for example p. 682 of Lepore (2007).

Note, nevertheless, that if this should be an objection (and Hacking, unlike Fodor and Lepore, does not intend to show that the proof-theoretic characterization is fundamentally flawed), the situation is not any different for standard Tarskian semantic definitions of logical constants. Or if you just think of the truth table for the conjunction, you also have to understand conjunction in advance in order to be able to use the table at all.

According to Došen, the logical constants are not fully defined by the Gentzenian rules because these rules lack two fundamental properties of definitions. He calls the first one Pascal's condition and by that he means that the defined expression be eliminable by what defines it. The second property is conservativity.

Now, for example (due, again to Došen 1989), in the single conclusion systems you cannot eliminate the conditional from the sequent A→B ⇒ C. Došen himself, nevertheless, points out that definition might not be the only ideal of explication we are striving to achieve, as many of the most interesting philosophical analyses are also not definitions by the strict criteria of Pascal's condition and conservativity. Should we, as inferentialists, be concerned by these remarks? Do they show that logical constants are not given just by these rules but that we need some sort of model-theoretic semantics, as well? Not quite. Having a model-theoretic semantics in addition to a system of deduction is surely an asset, as it can be in many ways easier to work with. But this does not mean that giving the Gentzenian rules for the constants fails to give a full answer to somebody asking what these constants are. Let us reconsider both the issue of conservativity and that of eliminability (as we can call Pascal's condition for the sake of brevity).

As far as conservativity is concerned, the example provided by Došen does not really pose a challenge. First of all, it should be clear that if we need to require the conservativity of logical constants, then it is sufficient that they be conservative as a whole with respect to the extra-logical part of the language. For instance, as is pointed out in Peregrin (2008)(p. 281), the purely implicative part of intuitionistic logic coincides with that of classical logic. Yet adding negation is conservative in the intuitionistic and not in the classical case. Yet the whole of the classical propositional logic is conservative with respect to the rest of the language and only this can be deemed to be a necessary condition for a logic to be able to make the inference rules explicit. Nevertheless, this consideration cannot really be used against Došen's example of making left weakening admissible by introducing the rules for conditional. But we can counter that conservativity can be breached to various degrees and some of them do not have to be seen as particularly damaging.

How about Pascal's condition? It is precisely the point of logical expressivism that with logic we can say something we previously could only do. Thus Pascal's condition would actually infringe on the main job logic is supposed to do. It can be surely useful to define a complex logical vocabulary from as small a group of primitive expressions as possible, yet should all the logical constants be eliminable, then no expression of rules which were only implicit so far can be achieved. Yet the example of the failure of the condition mentioned by Došen is remarkable; as for Došen himself, the main point of logic is that logical vocabulary should *internalize the meta*, as Peregrin puts it (Peregrin 2008, p. 269).[4] From this perspective, the fact that we cannot eliminate the conditional from the context of the sequent A→B ⇒ C might be seen as kind of a problem because in this case we cannot straightforwardly say what is being expressed. Nevertheless, this also is hardly a big issue, as it is natural to suppose that an expression can be introduced into a language for a purpose of making inference explicit and then can be used also in contexts where it does not play exactly this original role.

If we pause to think of conservativity a little more, we can see that matters do not have to be so strict as the mainstream logical expressivists put them. Clearly, something sufficiently similar to conservativity is required for the logical constants because the logical constants are supposed to express the structure of our language and not change it. Nevertheless, I think that this idea of making something explicit without changing it at all is too much of an abstraction because when a rule is implicit, it typically is to a great degree vague and imprecise. When making it explicit, we typically also change it, at least by making it more precise and decreeing more specifically in which cases it is to be applied. Thus, I doubt that full-blown conservativity is necessary for logic in general, though something sufficiently approaching it surely is.

To speak somewhat figuratively, the conservativity would be required if the notions we employ were static, while I believe they are dynamic. As according to inferentialism the inference rules are essential for the content of a concept, then with these rules the concept itself changes. Some of its changes would make no sense and in fact when accepting them, we would rather be speaking about a different notion. On the other hand, some changes can be said to develop the concept.

Nevertheless, to come back to the discussion about whether the inference rules really spell out what the logical constants are, I would say that they do, yet on the other hand the concept of an implication, negation, conjunction and so on can also develop, though clearly typically less quickly than some more mundane ones. And there is always something implicit about our usage of the logical constants in natural language, which is why any specific rules we are presented with cannot fully convince us that they completely capture what these constants are. They typically capture quite a lot of the fundamental features of, say, the conditional, yet something always seems to be left out, for example, the instance when even such fundamental rules as *modus ponens* seem to fail. The problem is not that we need something else besides the rules but rather that we have to appreciate the dynamic character of our language games and their implicit rules in general.

As well as in the case of Hacking, though, we have to say that Došen lacks a pragmatic account of what logic should be good for. We, on the other hand, pursue the thesis of logical expressivism and despite the ingenuity of Došen's proposal, we cannot straightforwardly claim that the logics he demarcates as real logics are exactly the ones apt to express implicit inference rules. Peregrin criticizes (in both Peregrin 2008 and 2014a) Došen's description of logical constants as punctuation marks, though he proposes to develop it, instead of rejecting it completely. He argues that the logical constants serve to denote some specific algebraic relations between the nodes of the inferential network of sentences. Take, for example, the conjunction. We can say that it is an inferential infimum, that is the greatest lower bound of the conjuncts. Or, again, the negation is the maximal incompatible, as every proposition which is incompatible with A implies the negation of A. Similar algebraic characterizations can be given also of the other logical constants (see Peregrin 2008, p. 290 for the account of this correspondence between calculi and algebras). Thus, the logical vocabulary enables us to find such algebraic nodes and express them; see Peregrin's characterization of the situation:

> There is a sense in which elements of a standard inferential structure do implicitly have their conjunctions, disjunctions etc. although they do not have them explicitly if there are no expressions within the language which would express them. They do have them implicitly in the sense that they form a (proto-)structure which can naturally be extended to a structure in which these elements are present. (Peregrin 2008, p. 290)

As we can see, Došen's view of logical constants as punctuation marks can be developed into a position which is already very close to logical expressivism and his demarcation thus also can, despite the appearances we already spoke of, be viewed as quite acceptable for logical expressivists. We only need to defend inferentialism against Došen's reservations that the Gentzenian rules cannot really spell out what the logical constants are. Besides Pascal's condition and conservativity we can adduce another – and I believe more important – reason why we should regard the Gentzenian rules as not being exactly definitions of logical constants, namely their static nature. I regard the logical constants as expressions which, together with all the other expressions, develop in a complicated and holistic manner. Thus, the very concept of making inference rules explicit develops and therewith also the concept of a conditional, of negation, disjunction and all the others. The validity of the rules guiding them has to be constantly revived by how we actually use them and thus the rules formulated in a sequent calculus, as well as in any other formal setting, cannot be exactly right because they present the constants in a petrified way, as something with a completely clear-cut shape.

Nevertheless, what keeps developing is nothing over and above the inference rules which can be captured in a sequent calculus. And some of the descriptions of our practices can be much better than others, as they capture the rules we indeed abide by more precisely and also because they might be better to work with in making the inferential structure of our languages explicit. As we already emphasized, logical theory can be good both by corresponding to what it is supposed to capture and also by changing it in a positive way, such as making it more simple.

7.1.3 On the import of structural rules

Došen's approach has one particularly neat and interesting property. Namely, it speaks of a given logical constant as having one meaning even across different logics. This brings us back to debates about Quine's bold, yet oversimplified, thesis that a change of logic means a change of meaning of logical constants. In Došen's framework (or rather in Gentzen's framework that he endorses), we can say that the connectives are all the same in both classical and intuitionistic logic. It is just one negation, conditional, conjunction and disjunction. Only the structural rules differ. Saying openly what Došen probably only thought and pointed at, Restall (2014) explicitly asserts that the connectives mean the same and therefore are the same across the systems which differ merely by their structural rules.

It seems an interesting question as to whether structural rules contribute to meanings of logical constants. If they do, then Quine would be right after all. If not, then we can speak of a strong plurality of logics, namely of that which countenances different logics which nevertheless speak of one and the same issue. But I believe this question is ultimately much less interesting and has problematic suppositions.

As the reader might have guessed from my argumentation against clear-cut meanings, I do not consider either of the alternative answers as felicitous and therewith also see the problem with the question. Every meaning lives in the practice of how we use a given expression and does not have a definite, clear-cut shape. Not only that the meaning is dynamic and thus moves in various directions, it rather is the movement itself. Competent users understand the trajectory of this movement and can operate with it. In some indirect sense, we can speak of meaning as if it were a clear-cut entity but then we never discuss all of its aspects. Clearly, meanings of logical constants across various logics are closely related. Došen points to a nice way in which we might understand their relationships. Indeed, we can in a simplified way even say that they have the same meaning.

On the other hand, the structural rules belong to the way we use the constants and thus also belong to their meanings. As I already noted earlier, every talk of meanings of individual expressions is a simplification. Now, different simplifications can be useful or illuminating in different contexts. We will speak of various kinds of logical pluralism in the last chapter. Yet I can already state in advance that against Quine I do not consider a slight difference in meaning as a hindrance for logical pluralism. Indeed, it is not a hindrance for the logicians who prefer different logics to discuss meaningfully and not talk past each other. Došen's approach enables us to see how closely at least some logics, those which can be captured in his framework, are related.

A somewhat more refined version of the thesis that connectives can share meanings is provided in Dicher (2017), where Bogdan Dicher argues, opposing the already discussed variety of pluralism due to Restall (2014), that the meaning of a logical constant typically includes some structural properties. By this, Dicher means the properties without which the constant cannot be even considered. For example, the sequent rules for negation typically need permission to have at least two formulae on at least one of the sides of the sequent. He calls these structural properties *intrinsic* for the given connective; the others, called by him *extrinsic*, are supposed to be unrelated to the behaviour of the constant itself, as they rather just indicate how it interacts with other logical constants. As sound as his insight is and although it certainly brings a more fine-grained version of the thesis that logical constants are the same across structurally different systems, one could still protest that even the so called extrinsic structural rules do indeed belong to the meaning of the given item.

It is useful to have a story about how the logicians adhering to different logics mean the same thing by the logical vocabulary they use. Yet it is hardly possible to get a story which would be invulnerable to any kind of attack in any context. And fortunately, such a story is not needed to enable pluralism to get off ground.

We saw that Došen's proposal for demarcation fares rather well from the perspective of logical expressivism, as the notion of logical constant as punctuation mark can be developed into that of logical constant as marking some important nodes in our inferential framework and thus making them explicit. Let us now, nevertheless, see some of the demarcations of self-avowed logical expressivists for comparison.

7.2 Expressivist demarcations

What do the important proponents of logical expressivism have to say about logical pluralism? Brandom himself remains surprisingly taciturn about the issue in both *Making It Explicit* and *Articulating Reasons* (Brandom 1994 and 2000). In fact, only a few hints at what he could consider as logic can be found in his major work, such as his eagerness to emphasize that his inferentialism is a development of what already Frege says in Begriffschrift (Frege (1879)); on the other hand, he also has strong reservations about the adequacy of the truth-functional conditional.

> This form of conditional, whatever its compositional virtues, is an extremely impoverished resource for the expression of properties of inference. (Brandom 1994, p. 112)

Yet these indications hardly suffice to let us know whether Brandom believed that some of the logics are privileged as an instrument of logical expression or if perhaps more of them can achieve such a goal equally well. We have to wait for his later book, *Between Saying and Doing*, to see him go as far as to explicitly mention the problem of logical pluralism. Yet, at the same time, Brandom points to a way of solving it as well:

> I am suggesting that standing in this complex, resultant meaning-use relation to every autonomously deployable vocabulary can serve as a partial answer to a central question in the philosophy of logic: the demarcation question. That question is, roughly, 'What is logic?' or, somewhat more carefully, 'What is logical vocabulary?', that is, 'What features should be taken as distinguishing some bit of vocabulary as distinctively logical vocabulary?' (Brandom 2008, p. 48)

The relation Brandom speaks of at the beginning of this quote is the relation of making the rules of inference explicit. Brandom tries to apply the strictest criterion possible for a group of expressions to count as logical constants, namely to be applicable universally to any vocabulary for the logical expression.

Brandom, as we already saw, mentions the relation of consequence and that of incompatibility between statements as the two fundamental relations which constitute the meaningfulness of our languages and which are to be rendered explicit by means of logic. The two relations are clearly very intimately interrelated, yet it is not entirely clear whether Brandom believes that they are even interdefinable. Peregrin is, on the other hand, inclined to see matters in this way.

Despite this possibility of interrelating them, developing logic from the concept of incompatibility led Brandom to classical logic as the core logic for making the implicit explicit and to the modal logic C^5 as its natural extension, while starting from the relation of consequence led Jaroslav Peregrin rather to intuitionistic logic and this time S5 as its natural extension. A succinct comparison of the two approaches was provided in Peregrin (2016). In this article it is shown that while the approach based on inference can be slightly modified (though in a less than natural way) to obtain rather classical logic, there is no such path available if incompatibility is taken as the basic concept.

I think that it is particularly laudable that Peregrin's and Brandom's demarcations target specifically such standard systems as classical logic, intuitionistic logic or the modal logics S5 and C. It would certainly be strange if logical expressivism forced us to abandon the logics we are used to working with, as then it would rather create a new notion of logic than explain the one we already have.

Nevertheless, I do not see how either Brandom's or Peregrin's demarcation can be seen as specifically expressionist. Surely, we can say that both are inferentialist in the sense that they base their demarcation, just as Hacking and Došen, on proof-theory, but still these demarcations could be done in exactly the same way from the point of view very different from logical expressivism. Let us therefore look for a demarcation which tries to exploit the insights of logical expressivism more.

7.2.1 Latest attempts

Ulf Hlobil develops a system which would be more general than, for example, classical or intuitionistic logic in that it would not in general be monotonic (remember that Brandom himself expressed his misgivings about monotonicity already in *Making It Explicit*). Thus in his article 'A Non-monotonic Sequent Calculus for Inferentialist Expressivist' he presents a system of logic which can easily be rendered intuitionistic or classical by the addition of further rules. He thus claims the following:

> The system I have presented can be viewed as a 'mother-logic' that gives rise to intuitionism or classical logic under special circumstances. (Hlobil 2016, p. 104)

A specifically expressivist and anti-formalist trait of his system is that it countenances the possibility of there being (not necessarily monotonic) relations of consequence and of incompatibility among logically atomic formulae. He thus gets this general expressivist idea of inferential relations between atomic formulae into the logical system itself. Hlobil continues in the direction of looking for more adequate expressivist logic in his article 'When Structural Principles Hold Merely Locally' (see Hlobil 2017). There he discusses the possibility of expressing in which cases the structural rules hold. His motivation is to have a system which is not in general monotonic (which under some standard conditions regarding the nature of the consequence relation means that the rule of cut cannot hold in general either, as that would lead to monotonicity), yet which has the expressive power to make explicit where the monotonicity holds. The idea is to modify the consequence relation and thereby say that formulae from a given set of formulae can be added to the premises under the preservation of the consequence relation between the original premises and the conclusion. More precisely we define in the following way (where L_0 is the set of original formulae and $\vdash_0$ is the original consequence relation):

$$X \subseteq P(L_0)^6 \text{ and } \forall \Delta \in X(\Delta, \Gamma \vdash_0 p), \text{ then } \Gamma \vdash^{\uparrow X} p.$$

Thus Hlobil's logic can make explicit what other logics typically leave out of the picture and accommodates Brandom's reasons for holding that the relation of consequence is in general not monotonic. Generally speaking, he opens the door for similar considerations about making explicit the local validity of any structural rules, not only of monotonicity. This is a real step into doing logic in a genuinely expressivist way, as this project of making the validity of structural rules explicit is something which could hardly be made sense of without acceptance of the Brandomian outlook on the purpose of logic. Hlobil thus gives much more flesh to Peregrin's dictum of *internalizing the meta*.

7.2.2 Structural rules – Does logic need them?

By countenancing Hlobil's system which lacks monotonicity, one might wonder about the merits of structural rules in general. Which ones are necessary for something to be a logic? To what degree? Clearly, the more standard view would be that structural rules such as weakening, contraction, exchange or transitivity of the relation of logical consequence are essential for deductive reasoning and for logic. For example, Beall and Restall, despite their advocacy of logical pluralism, refuse to consider substructural logics as genuine logics. On the other hand, the specialists in and fans of substructural logics will naturally see this as too close-minded a stance and might rather consider structural rules as hindrances to the study of phenomena which belong to deductive reasoning, such as reasoning about sorites paradoxes which invite dropping transitivity of consequence. In fact, even such a seemingly undisputable structural feature as reflexivity of consequence (that every formula is a consequence of itself, that is, $A \vdash A$) is not valid in some systems, as can be read in Zardini (2018).

I do not side with either party. In a way, supporters of substructural logics are right to pursue their endeavours given that no inference rule is beyond the reach of criticism. I regard meaning of any expression, including logical expressions, as dynamic. This leads me to the view I call *logical dynamism* and to which I will return later. I do not see any reason why structural rules should not be doubted, but at the same it should be said that historically they are well entrenched. Countenancing systems which break them means stretching the notion of logic. It is disputable to what degree such stretching can be useful, yet in principle it is justifiable. I hope this will be clearer when I get to explaining logical dynamism.

7.2.3 Dialogical approaches

There are further approaches related to inferentialism and logical expressivism which should be at least mentioned here. A more thorough exposition and deeper analysis of these are, nevertheless, not to be found here. For one thing, for all their own value, I am not sure to what degree they are relevant to our issue of the plurality of logics. And furthermore, it would be too great a digression full of technical detail.

These approaches are all based on the view that logic and reasoning are at home in dialogue much more than in isolated musings of an individual mind. This insight is also fundamental to the approach that I defend here, as is clear from the Wittgensteinian insistence on the social character of all rules, including those of logic. Let me now briefly mention what options are on the table.

There are two classical kinds of game-theoretic semantics. One of them treats logic and meaning in general as a single player game, the second one as a game for two players, that is indeed as a matter of dialogue. The first approach can be found in Hintikka and Kulas (1983) and Hintikka and Sandu (1997) and takes the meaning of logical expressions to consist of rules which establish how one can prove a given statement containing them. The partner in discussion is not explicitly considered; the statement to be proven is considered as isolated. If one wants to have an image of an opponent, then it is usually claimed that the opponent is the nature or the world which decides about our success or failure at establishing the claim in question.

The other approach is based on there being explicitly a proponent and an opponent of a given thesis. The proponent tries to prove a given formula, while the opponent tries to reject it. Depending on what strictures you put on the possible moves in such a game, you can define either classical or intuitionistic logic in this way. Both these approaches, although they have something in common with our approach, can be conceived also without embracing either inferentialism or logical expressivism. An approach more closely related to Brandom's doctrines was proposed under the name *ludics*. This approach is based on seeing proofs in sequent calculus of linear logic as dialogues. This approach models not only dialogue in which one party tries to win over the other and thus covers a broader class than the approaches just mentioned. It also captures formally the pragmatist tenets of Brandom's philosophy, in particular his insistence that practice precedes explicit theory and formulation. This approach is presented in Lecomte (2011 and 2013). The linear logic on which it is based is substructural logic, presented for the first time in Girard (1987). Going substructural is a feature ludics has in common with Hlobil. It should be mentioned that also Danielle Porello (2012) goes in this direction, as he also bases his variation of Brandom's incompatibility semantics on linear logic.

8

Pluralism or monism?

In this closing chapter, we will summarize what conclusions regarding the plurality of logics we have arrived at and, in particular, consider the resemblances with and differences from positions of other authors who consider themselves as logical pluralists. Furthermore, we will also consider the question as to whether logic is in some interesting sense exceptional or whether it is on equal footing with other disciplines, which entails being revisable in the light of similar reasons which can make us revise our, for example, zoological theories.

8.1 Varieties of pluralism

Lots of authors are self-avowed logical pluralists and they mean lots of different things by claiming that more than one logic is in some sense correct or acceptable. Some of the varieties of pluralism can be rather innocuous; others can be very controversial. The thesis of logical pluralism thus needs to be rendered more precise in order to be interesting. We cannot hope to list all the possible forms of logical pluralism one can think of, perhaps not even all those that have actually been thought of. Nevertheless, let us revise at least some of the most fundamental forms.

8.1.1 Linguistic vs. non-linguistic pluralism

In their *Logical Pluralism*, Beall and Restall base their stance on the possible different understandings of what logical consequence amounts to. All the different understandings must, nevertheless, still have something in common. They call this the *Generalized Tarski thesis* and it runs thus:

> An argument is valid if and only if, in every case$_x$ in which the premises are true, so is the conclusion. (Beall and Restall 2006, p. 29)

Their pluralism stems from the possibility of understanding the notion of *case* differently (hence the subscribed x). We can countenance complete and consistent cases which, according to Beall and Restall, lead us to classical logic. If, on the other hand, we countenance incomplete cases, we get intuitionistic logic. And again, allowing also for the inconsistent cases, we obtain relevance logic. Maybe other logics can be opened up in this way, yet the authors claim that it is only the three mentioned ones that they have managed to legitimize. Their view is therefore a form of pluralism, though a very restricted one.

They contrast this position with its predecessor, endorsed by Carnap and known as *Toleranzprinzip*. According to Carnap, many logics are possible, as they stem from different stipulations of inference rules. We can just choose which rules we accept, say, for negation. Choosing different rules means using a different language. According to Carnap there is no need to prefer any language to any other, as can be read in this famous quote:

> In logic, there are no morals. Everyone is at liberty to build his own logic, i.e. his own form of language, as he wishes. All that is required of him is that, if he wishes to discuss it, he must state his methods clearly, and give syntactical rules instead of philosophical arguments. (Carnap 1934, p. 17)

We can thus distinguish Carnap's pluralism from Beall's and Restall's by calling it linguistic, as opposed to non-linguistic pluralism. For instance, according to linguistic pluralism, classical and intuitionistic logic attach different meanings to the negation and disjunction signs, while according to non-linguistic pluralism these two logics differ, although they use the signs with the same meanings. Beall and Restall apparently find their non-linguistic pluralism more interesting and convincing but they still regard Carnap's pluralism as a worthy forerunner of their own conception. Other authors are more critical towards *Toleranzprinzip*. Indeed, we have already discussed Quine's view, namely that changing the rules of logic means changing the subject in the sense of not talking about logic anymore. Obviously, he thus presupposed that linguistic pluralism is not a logical pluralism. We have already declared Quine's view too extreme for reasons which can be once again summed up by a quote from Hartry Field:

> On some readings of 'differ in meaning', any big difference in theory generates a difference in meaning. On such readings, the connectives do indeed differ in meaning between advocates of the different all-purpose logics, just as 'electron' differs in meaning between Thomson's theory and Rutherford's; but Rutherford's theory disagrees with Thomson's despite this difference in meaning, and it is unclear why we shouldn't say the same thing about alternative all-purpose logics. (Field 2009, p. 345)

It has to be admitted though that Carnap's view, albeit, pace Quine, genuinely pluralistic, seems prima facie as a less bold version of pluralism. Furthermore, it has its problems which partly invite criticism of a Quinean sort. One problem is that Carnap presupposes complete arbitrariness of logic. Quine came up with interesting reasons against this view already in Quine (1936), where he argues that were the logical rules merely stipulated by conventions, we would still need some rules for applying these conventions and these rules would necessarily be of a logical kind, that is it will be such rules as should be, according to Carnap, stipulated by the very convention.

Indeed, the Carnapian view relies on a firm boundary between analytic and synthetic statements which was rendered obsolete by Quine. We cannot just postulate a language and its logic out of the blue. Yet this criticism should not dissuade us from what remains viable in the Carnapian line of thought. It is true that, taken literally, this line of thought would mean that anything at all could be regarded as logic. Carnap thus wants to foster a quite inebriating sense of freedom:

> The first attempts to cast the ship of logic off from the terra firma of the classical forms were certainly bold ones, considered from the historical point of view. But they were hampered by the striving after 'correctness'. Now, however, that impediment has been overcome, and before us lies the boundless ocean of unlimited possibilities. (Carnap 1934, p. xv)

But how could we then recognize something as a proposal of alternative logic at all? We can be open to there being various legitimate logics which one can propose, but still they all have to agree on at least some principles in order to be regarded as proposals of logic at all. And that is exactly the way to redeem what is valuable in Carnap. We indeed have some freedom, but it is restricted. We could also say that we can abandon Carnap's attempt to open up the room for what is merely a *negative freedom* and rather try to formulate what a *positive freedom* in logic could amount to. We cannot completely choose the rules of logic or change the rules we already use but, invoking again the Neurathian ship, we can choose some of the rules when we regard many others as fixed. Nevertheless, there seems to be no reason to regard any of the rules as unrevizable in any context whatsoever. Even though it is much more restrained than Carnap imagined, we have acquired some freedom by the development of various logics. They can be seen as proposals of different languages and therewith as proposals to modify the language we use.

8.1.2 Beall and Restall

Now, how about Beall and Restall's pluralism, how are we to assess it in comparison with Carnapian pluralism? Just as in the previous case, we can retain something very good from it while there is also some one-sidedness to it. On the one hand, they claim that their pluralism is more substantial but also that it is more plausible than the Carnapian one. Restall (2002) argues extensively that divergence in logic does not have to mean divergence in language. As we have so far argued that having different legitimate languages can lead to an interesting form of logical pluralism, we should concur with Restall that it is not the only route. When Field compares the disputes about logical laws to the disputes about the properties of an electron between Thomson and Rutherford, he emphasizes that when two disputing parties endow some important expressions with different meanings, their debate can still be substantial. On the other hand, the same debate between Thomson and Rutherford can also be seen as concerning purely matters of fact. One and the same dispute can be described in various ways, some making it appear as rather a dispute concerning language, others rather as a factual dispute. And Beall and Restall are right in claiming that there is no reason why we should think that any logical dispute has to be regarded as purely linguistic. This is also admitted by Teresa Kouri Kissel (2018), who, nevertheless, doubts whether one can take all the three logics which Beall and Restall countenance as real logics, that is classical, intuitionistic and relevance logic, as having all the same meanings of connectives.[1]

In this respect, we can claim that Beall and Restall are right. Yet they frame their version of logical pluralism as one which is not linguistic at all. When a relevantist thus refuses the *ex contradictio quodlibet* law, while a proponent of classical logic claims that it is valid, they understand this as a dispute about two different understandings of the notion of entailment. When they thus discuss the validity of the inference A∧¬A⊨B, then, according to Beall and Restall, it is really about the ⊨ that they discuss (because ⊨ implicitly contains a reference to a specific understanding of *case*). Yet, how can we decide whether this is really so or whether the debate is rather focused on ∧ and ¬? It is true that we can try asking the participants and sometimes we can have good reasons for deciding to see the dispute in one way or another. Yet I am afraid that in many cases such decisions cannot be made rationally and we can analyse the same dispute in both ways with equal legitimacy. Their claim that there can be a legitimate pluralism which countenances different legitimate logics with the same meanings of logical constants is therefore vague and too radical. Any reasonable pluralism, I think, has to be of a kind somewhere between that of Carnap and that of Beall and Restall.

Can we, nevertheless, claim that the less a pluralism is about the meanings of logical constants, the more substantial and interesting it is? There seems to be a hidden supposition behind such a claim, namely that linguistic disputes are in general less important or substantial than factual ones. I think such a principle can be accepted, though as a defeasible one. In general, it is very plausible, even though we can be in dispute about very important linguistic questions and about very unimportant factual ones. On the one hand, it would be very consequential if we agreed to drop the present perfect tense in English; on the other hand, it can hardly be of much interest to find out how many hairs there are on Donald Trump's head. In general, though, the principle does not lead us astray. We can thus say that Beall and Restall open up a pathway towards a more interesting kind of logical pluralism.

Nevertheless, as it is hardly possible – putting perhaps some trivial cases aside – to characterize an interesting dispute as merely linguistic or utterly factual, Beall and Restall do not fulfil their ambition to make their pluralism an utterly non-linguistic matter. In fact, this argument applies to a broader class of approaches which Stewart Shapiro characterizes in the following way:

> We vary the logic, within a single semantic/logical framework, by varying something that is, supposedly, unrelated to meaning, the class of interpretations, the designated values, the structural rules, etc. (Shapiro 2014, p. 19)

Thus it is not only the logical pluralism of Beall and Restall (2006) but also a proof-theoretic variations on it from Restall (2014) and its refinement due to Dicher (2017) which only partly succeed at opening a plurality of logics without varying meanings of logical expressions. Similar reasoning applies also to Hjortland (2013).

8.2 Further distinctions

Although the distinction we have just discussed is the most mentioned, there are a few other interesting distinctions between different kinds of logical pluralism which we can review now. One distinction will be the one between logical pluralism regarding the demarcation of logical constants and the one concerning the same logical constants. The other distinctions will be taken from an article by Matti Eklund, concerning whether there is a plurality of actual uses of logical expressions or the plurality of logics which are good for some purpose independently of whether we use them or not.

8.2.1 Logical constants once more

We have already encountered the problem of logical constants and, before considering specific proposals to solve it, we had dedicated some space to establish that it is a legitimate problem. We defended it against the Quinean thesis that a deviant logician always changes the topic. It is clear also from our discussion of Carnap's Toleranzprinzip that we do not need to dwell on this anymore. Yet, although it can be reasonable to distinguish the problem of logical constants as a part of the broader problem of deciding which logical systems are genuine logics, that does not mean we can always easily decide whether two given logics differ rather in their choice of logical constants or in their analysis of the same constants.

Roy Cook distinguishes, among other varieties of logical pluralism, also a pluralism regarding the possible ways to draw the division between logical and non-logical vocabulary in one and the same language.[2] This version is thus clearly distinct from the pluralism of Beall and Restall as it is linguistic, yet also differs from Carnap's account. While Carnap countenances the possibility to use different languages with different logics, this version considers just one language and claims that there are more possibilities to divide logical and non-logical vocabulary. This pluralism regarding the divide is endorsed by Achille Varzi (2002), yet we have also seen lots of pluralist tendencies in authors convinced, contrary to Varzi, that there is a unique optimal way to demarcate logical constants, as, for instance, Došen reckons with the possibility of accepting different structural rules while sticking with the same divide between logical and extra-logical vocabulary. Obviously, the two kinds of pluralism can be combined. We have already endorsed a more sober version of the Carnapian pluralism. Can we in some ways endorse also the pluralism regarding the divide between logical constants and extra-logical vocabulary? The answer is unsurprisingly yes, even though we have been sympathetic to some of the actual demarcations; these demarcations themselves, be they by Hacking, Došen, Peregrin, Brandom or Hlobil, did all allow for some openness to the notion of logical constant. Again, then, we have discovered some freedom though a limited one, just as with our adaptation of Carnapian pluralism. The freedom is even more present in our account, which emphasizes that every notion, including the very notion of logic, is capable of development, as there is no reason why we should think that this development cannot influence also our understanding of which expressions are necessary as tools for logic as an instrument of making inference rules explicit, that is our understanding of what is a logical constant.

8.2.2 Eklund's projects

Matti Eklund manages to distinguish as many as eight possible kinds of logical pluralism and as his systematization is very insightful, we should consider if our approach does fall under one of his categories and to what degree the different kinds of pluralism can be maintained independently of each other. Ultimately, I think, they all more or less collapse.

Eklund's article is somewhat sceptical in its spirit, as it shows how the various kinds of pluralism either fail to be of much interest, as they are trivial, or are hard to substantiate. Nevertheless, he emphasizes that any problems to give logical pluralism a cogent shape necessarily ail also the opposite thesis of logical monism:

> Logical pluralism – my explicit topic – is a contentious doctrine. But the problems regarding making sense of logical pluralism are equally problems regarding making sense of logical monism. (Eklund 2017, p. 451)

Indeed, if we consider logical monism as a negation of the thesis of logical pluralism, namely that there is more than one correct logic, then obviously logical monism can be made sense of only if it can be made of logical pluralism, as you can hardly negate anything which is not already a meaningful assertion. And at least prima facie, logical monism and logical pluralism appear to be in this relation, that is that monism is the negation of pluralism.

The first of Eklund's distinctions does not need to be dwelled upon, as it is that between Carnapian pluralism and the pluralism of Beall and Restall. We have already commented on what we regard as viable in both approaches and have also argued that they in general have to collapse. Nevertheless, Eklund furthermore divides both of these approaches into four separate kinds, or rather three kinds of which the last one again can be divided into two distinct branches. They are the following:

1. mapping pluralism
2. actual language indeterminacy pluralism
3. normative pluralism, which is divided into
    (a) purpose pluralism
    (b) goodness pluralism

Eklund relates these possible kinds of pluralism to different projects a logician might be interested in pursuing. In the case of mapping pluralism, one can be merely interested in studying different possible languages and their relations of logical consequence. And as there are more such languages with distinct relations of logical consequence, we arrive at a version of logical pluralism. Such a pluralism, Eklund believes, is hardly controversial, as clearly we can analyse more than one possible language. I concur that such a construal of logical pluralism is rather anodyne, yet it still does not have to be completely vacuous. This is because when we speak of possible languages we study, we must possess some idea of what makes something a language and it is reasonable that anything we can consider as language must have some logical vocabulary and relation of logical consequence. Now it might be a legitimate object of discussion how flexible our notion of language is and how that flexibility depends on the flexibility of the notion of logic.

In the case of actual language indeterminacy pluralism, one could be interested in the actual language project, studying the properties of logical vocabulary in the language we actually use. In the course of this study, we can find out that our ordinary practices leave some of the properties of logical vocabulary underdetermined which yields an indeterminacy pluralism. Eklund believes such a thesis can hardly be of much philosophical interest. A similar feeling is echoed in Field, who, talking about the possible indeterminacy of the English word implies, claims:

> But personally I find it hard to get excited about issues related to the extent of indeterminacy in English words. (Field 2009, p. 345)

Of course, questions about nuances in the meanings of any words of any language are of particular interest only for linguists and not for logicians, but the matter is put inappropriately as a problem of merely contingent linguistic affairs by both Eklund and Field. Rather than the actual meaning of the logical vocabulary of English, we can be interested in that part of their meaning, if there be such, which they must share with all their equivalents from other languages and which makes a given expression logical in the first place. When we then claim that any system of logical vocabulary is bound to be in an interesting sense underdetermined by its use, I think we are at least gesturing at what might be an interesting version of logical pluralism and one which I think my account spells out. We can see that the actual language project cannot be held so neatly apart from the mapping project as Eklund seems to imagine. He presents both of these approaches in a rather uncharitable light, yet when we try to make them plausible, we see that they tend to blend into one project. When we study what indeterminacies are bound to accompany a given piece of English logical vocabulary, then we come close to the study of what possible alternative rules this very expression could obey.

The first kind of normative pluralism, namely purpose pluralism, simply claims that logic can be put to different uses, and different logics can be good for different purposes. Indeed, this is something commonly claimed by authors who endorse logical pluralism, yet I concur with Eklund that in such a general form the thesis is too vague and threatened by triviality. Yet, just as with the previous two projects, one can think of a more interesting version of the account than the one Eklund presents. It would be more interesting to sustain that, given some important purposes of logic, these purposes are bound to be again to some degree open to various precisifications. Indeed, we claim that the chief purpose of logic is to make inference rules explicit and that this very notion of making a rule explicit can develop, just as any other notion we might have. And there are different ways in which it can be developed.

Finally, the goodness pluralism claims that given some specific purpose of logic, more than one logic can be equally good for it. Eklund finds only this kind of pluralism promising yet admonishes that we have to first clarify what the important purpose of logic could be. He is therefore also afraid that for many of the purposes one would suppose logic should fulfil, a system of quick but dirty rules could be applied rather than something resembling the logics we know.[3] Yet obviously, we have an answer to what the purpose of logic should be: namely that given by logical expressivism, which is beyond the reach of the worries regarding dirty but quick rules, as according to logical expressivism, logic is not primarily supposed to enable reasoning or help us acquire as many true beliefs as possible (in the shortest time possible?) but rather makes inference rules explicit. But the idea of the purpose and the idea of what is best for its fulfilment are obviously interdependent and can influence each other in their mutual development. That means that the purpose pluralism again cannot be clearly divided from the goodness pluralism, at least when we put enough flesh on the bones of both these approaches to make them reasonable.

We should also remark that the questions about the purpose of logic cannot be divorced from the questions about what makes some actual vocabulary logical, nor from the question about what possible shapes logical vocabulary could have. Overall, then, we see that the normative project cannot be separated from either the actual language project or the mapping project. I therefore conclude that the varieties of pluralism identified by Eklund actually have to collapse if we try to make them plausible. Eklund is probably right that the formulation of logical pluralism in terms of goodness pluralism is the most fortunate one of those he offers, yet it has to involve all the other kinds of pluralism as well.

8.3 Is logic exceptional?

If one wants to present an interesting form of logical pluralism, it is natural to present it coupled with the thesis that logic is in some important sense not exceptional. This thesis can take more shapes but generally revolves around the idea that logic cannot play such a foundational role with respect to our rationality that it cannot be revised, at least not without profound damage caused by such a revision. Logical pluralism, as we understand it, contains this potentially controversial claim that logic is somehow revisable. In the case of other disciplines, such as geology or zoology, nobody would seriously want to doubt that they are revisable; we can imagine scenarios where a single important empirical finding could induce deep revisions in such empirical disciplines, though we can expect that the more fundamental the revision, the more difficult its implementation. In the case of logic, though, one might feel that it cannot be easily changed, as it is too fundamental for our reasoning as such.

On the other hand, the very development of various different logics looks like a solid defeasible evidence for the thesis that logic can be changed and is therefore not in some interesting sense really special. Ole Hjortland (2017) calls such a view, per the title of his article, 'Anti-Exceptionalism about Logic'. Such a view obviously is not unprecedented; in fact it is only a development of what is already present in Quinean holism. Quine himself proposes to extend his thesis that no individual statement is unrevisable even to logical statements (a position he, as we know, later abandoned to embrace complete irrevisability of classical logic). Hjortland wants to give more flesh to the bones of this proposal and reviews the criteria which decide about the rationality of choosing a given system of logic. He claims that we choose logic by abductive criteria and considers two authors who tried to promote their preferred logic by such criteria, namely Timothy Williamson and Graham Priest. Both of them believe that no logic has a privileged status, yet while Williamson argues that abductive criteria after all favour classical logic and that abandoning it is typically a very bad idea, Priest – together with Hjortland – argues that there still might be good reasons to go non-classical.

Hjortland showcases the difference of their approach on their stance towards semantic paradoxes. When we consider the liar paradox, we see that classical logic cannot coexist together with a truth predicate obeying the Tarskian disquotation. The question, then, is which of the two we should prefer to abandon:

> Thus although the restriction of classical logic involves a loss of both simplicity and strength, it compensates us by saving the simplicity and strength of unrestricted disquotation. Saving the simplicity and strength of unrestricted

classical logic forces us to sacrifice the simplicity and strength of unrestricted disquotation. Which is the better deal? (Williamson 2017, p. 21)

Williamson has a peculiarly straightforward view of logic, namely that it is simply a discipline which deals with the most general truths. Such a simple characterization seems to him more appropriate than those ascribing to logic a specific topic with which it deals, be it deductive reasoning, its analogues in our languages or something else. Williamson's view very much resembles that of Sher, against which we already argued at sufficient length. With this view all of Williamson's abductive arguments which are based on it must go. For example, he claims that logic is much more general than the theory of truth predicates (which deals only with linguistic truths, not with the most general ones) and thus should be mutilated much less; he even compares modifying logic instead of the theory of truth to modifying physics rather than some very parochial part of economy when they clash (Williamson 2017, p. 21).

Putting his view of logic as a discipline concerned with the most general truths aside, Williamson offers a very Quinean defence of classical logic as it is overall a very simple, elegant and powerful system and no other system combining these qualities in such a way is in sight. Williamson furthermore stresses that his preference of classical logic is not based on the Quinean conservative maxim of minimal mutilation:

> The case may indeed be strengthened by reference to the track record of classical logic: it has been tested far more severely than any other logic in the history of science, most notably in the history of mathematics, and has withstood the test remarkably well. Nevertheless, the initial case for classical logic would be quite powerful, even if we had only stumbled across that logic a few weeks ago. (Williamson 2017, p. 19)

On the one hand, the reasons Williamson adduces are in general rather vague; for example it is not clear how to compare the simplicity of logics. Yet this last quote has something to sympathize with; indeed, the prominence of classical logic cannot be a mere accident. Still, the overall spirit seems to be too radical in Williamson, just as it was in the Quine of *Philosophy of Logic*. Logic indeed can be revised and besides Williamson's arguments to remain classical, those given by Priest (in Priest 2006 and 2014) for non-classical resolution of semantic paradoxes are also legitimate.

Overall, though, the abductive criteria just do not seem to pinpoint only a single, best logic. Many of the criteria are too vague: for instance, simplicity and elegance. Of others we are not sure how valuable they are or even if they are an asset or drawback, such as compactness (it might seem natural but maybe we want our logic to capture reasoning which needs infinitely many premises). Overall there are good reasons to be pluralist if one is an anti-exceptionalist about logic.

8.3.1 Logic and truth, logical and aletheic pluralism

Williamson and Priest offer a good pretext to introduce one further strand of recent or contemporary thought on the plurality of logics, namely that which links them to the purported plurality of truths. The intuitive appeal of the idea that we deal with different kinds of truths in different domains or contexts led some authors to formulate the doctrine of *aletheic pluralism*. Inspired, among others, by Wright (1992), the doctrine has attained, just as logical pluralism, a rich variety of forms and defences. Among the more recent ones, particularly Lynch (2008, 2009) and Pedersen (2014) were influential. We will dwell on the issue of aletheic pluralism only insofar as it is connected with logical pluralism.

The link that comes to mind immediately is that logical consequence is defined as a preservation of truth and, therefore, should there be a plurality of truths, then there must be one of logics. While the conventional understanding of logical consequence as a necessary and formal preservation of truth has got not only a fine tradition but also many good reasons on its side, it is not the only way we can understand the relation between truth and logical consequence. Peregrin, for instance, offers an opposite view, as he sees consequence as primitive (constituted by rules) and truth subsequently extracted from consequence as that which is transmitted by inference rules. Peregrin states the following:

> Instead of saying that consequence is a relation of truth-preservation, we can say that truth is that property that is preserved by consequence, i.e. by our loosely-criterial inference. We may perceive the moves of the game of giving and asking for reason as a matter of handing down, by means of sentences, a specific stuff – the truth. (Just like in the tag game, where although the point is simply to touch another person rather than to give them anything,

it is very natural to perceive it as the handing down of something, 'the tag'.) (Peregrin 2014a, p. 116)

Needless to say, from my inferentialist perspective, I find Peregrin's approach much more persuasive. On the other hand, perhaps both of the views can be combined in the claim that truth and consequence mutually influence one another. In this sense, it is reasonable to expect that logical and aletheic pluralism support each other. Whether you come from consequence to truth or the other way round, plurality on one side provokes plurality on the other. Although my preferred path to pluralism is rather through the open-endedness of the rules of inference, my view is not in conflict with seeing logical pluralism linked to aletheic pluralism by means of mutual support.

There are, nevertheless, strong objections to linking the two pluralisms. Kevin Scharp (2018) notes that if we want to prevent liar paradox and its kins by invoking the plurality of logics and truths, we typically encounter an analogous paradox at a higher level, often called *revenge*. As soon as we can form higher-level predicates such as *true in context 1* (let us say that we countenance three basic contexts to which different notions of truth and logical consequence pertain), we can form paradoxical statements. The issue of different contexts or domains for different truth predicates or consequence relations raises serious concerns. I share the doubts of Rosanna Keefe (2018) about the boundaries between the different domains. She points out that, for example, a typical ethical inference features factual statements which are typically considered as pertaining to a different domain (with a different truth predicate or a consequence relation or both).

Keefe thus casts doubt on pluralism based on a division into domains. Her main criticism is that it cannot explain *mixed inferences*, that is inferences consisting of statements pertaining to different domains. There are other strategies as to how to deal with this issue. Michael Lynch, the proponent of domain-specific logical and aletheic pluralism, advocates opting for the intersection of all the logics of all the domains to which the statements forming a given mixed inference pertain.[4] That is prima facie a plausible approach, yet the problems it faces show its limits. Charles Wrenn (2018) complains that this approach, which he calls *modesty*, rules valid inferences as invalid and thus he pleads for *immodesty*. Although it is not straightforward which inferences should be counted as valid by a plausible account of consequence, Wrenn's complaint is very natural.

Wrenn also warns that in this way logical pluralism is lost, he speaks of a merely *virtual* logical pluralism, as we can simply intersect all the logics that we use in all the possible contexts and proclaim that this is the one true logic. Maybe a somewhat weak logic but a truly universal one, in the manner in which Neil Tennant understands his *core logic*.[5] In fact, both Rosanna Keefe and Roy Cook claim that the apparent differences between logics might be illusory.[6] It might seem that in Domain 1 we use Logic 1 and in Domain 2 we use Logic 2, yet perhaps the first logic is stronger than the second one and therefore we can say that it is the weaker Logic 2 which we use in both domains, only in Domain 1 we can use also extra-logical principles when inferring. When the first logic is classical propositional logic and the second intuitionistic logic, then we are free to say that the real logic of both domains is the weaker one, that is intuitionistic logic, and that we can use the law of the excluded middle or the law of double negation simply because in that domain it happens to be true due to extra-logical reasons. Cook is interested in this option, as it opens the possibility to separate logical and aletheic pluralism. We can imagine that there are three domains, D1, D2 and D3; and two truth predicates, T1 (let us call it constructive truth) and T2 (let us call it Platonistic truth); and two logics, L1 (intuitionistic propositional logic) and L2 (classical propositional logic). Now, we can imagine that in D1 we have T1 and L1, in D2 we have T2 and L1 and, finally, in D3 we have T2 and L2.[7] This, for Cook, demonstrates that a given truth predicate does not force one specific logical consequence relation and vice versa. Ergo, logical and aletheic pluralisms are independent theses, at least as far as they are linked to countenancing different domains. Rosanna Keefe uses a similar strategy to get rid of this kind of pluralism in favour of effective monism or, what Wrenn calls, mere *virtual logical pluralism*. A slight methodological difference between Cook and Keefe is that while Cook attributes the appearance of having a stronger logic merely to the truth of further general premises, Keefe prefers to speak of further valid extra-logical inference rules. She calls this *suppressed rule strategy* in contrast with *suppressed premise strategy* on p. 444 of Keefe (2018).

These discussions show that one can opt for regarding some principle we use in reasoning as external to logic, which can again reduce the plurality. In fact, it can make logical pluralism collapse into logical monism, as many authors are afraid of, among others Gillian Russell, who speaks of the resistance of logical pluralism not only to logical monism but also to logical nihilism in G. Russell

(2018b). While it is possible to settle for a weaker logic by proclaiming some principles as extra-logical and there are no principled limits to this procedure, it is somewhat artificial when these principles are rules which guide the behaviour of logical vocabulary. It seems, nevertheless, that these authors regard logical inference rules as instruments for expanding our knowledge, while I side with logical expressivism and see them rather as means for making explicit the extra-logical inference rules which constitute our languages. Thus, dilemmas of this sort are not so pressing for my approach.

Furthermore, I doubt that we ever have all the possible contexts and kinds of mixed inferences at hand so that we could put forward a complete list containing them all. Rather, these contexts come into existence as we go along and logic, as well as the rules it makes explicit, is dynamic. This means that we can never reach the intersection of all logics from all appropriate contexts or domains. But this is already foreshadowing my response to logical pluralism and monism (and nihilism, for that matter), which I call *logical dynamism*. We will get back to it after clarifying a few extant points.

8.3.2 Having and changing a logic

The debate about which logic is best or which logic we actually use rests on an important assumption that it is reasonable to say of somebody that he or she indeed uses a given logic and/or can change it if there are rational arguments in favour of such a shift. Williamson, again just as Quine, seems to be very much convinced that we already in some important sense use classical logic, although they part ways when Quine seems to indicate that we actually cannot change it while Williamson is happy to merely assert that any such change would be overall an irrational decision. Yet does it make sense to say of anyone that he is reasoning classically? Or non-classically, according to any of the non-classical logics?

We can thus reasonably ask two questions. The first one is who has a given logic and what does his or her having a logic mean. The other question is then who and in what sense can change a logic. The question regarding changing is obviously dependent on the one regarding the having, so let us start with pondering on what it means to have a logic. Who, then, has a logic? Being acquainted with logic as it lives in academia, we can easily picture two logicians disputing whether, say, classical or intuitionist logic is somehow better. Such a picture surely suggests that one of them is reasoning classically, the other one intuitionistically. Yet with the lessons of the later Wittgenstein in mind, we know that such a statement is problematic, as no rule can be private. Of course, an individual can to some degree decide which rules he or she will follow, yet this means deciding to which community following the rules he or she will belong. Therefore, only a community can be a candidate for having one or another logic; the two disputing logicians can be said to differ in their reasoning at best only by their being members of different communities.

Can a community then be described as following, for example, classical rather than intuitionistic logic? On the one hand, we know from Wittgenstein's remarks about rule following that any observable behaviour leaves something in the interpretation open; that is it does not uniquely determine which rules we should describe the members of the community as following. Of course, the overt behaviour should determine quite a lot, at least enough as to enable someone to learn how to follow the given rules. We can thus typically observe that in a given community, people usually infer the statement B from statement A and in such a case it would be clearly wrong to say that they infer the negation of B instead. Yet the differences between serious logical systems typically are not of this radical kind. When logicians are in dispute about the law of the excluded middle, the intuitionist just denies that $B \vee \neg B$ is always true or can be inferred from any premises whatsoever. Yet this does not prevent the intuitionist from agreeing that $B \vee \neg B$ is true for almost all of the possible statements which we substitute for B. It is only in some specific cases in mathematics that the dispute arises and therefore one can very well fail to gather evidence for ascribing either classical or intuitionistic logic to a given community. Besides this, it is always a non-trivial affair to determine an acceptable logical form of the statements people make such as, for example, whether a given controversial statement should indeed be formalized as an instance of the law of the excluded middle and therewith the dispute as being between classical and intuitionistic logic in the first place. It thus hardly makes sense to claim that someone is reasoning intuitionistically, classically or otherwise in general. Rather we have to specify the area of discourse, such as mathematics, where the differences become salient. The talk of reasoning with a certain logic and therewith also the talk about possibly changing one's logic are thus quite problematic and unfortunate, according to our analysis. Therefore, when authors such as Williamson speak about the costs of abandoning classical logic, whether they encourage it or not, their talk is largely unintelligible or at least wants to say more than it possibly can.

When we discuss the liar's paradox and the possibilities to cope with it either by using non-classical logic or by restricting the truth predicate, one can get the impression that the paradox could perhaps serve as an evidence against our logic and lead us to revising our logic and for example reason non-classically also when something other than the liar paradox is the issue. Yet it is rather the case that we just decide what logic to use for the liar paradox itself, as it should first be argued for the thesis that the differences between various logics are salient also for some other issues than paradoxes. This is, of course, very well possible but still by no means self-evident.

To sum up, I claim that it does not make much sense to say of anyone that he or she is in fact reasoning according to classical logic, as well as intuitionistic or any other logic. If we cannot ascribe any logic to our reasoning, do we have to conclude that our reasoning is illogical? That would be obviously absurd. Strawson famously concludes his article 'On Referring' by claiming that ordinary language has no logic.[8] This statement has been criticized by Peregrin and Svoboda (see Peregrin and Svoboda 2017, pp. 110–11), who interpret him as claiming that ordinary language is basically chaotic and does not obey any rules, which is contrary to their – and my – view, according to which language is constituted just by appropriate rules. Strawson probably wanted to say, or at any rate should have wanted to say, that the logic of our natural languages does not correspond to any of the specific logical systems because their differences are just not important in the ordinary use of language.

8.3.3 Logical nihilism

Some authors interpreted Strawson's assertion that ordinary language has no exact logic as leading to the conclusion that no logic is correct. We have already mentioned this doctrine, which goes under the name of *logical nihilism* and has been defended, for instance, in G. Russell (2017, 2018a, 2018b), Cotnoir (2018) and Franks (2002). This view has already been criticized in Dicher (in press). Gillian Russell argues that in some context and in some sense every logical rule fails. There are familiar examples such as the law of the excluded middle, but Russell tries to undermine even such unshakable principles as conjunction elimination, that is inferring A from $A \wedge B$. She does this by introducing a special expression which is true in conjunction but not when it is free-standing. Bogdan Dicher argues that a more natural counterexample should be found but I find such a requirement too vague. Language is not a closed system and it keeps integrating new expressions all the time. Dicher further argues that this might show that a given logical law is invalid yet this does not make all logical laws invalid at the same time. Therefore, the relation of logical consequence is not empty, as Russell suggests. This might be true, but still casting doubts on any single logical law suffices for casting doubts on any logical system. But as every logical rule is in some sense wrong, it is also typically in some sense also right, at least in the serious logics. If we do not believe that language lives in anarchy but only in a very complicated and dynamic system, we cannot say that no rules hold. Yet when a rule holds this does not mean that we have to follow it at every occasion and under any interpretation of the occasion that is thinkable. The same action, in our case every inference, can be seen both as breaking a given rule and as following it, though maybe under a somewhat unorthodox interpretation.

Logical nihilism does a good job at showing us what logical systems are not. They do not purport to show us one true relation of logical consequence, nor a collection of true logical consequence relations. Thus logical nihilism hits not only naive forms of logical monism but also many forms of pluralism, quite obviously Beall and Restall's who claim that they have identified exactly three true logics. On the other hand, the message of logical nihilism is not as novel nor controversial as its proponents might want us to believe. Dicher is right to remind us that some discrepancy between formal logical systems and everyday reasoning had been countenanced already in Frege, who compared reasoning in formal systems to using a microscope as opposed to the naked eye to, which he compared reasoning in natural language. Yet I think this admonition is easy to forget. It is arguable whether even Frege was not a culprit at certain stages of his development. How to sum up my assessment of logical nihilism? While it is true that no system is exactly correct, this is not so much because there is no logic but rather because logic is dynamic. And we should not regard logical systems as attempts to capture this logic.

8.3.4 The logic we in fact use and the logic we should use

When discussing logical pluralism, it is legitimate to ask whether the purported plurality should pertain rather to the logic we use or to the logic we should use.

The considerations we have just gone through enable us to give an answer to this question. As in other cases, rather than siding in one or the other party in the controversy, I doubt the cogency of the controversy.

As it is very problematic to attribute one or another logic to a given person, so it is equally problematic to speak of the logic that one should use. If you cannot effectively decide what logic one is actually using, you also cannot decide whether a proposed logic has actually been implemented. For this reason both answers to the question of which plurality I am opting for are unsatisfactory from my point of view.

Maybe this looks simply too extreme and extravagant. Can I at least say that my pluralism should pertain to something between the logic we actually use and the logic we should use? I believe even this is not a viable solution. It is true that every rule and meaning is dynamic and tends to continually transcend itself. There is always a potential to develop into new contexts. This means that any rules, including the logical ones, always go into new directions of their modifications which we can adopt. Whether we indeed should adopt them can be an issue up for discussion yet in many cases it remains underdetermined. It is simply up to us to choose which development to endorse. But we should also not forget that rules are never fully under our control. Therefore any control we have over their development must be only partial and imperfect. In this way, even if we wanted to deal rather with the logic we actually use as opposed to that which we should use, we could not restrict our attention in this way. In order to remain cogent, we would have to deal with the logic we should use as well. On the other hand, if the logic we should use would radically differ from the one we in fact use, it would hardly be intelligible as a logic at all.

The two options thus cannot be distinguished in a very useful manner. But rather than opting for something in between, I choose a different way of looking at the plurality of logical systems. I see them as showing both what is already in a way implicit and hidden in the actual usage of logical vocabulary and what can be potentially further developed. This is another teaser for logical dynamism which we will get to soon.

8.3.5 Ways of being exceptional

Is logic exceptional, according to our view? On one very crude understanding it is. It is a discipline with its specific role in the whole of our cognitive activities, namely that of making inference rules explicit. But the anti-exceptionalist thesis by Hjortland obviously focuses rather on the possibility to revise logic. We have clearly diverged from this view by showing that the talk about changing one's logic does not make good sense. On the other hand, we clearly are not exceptionalists in the sense of urging that we have to keep obeying the exact same logical rules all the time. There remains a lot of room for sympathy with both exceptionalism and anti-exceptionalism.

The role which we ascribe to logic, namely to make inference rules explicit, makes it a discipline which is foundational to all the discourse, yet the discourse can work independently of it. A language becomes meaningful only by means of logical relations between statements; on the other hand, we can infer conclusions from premises and therewith argue and reason without making the constitutive rules explicit. Changing the tools of logical expression, and therewith also the nature of constitutive relations, is thus no small enterprise and typically we should prefer changing something less fundamental than logical laws. But we can change them if we want to and they can also change by our usage without our giving explicit approval to such a change, sometimes perhaps even to our unpleasant surprise. A change of logic means a change of some logical concepts, such as that of negation or disjunction. How can such changes be affected by our logical systems?

8.3.6 Stability of concepts

We have found the notion of adopting a given logic highly problematic, so we cannot say that we can simply agree to use classical logic in our reasoning from now on. On the one hand, we already mentioned that it would be quite difficult, perhaps impossible, to decide whether we have succeeded in adopting it as the differences between being a classical and, for example, intuitionistic logician cannot really be decided on the basis of observing the overt behaviour of language users.

But surely we can agree to use a given expression in one way rather than in another, no matter if it is logical. Indeed, not only can we do this, it is actually being done in mathematics, where the mathematicians agree to use their preferred, mostly classical, sometimes intuitionistic logic and sometimes another logic yet. This is due to the fact that they do not agree to reason according to their favourite logic in all discourse whatsoever but only when dealing with mathematics where the differences between various logics become important. The mathematicians adapt the logical concepts constituted in natural languages into their mathematically precise form. Now in the area of mathematics, interesting discussions can and indeed have taken place regarding the respective merits of various logics when used to make mathematical reasoning explicit. I doubt that for any other area of discourse than mathematics have the differences between logical systems been important in this way.

But do the logical concepts as we have them in our natural languages remain intact by the development of logical systems? I think we do not have to be so sceptical. Attempts to make the logical vocabulary of our ordinary discourse behave like that of some specific systems might have an unclear meaning and can also be difficult to realize, yet this does not entail that the systems cannot influence the way we reason and make inference rules explicit. To use a somewhat evasive expression, they surely can at least inspire us to use the logical vocabulary in some specific way. The logical concepts of negation, disjunction, general quantification, entailment and so on themselves grow from the ordinary ones; they are contained in them as their possible developments and sharpenings. On the other hand, by being presented with the interesting sharpenings, we understand the original concepts better and can use them more adroitly. Not only logicians but anyone who has passed at least an elementary course in formal logic, typically containing the basics of classical logic, becomes to some degree more attentive to the use of logical concepts in everyday discourse and can occasionally even modify it.

Compare this to any other concepts which can receive more than one interesting sharpening. Philosophers have developed various ethical systems which give different accounts of what makes an action moral. Thus we have the Aristotelian, Kantian, utilitarist and other accounts. Now, their concepts of morality all have some common root to be found in ordinary usage of moral vocabulary. One can have one's own preference – for example, think that Kant's ethics makes particularly good sense – yet still this does not mean that the original vague concepts just get replaced by the Kantian ones. However, by being confronted with these theoretical elaborations, we can reason about morality more aptly than we would naturally be able to. We can occasionally also agree to settle on the Kantian or utilitarist or other theoretical understanding of the terms for a purpose of a given discussion.

Once the theories, be they logical, ethical or different yet, influence our understanding of the fundamental concepts of logic or ethics, we can then again modify our understanding of evaluating such theories. For our case this means that we can change our criteria of what is a good logical system. Therefore, we see that our ordinary logical concepts and the theoretical concepts developed by various logics can influence each other. In fact, the measure to which they influence each other is the measure of success and importance of logic as a theoretical discipline. The influence on the ordinary concepts cannot be particularly great due to their relative fundamentality. But it is still there. In this sense, then, our position is anti-exceptionalist.

8.4 Logical dynamism

Now we can finally formulate our position and explain in which sense it is pluralist and monist at the same time. Our position is best called *logical dynamism*. This is because it emphasizes the ability of logic to develop. This development is twofold.

The logical concepts we have and use in ordinary discourse can change, though typically only very little, as they are so basic for our concept of language and rational discourse as such. The change either can be completely uncontrolled or can be to some degree influenced by us, when we develop and study various logical systems. The development of logical systems enhances our mastery of logical concepts. At the same time it enables us to use them in a more flexible manner, as we can adapt them according to the diverse systems for given arguments. We can use them more precisely and specifically. It is only by having the plurality of logical systems that this ability of having at least some control over the specific shape of logical concepts is attained by us.

Our view has some affinity to logical monism. Logic is a system of concepts which has a specific purpose, namely to make inference rules explicit. As concepts have to be shared, we share in fact one logic which underlies our logical competence. Unlike more orthodox monists, though, we do not believe that this one logic has to have a specific shape of any of the known logical systems. It is rather dynamic in its nature; the very logical concepts we need to be acquainted with in order to learn to use any of the plurality of logical systems have to remain to a great degree implicit and also dynamic, as they can develop, partly inspired by the logical systems which are much more explicit and sharply defined. Yet as there are many logical systems, so there are many shapes which our logical concepts and with them our overall logical capacity can develop into. This is the fundamental pluralist feature of our dynamist approach to logic.

I like very much the variety of pluralism which was developed by Stewart Shapiro and which he calls *eclectic approach* in Shapiro (2014). It is true that he does not settle for a very clear and definitive explanation of what this approach consists in, but I think he remains somewhat open-ended on purpose and for good reasons. The main feature of his approach is, as I see it, that it is ungrudging in its pluralism. Being mainly focused on logic in mathematical discourse, Shapiro extensively and persuasively argues that different mathematical practices and theories are best understood as founded on different logics. The prima facie attitudes of mathematicians who consider themselves as intuitionists, classicists and otherwise thus make sense and it is better to accept them than to grudgingly try to explain them away. Many authors attempt at either explaining away or at least severely limiting the apparent logical pluralism. The most severe example of an attempt to try and explain it away might be Quine with his thesis that 'deviant logicians only change the subject when they want to change the doctrine' (Quine 1986, p. 80). A typical example of limiting logical pluralism is the view of Beall and Restall who want to delimit what can yet constitute a legitimate logic in Beall and Restall (2006), and declare the other systems as non-logics.

Shapiro remains ungrudging and I believe I can join him and strengthen his position. We can admit the various perspectives and let a thousand flowers bloom when we acknowledge how much they have in common. The monist strait in logical dynamism enables us to do as much. In this sense logical dynamism is a development of a particularly strong and unapologetic form of logical pluralism.

Furthermore, the logical systems can and in fact do inspire new systems to come. As the algebraic study of classical logic made some properties of conjunction explicit, it opened the door for the development of substructural logics which have two kinds of conjunctions, depending on which structural rules they obey. In the same manner, the study of the two standard first-order quantifiers inspired the development of new kinds of quantifiers by Lindström, Tarski, Sher and others. These new systems can then be again inspiring for us in our use of fundamental logical concepts. Of course, due to the increasing complexity of these enriched systems, such an influence will probably not become very significant as they are difficult to implement. It is a fact that the many logical systems that have been contrived are at the moment rather just plain possibilities of modifying our logical practice. Our ordinary logical concepts do not seem to be in harsh need of being modified in some significant way, as they enable us to make inference rules explicit and marshal our reasoning rather well. But just as classical logic has made its way into classrooms and is a part of the curricula of well-educated people who are not professional logicians and thereby makes many people more conscious of how they reason logically, maybe other systems will spread in a similar way and indeed induce some changes in our daily reasoning. Such changes probably will be rather modest, yet could still serve to advance our rationality.

Conclusion

The synopsis I offered in the introduction was supposed to prepare the reader to look for continuity between the chapters which discuss topics many would probably not be inclined to connect. The links between the parts could have certainly been rendered more clearly, yet I hope that the reader has nevertheless succeeded to perceive one, though not always straightforward, line of thought.

Logical dynamism as the main fruit of this work has so far only been arrived at and has therefore been rather programmatically stated than developed. Though vagueness in the stated thesis is, in general, reproachable, it is only natural to reckon with it when the issue is as general as that of logical dynamism. Nevertheless, I hope more flesh can be put on the bones of my approach. This can be done by using it as a method for the study of the history of logic, namely by paying special attention to the historical development of logical concepts as instruments for the expression of inference rules. Furthermore, and perhaps more importantly, the emphasis on the dynamic aspect of meaning, and not only of logical expressions, can be developed in inferentialist philosophy.

Notes

Chapter 1

1. Brandom (1994).
2. See page 49 of Brandom (2000).
3. Namely from Wittgenstein (1953) and Kripke (1982).
4. B. Russell (1923).
5. The expositions of the respective thought experiments can be found in Kripke (1982), Quine (1960) and Davidson (1973).
6. Quine (1951).

Chapter 2

1. Turbanti (2017).
2. See Quine (1986).

Chapter 3

1. From the historical perspective much more should be said about how much the logic he used was indeed that of Aristotle or rather its Port Royal reconstruction. Yet this will not be our concern here.
2. 'Da die Logik diesen sicheren Gang schon von den ältesten Zeiten her gegangen sei, läßt sich daraus ersehen, daß sie seit dem Aristoteles keinen Schritt ruckwärts hat tun dürfen, wenn man ihr nicht etwa die Wegschaffung einiger entbehrlicher Subtilitäten, oder deutlichere Bestimmung des Vorgetragenen als Verbesserungen anrechnen will, welches aber mehr zur Eleganz, als zur Sicherheit der Wissenschaft gehört. Merkwürdig ist noch an ihr, da sie auch bis jetzt keinen Schritt vorwärts hat tun können, und also allem Ansehen nach geschlossen und vollendet zu sein scheint' (Kant 1954 [1787], B VII). English translation: 'That from the earliest times logic has travelled this secure course can

be seen from the fact that since the time of Aristotle it has not had to go a single step backwards, unless we count the abolition of a few dispensable subtleties or the more distinct determination of its presentation, which improvements belong more to the elegance than to the security of that science. What is further remarkable about logic is that until now it has also been unable to take a single step forward, and therefore seems to all appearance to be finished and complete' (Kant 1998, B VII).

3 English translation: 'If "I know etc" is conceived as a grammatical proposition, of course the "I" cannot be important. And it properly means "There is no such thing as a doubt in this case" or "The expression I do not know" makes no sense in this case. And of course it follows from this that "I know" makes no sense either' (Wittgenstein 1969, aphorism 58).

4 'Being finite and relatively short living creatures, we cannot hope to establish all our knowledge directly, but have to resort to such indirect means as inference to obtain a considerable portion of our knowledge' (Sher 2008, p. 313).

5 'Nur so viel scheint zur Einleitung, oder Vorerinnerung, nötig zu sein, daß es zwei Stämme der menschlichen Erkenntnis gebe, die vielleicht aus einer gemeinschaftlichen, aber uns unbekannten Wurzel entspringen, nämlich Sinnlichkeit und Verstand, durch deren ersteren uns Gegenstande gegeben, durch den zweiten aber gedacht werden' (Kant 1954 [1787], A16/B30). English translation: 'All that seems necessary for an introduction or preliminary is that there are two stems of human cognition, which may perhaps arise from a common but to us unknown root, namely sensibility and understanding, through the first of which objects are given to us, but through the second of which they are thought' (Kant 1998, B30).

6 Note the Kantian motif in Wittgenstein: 'Jedes Ding ist gleichsam in in einem Raume möglicher Sachverhalte. Diesen Raum kann ich mir leer denken, nicht aber das Ding ohne den Raum' (Wittgenstein 1921, 2.013). English translation: 'Each thing is, as it were, in a space of possible states of affairs. This space I can imagine empty but I cannot imagine the thing without the space' (Wittgenstein 1961, 2.013).

7 See Helmholtz (1870) for the original presentation of the thought experiments and also my article Arazim (2012) for a discussion of these.

8 'Nehmen wir aber zu den geometrischen Axiomen noch Sätze hinzu, die sich auf die mechanischen Eigenschaften der Naturkörper beziehen ... dann erhält ein solches System von Sätzen einen wirklichen Inhalt, der durch Erfahrung bestätigt oder widerlegt werden, eben deshalb aber auch durch Erfahrung gewonnen werden kann' (Helmholtz 1870, p. 30). English translation: 'But if to the

geometrical axioms we add propositions relating to the mechanical properties of natural bodies, ... such a system of propositions has a real import which can be confirmed or refuted by experience, but just for the same reason can also be got by experience' (Helmholtz 1876, p. 320).

9   More on the conflicting tendencies in Helmhotz's thought can be found in the third chapter of Coffa (1993).
10 English translation: 'Is it maybe in my power what I believe? or what I unshakeably believe? I believe that there is a chair over there. Can't I be wrong? But, can I believe that I am wrong? Or can I so much as bring it under consideration? – And mightn't I also hold fast to my belief whatever I learned later on?! But is my belief then grounded' (Wittgenstein 1969, paragraph 173)?
11 'Die Sätze, die für mich feststehen, lerne ich nicht ausdrücklich. Ich kann sie nachträglich finden wie die Rotationsachse eines sich drehenden Körpers. Diese Achse steht nicht fest in dem Sinne, daß sie festgehalten wird, aber die Bewegung um sie herum bestimmt sie als unbewegt' (Wittgenstein 1984 [1969], paragraph 152). English translation: 'I do not explicitly learn the propositions that stand fast for me. I can discover them subsequently like the axis around which a body rotates. This axis is not fixed in the sense that anything holds it fast, but the movement around it determines its immobility' (Wittgenstein 1969, paragraph 152).
12 English translation: 'It is always by favour of Nature that one knows something.' (Wittgenstein 1969, paragraph 505).

Chapter 4

1   For example in Sellars (1953), Brandom (2000) and Peregrin (2014a).
2   A similar worry was formulated succinctly by John McDowell, who asked whether the system of our concepts does not merely spin in the void (see McDowell 1994).
3   Wittgenstein introduces this thought in paragraph 85 of Wittgenstein (1953).
4   English translation: 'I believe that I can best make the relation of my ideography to ordinary language clear if I compare it to that which the microscope has to the eye. Because of the range of its possible uses and the versatility with which it can adapt to the most diverse circumstances, the eye is far superior to the microscope. Considered as an optical instrument, to be sure, it exhibits many

imperfections, which ordinarily remain unnoticed only on account of its intimate connection with our mental life. But, as soon as scientific goals demand great sharpness of resolution, the eye proves to be insufficient. The microscope, on the other hand, is perfectly suited to precisely such goals, but that is just why it is useless for all others' (Frege 1967, p. 6).

5 English translation: 'But since the mere form of cognition, however well it may agree with logical laws, is far from sufficing to constitute the material (objective) truth of the cognition, nobody can dare to judge of objects and to assert anything about them merely with logic' (Kant 1998, A60/B85).

6 We could also specify a given language and the rules for forming formulae in that language.

7 Susan Hack on p. 3 of Haack (1978) mentions Brouwer as the proponent of the first thesis, Dummett as that of the second one. She thus calls Brouwer a local reformist, while calling Dummett a global reformist with respect to classical logic.

8 The language which the linguist is at pains to understand.

9 Donald Davidson expressed this in his article 'On the Very Idea of Conceptual Scheme': 'Since charity is not an option but a condition of having a workable theory, it is meaningless to suggest that we might fall into massive error by endorsing it' (Davidson 1974, p. 19).

10 'The canon save the obvious bans any manual of translation that would represent the foreigners as contradicting our logic' (Quine 1986, p. 83).

11 See Shapiro (2015) and Waismann (1945).

12 Especially in section 1 (pp. 127–33) of the indicated chapter, he compares the situation of a classically trained mathematician who is introduced to smooth infinitesimal analysis based on intuitionistic logic. At first the theory seems to him quite absurd, but then it is natural for him to realize that the other mathematicians endow the logical vocabulary with different meanings. On the other hand, when two logicians or mathematicians discuss doing mathematics classically and intuitionistically and compare what theorems do and which do not hold in each case, it makes perfect sense to say that the theorems have the same meanings in that conversation. The issue of sameness of meaning even of logical vocabulary is thus, as Shapiro contends, context dependent.

Chapter 5

1 'Underlying our whole construction is the division of all terms of the language discussed into logical and extra-logical. This division is certainly

not quite arbitrary. If, for example, we were to include among the extra-logical signs the implication sign, or the universal quantifier, then our definition of the concept of consequence would lead to results which obviously contradict ordinary usage. On the other hand no objective grounds are known to me which permit us to draw a sharp boundary between the two groups of terms. It seems to me possible to include among logical terms some which are usually regarded by logicians as extra-logical without running into consequences which stand in sharp contrast to the ordinary usage' (Tarski 1936, p. 418).

2 If we want to follow the traditional division, at least in its basic tenets, and regard the notion of syncategorematic vocabulary at least as an approximation of the notion of logical constants.
3 More details can be found on p. 569 of McGee (1996).
4 $\aleph_1$ denotes, as is standard in set-theory, the first infinite cardinality (number, if you want) strictly greater than that of the set of all natural numbers.
5 From the merely historical perspective, let us remind ourselves that this approach was developed mostly independently from Tarski. Sher herself discovered that Tarski propounded a very similar approach only while she was already working on the development of her unrestricted logic. This means that, with respect to the invariance criterion, Tarski is important mostly for the clarity and intelligibility of his exposition.
6 Tarski writes: 'Now suppose we continue this idea, and consider still wider classes of transformations. In the extreme case, we would consider the class of all one-one transformations of the space, or universe of discourse, or "world," onto itself' (Tarski 1981, p. 49).
7 We should note, however, that Etchemendy claims that the Quinean attack on the synthetic/analytic distinction should be rejected because Quine is also a victim of a mistaken conception of logic. It is, according to Etchemendy in Etchemendy (2008, p. 299) because Quine is beholden to classical logic with Tarskian semantics that he cannot reasonably draw the line between the analytic and the synthetic.
8 And to generalize from the case of logic, I think that any explanation of a complicated concept should as much as possible grow from the established usage, as a failure to do so can hardly end up short of changing the topic.
9 Arguments that logic should be the most general and most formal discipline, proposed, according to Bonnay, respectively by Tarski and Sher.
10 Meaning logical according to Feferman.
11 An interested reader should read Bonnay (2006).
12 The abbreviation, obviously, meaning first-order logic.

Chapter 6

1. The rules are presented in the form which is to be found in Švejdar (2002).
2. See 5.4611 of Wittgenstein (1921).
3. Logic being about 'constitutive norms for thought as such' (MacFarlane 2000, p. iii).
4. I am indebted to the talks by Martin Kusch on Wittgenstein for my views presented here.
5. It seems to me that this also should make us suspicious about MacFarlane's thesis that the three senses of formality he mentions are independent of each other, so that there is no entailment between them. But let us not pursue this further.
6. A theory claiming that entities from the actual world have their counterparts in other possible worlds which make statements about what is possible true. Thus, for example, Hubert Humphrey, who ran for American presidency and lost in the general election to Richard Nixon, could have won because his counterpart in another possible world won (in that world).
7. See the first chapter of Kolman (2008) for a presentation of this historical development.
8. For a motivation to embrace paraconsistency, see Carnielli and Rodrigues (2016).
9. See Brandom (1994 and 2000).
10. Note that this is in line with what was originally Frege's or even Kant's insight, namely that a word can be meaningful only thanks to its occurence within sentences.
11. For a concise explication of the necessity of this distinction, see the chapter about Wittgenstein from Peregrin (2014b).
12. A distinction, which, as he notes in Peregrin (2007) is akin to that made by Searle between the rules which are *constitutive* and those which are merely *regulative* for a certain practice (see Searle 1969, p. 34).
13. I suspect a suitable alternative expression would be quite difficult to find. Should we say *stating the rules*, it would be a little bit less misleading but also much less inspiring.
14. The period before and after the word 'triangular' is a means by which Sellars designtes the inferential role of a given expression.

15 English translation: 'We are like sailors who have to rebuild their ship on the open sea, without ever being able to dismantle it in dry-dock and reconstruct it from its best components' (Neurath 1983, p. 92).
16 In Hanna (2006) he even encourages us to look for that logic, also by means of the psychological study of our reasoning. Obviously, such an approach is very alien to the one pursued here.
17 Though, for example, the epistemic logics focus on a specific, delimited area of discourse. Yet I suspect that so far they have not been able to influence the talk of knowledge, ignorance or ascription of beliefs as much as classical and intuitionistic logic influenced reasoning in mathematics. Similarly, quantum logic can be seen as an attempt to create a new logical framework for physics, yet not a particularly successful one.

Chapter 7

1 A summary of which can be found in MacFarlane (2005).
2 See Popper (1946a, 1946b) and Kneale (1956).
3 On page 290 of the discussed article Hacking quotes: 'The representation of logic as concerned with a characteristic of sentences, truth, rather than of transitions from sentences to sentences, had highly deleterious effects both in logic and in philosophy' (Dummett 1973, p. 432).
4 Ascribing to logic the purpose of internalizing the meta is obviously very close to logical expressivism. I would even say that it can be seen as a somewhat more mathematical reglementation of the thesis of logical expressivism.
5 Logic C was presented by Carnap (1947). For a presentation of this logic and its comparison with the S5 logic, see Punčochář (2010).
6 Denoting the powerset, that is the set of all subsets of L_0.

Chapter 8

1 Kissel points out that while the models of classical logic can be seen as special cases of both relevance and intuitionistic models, intuitionistic models cannot be considered as special cases of the relevant ones, nor the other way round, due to the properties of the relations on possible worlds or information states.
2 See Cook (2010), pp. 496–9.
3 See Eklund (2017), p. 444.

4   See Lynch (2009), p. 102.
5   See, for example, Tennant (2018).
6   See Keefe (2018) and Cook (2018).
7   Adapted from pages 368–9 of Cook (2018).
8   'Neither Aristotelian nor Russellian rules give the exact logic of any expression of ordinary language; for ordinary language has no exact logic' (Strawson (1950), p. 344).

References

Arazim, P. (2012). Pluralism in geometry. *Miscellanea Logica*, IX (1): 7–21.

Arazim, P. (2015). Model theory and foundations of logic. *Miscellanea Logica*, X (1): 7–21.

Arazim, P. (2017). Logical space and the origins of pluralism in logic. *Miscellanea Logica*, XI (1): 7–26.

Aristotle. (1997). *Prior Analytics*. (Translated and commented by G. Striker). Oxford: Oxford University Press.

Austin, J. L. (1962). *How to Do Things with Words*. 2nd edn. M. Sbisa and J. O. Urmson (Eds), Oxford: Oxford University Press.

Beall, J. and Restall, G. (2006). *Logical Pluralism*. Oxford: Oxford University Press.

Belnap, N. (1962). Tonk, plonk and plink. *Analysis*, 22 (6): 130–4.

Beltrami, E. (1868). Saggio di interpretazione della geometria non euclidea. *Giornale di Matematiche*, 6 (1): 284–322.

Beziau, J.-Y. (2007). *Logica Universalis: Towards a general theory of logic*. Basel: Birkhauser.

Bonnay, D. (2006). 'Qu'est-ce qu'une Constante Logique?' (Unpublished doctoral dissertation). Paris: Université Paris 1.

Bonnay, D. (2008). Logicality and invariance. *Bulletin of Symbolic Logic*, 14 (1): 29–68.

Boolos, G. (1975). On second-order logic. *Journal of Philosophy*, 72 (16): 509–27.

Brandom, R. (1994). *Making it explicit*. Cambridge, MA: Harvard University Press.

Brandom, R. (2000). *Articulating reasons*. Cambridge, MA: Harvard University Press.

Brandom, R. (2008). *Between saying and doing*. New York: Oxford University Press.

Carnap, R. (1934). *Logische Syntax der Sprache*. Wien: Springer. (English translation: *The Logical Syntax of Language*, London: Kegan, Paul, Trench Teubner & Co, 1937.)

Carnap, R. (1947). *Meaning and necessity*. Chicago: The University of Chicago Press.

Carnielli, W. and Rodrigues, A. (2016). Paraconsistency and duality: Between ontological and epistemological views. In P. Arazim and M. Dančák (Eds), *The Logica Yearbook 2015* (39–56). London: College Publications.

Coffa, A. J. (1993). *The Semantic Tradition from Kant to Carnap: To the Vienna Station*. Cambridge: Cambridge University Press.

Cook, R. (2010). Let a thousand flowers bloom: A tour of logical pluralism. *Philosophy Compass*, 5 (6): 492–504.

Cook, R. (2018). Pluralism about pluralisms. In J. Wyatt, N. Pedersen & N. Kellen (Eds), *Pluralisms in truth and logic*. London: Palgrave Macmillan.

Cotnoir, A. J. (2018). Logical nihilism. In J. Wyatt, N. Pedersen & N. Kellen (Eds), *Pluralisms in truth and logic* (301–29). London: Palgrave Macmillan.

Davidson, D. (1973). Radical interpretation. *Dialectica*, 27 (1), 314–28.

Davidson, D. (1974). On the very idea of conceptual scheme. *Proceedings and Addresses of the American Philosophical Association*, 47 (1), 5–20.

Descartes, R. (1996 [1641]). *Meditations on first philosophy*. (Translated by J. Cottingham). Cambridge: Cambridge University Press.

Descartes, R. (1965). *Discourse on method, optics, geometry, and meteorology*. (Translated by Paul J. Olscamp). Indianapolis: Bobbs-Merrill.

Descartes, R. (1999). *Discourse on method and related writings*. (Translated by Desmond M. Clarke). London: Penguin.

Dicher, B. (2017). A proof-theoretic defense of meaning-invariant logical pluralism. *Mind*, 125 (499), 727–57.

Dicher, B. (in press). Requiem for logical nihilism, or: Logical nihilism annihilated. *Synthese*.

Dogramaci, S. (2017). Why is a valid inference a good inference? *Philosophy and Phenomenological Research*, 94 (1), 61–96.

Došen, K. (1980). 'Logical constants: An essay in proof theory'. (Unpublished doctoral dissertation). Oxford: University of Oxford.

Došen, K. (1989). Logical constants as punctuation marks. *Philosophy and Phenomenological Research*, 30 (3), 362–81.

Dummett, M. (1973). *Frege: The philosophy of language*. London: Duckworth.

Dummett, M. (1976). Is logic empirical? In *Truth and other Enigmas* (269–89). Cambridge, MA: Harvard University Press..

Dummett, M. (1977). *Elements of intuitionism*. Oxford: Oxford University Press.

Dummett, M. (1978). *Truth and other Enigmas*. Cambridge, MA: Harvard University Press.

Eklund, M. (2017). Making sense of logical pluralism. *Inquiry*, 60 (3), 433–54.

Etchemendy, J. (1990). *The concept of logical consequence*. Cambridge, MA: Harvard University Press.

Etchemendy, J. (2008). Reflections on consequence. In D. Patterson (Ed.), *New Essays on Tarski and Philosophy* (263–99). Oxford: Oxford University Press.

Feferman, S. (1999). Logic, logics, and logicism. *Notre Dame Journal of Formal Logic*, 40 (1), 31–54.

Feferman, S. (2010). Set-theoretical invariance criteria for logicality. *Notre Dame Journal of Formal Logic*, 51 (1), 3–20.

Field, H. (2009). Pluralism in logic. *Review of Symbolic Logic*, 2 (2), 342–59.
Franks, C. (2014). Logical nihilism. In P. Rush (Ed.), *Metaphysics of logic* (109–27). Cambridge: Cambridge University Press.
Frege, G. (1879). *Begriffschrift*. (Translated in Frege (1967)). Halle: Nebert.
Frege, G. (1884). *Die Grundlagen der Arithmetik*. Jena: hrsg. von Christian Thiel.
Frege, G. (1892). Über Sinn und Bedeutung. *Zeitschrift für Philosophie und philosophische Kritik*, 25–50.
Frege, G. (2017 [1918]). Der Gedanke. eine logische Untersuchung. *Beiträge zur Philosophie des deutschen Idealismus*, 39, 58–77.
Frege, G. (1967). Begriffschrift, a formal language, modelled upon that of arithmetic, for pure thought. In J. van Heijenoort (Ed.), *From Frege to Gödel: A source book in mathematical logic*. (Translated by S. Bauer-Mengelberg). Cambridge, MA: Harvard University Press.
Gentzen, G. (1935). Untersuchungen über das logische Schliessen. *Mathematische Zeitschrift*, 39, 176–210.
Girard, J.-Y. (1987). Linear logic. *Theoretical Computer Science*, 50 (1), 1–102.
Haack, S. (1974). *Deviant logic*. Cambridge: Cambridge University Press.
Haack, S. (1978). *Philosophy of logics*. Cambridge: Cambridge University Press.
Hacking, I. (1979). What is logic? *Journal of Philosophy*, 76 (6), 285–319.
Hanna, R. (2006). *Rationality and logic*. Cambridge, MA: MIT Press.
Harman, G. (1986). *Change in view*. Cambridge, MA: MIT Press.
Hegel, G. W. F. (1807). *Phänomenologie des Geistes*. Bamberg/Wurzburg: Verlag Joseph Anton Goebhardt. (Translated by A. V. Miller (1977). *Phenomenology of spirit*. Oxford: Oxford University Press.)
Helmholtz, H. v. (1870). Über den Ursprung und die Bedeutung der geometrischen Axiome. *Vorträge und Reden*, 2, 1–31, Braunschweig: Vieweg. (English translation in Helmholtz (1876).)
Helmholtz, H. v. (1876). On the origin and meaning of geometrical axioms. *Mind*, 1 (3), 301–21.
Hilbert, D. (1899). *Grundlagen der Geometrie*. In *Festschrift zur Feier der Enthüllung des Gauss-Weber-Denkmals in Göttingen*. Leipzig: Teubner.
Hintikka, J. & Kulas, J. (1983). *The game of language: Studies in game theoretical semantics and its applications*. Dordrecht: D. Reidel.
Hintikka, J. & Sandu, G. (1997). Game-theoretical semantics. In A. van Benthem Johan ter Meulen (Ed.), *Handbook of logic and language* (361–410). Amsterdam: Elsevier.
Hjortland, O. (2013). Logical pluralism, meaning invariance and verbal disputes. *Australasian Journal of Philosophy*, 91 (1), 355–73.
Hjortland, O. (2017). Anti-exceptionalism about logic. *Philosophical Studies*, 174 (3), 631–58.

Hlobil, U. (2016). A nonmonotonic sequent calculus for inferentialist expressivists. In P. Arazim & M. Dančák (Eds), *The logica yearbook 2015* (87–105). London: College Publications.

Hlobil, U. (2017). When structural principles hold merely locally. In P. Arazim & M. Dančák (Eds), *The logica yearbook 2016* (65–84). London: College Publications.

Husserl, E. (1913). *Logische Untersuchungen*. Halle: Niemeyer.

Kant, I. (1954 [1787]). *Kritik der reinen Vernunft*. Hamburg: Felix Meiner. (English translation in Kant (1998).)

Kant, I. (1998). *Critique of pure reason*. (Translated by Paul Guyer and Allen W. Wood). Cambridge: Cambridge University Press.

Keefe, R. (2018). Pluralisms: Logic, truth and domain-specificity. In J. Wyatt, N. Pedersen & N. Kellen (Eds), *Pluralisms in truth and logic*. London: Palgrave Macmillan.

Kissel, T. K. (2018). Connective meaning in Beall and Restall's logical pluralism. In J. Wyatt, N. Pedersen & N. Kellen (Eds), *Pluralisms in truth and logic* (217–35). London: Palgrave Macmillan.

Kneale, W. (1956). The province of logic. In L. H. D (Ed.), *Contemporary British Philosophy* (237–61). London: George Allen and Unwin.

Kolman, V. (2002). *Logika Gottloba Frega*. Praha: Filosofia.

Kolman, V. (2008). *Filosofie čísla*. Praha: Filosofia.

Kolman, V. (2009). Filosofie jako vyslovování nevyslovitelného. *Filosofie Dnes*, 1 (1), 33–46.

Koreň, L. (2014a). Quantificational accounts of logical consequence I: From Aristotle to Bolzano. *Organon F*, 21 (1), 22–44.

Koreň, L. (2014b). Quantificational accounts of logical consequence II: in the footsteps of Bolzano. *Organon F*, 21 (3), 303–26.

Koreň, L. (2014c). Quantificational accounts of logical consequence III: The standard model-theoretic account: quantificational accounts triumphant? *Organon F*, 21 (4), 492–515.

Kripke, S. (1972). *Naming and necessity*. Cambridge, MA: Harvard University Press.

Kripke, S. (1982). *Wittgenstein on rules and private language: An elementary exposition*. Cambridge, MA: Harvard University Press.

Lecomte, A. (2011). *Meaning, logic and ludics*. London: Imperial College Press.

Lecomte, A. (2013). Ludics, dialogue and inferentialism. *The Baltic International Yearbook of Cognition, Logic and Communication*, 8 (1), 1–33.

Lepore, E. (2007). Brandom beleaguered. *Philosophy and Phenomenological Research*, 74 (3), 677–91.

Lindenbaum, A. & Tarski, A. (1983). On the limitation of the means of expression of deductive theories (translated by J. H. Woodger). In J. Corcoran (Ed.), *Logic, Semantics, Metamathematics* (384–92). Indianapolis: Hackett.

Lindström, P. (1966). First order predicate logic with generalized quantifiers. *Theoria*, 32 (3), 186–95.

Lynch, M. (2008). Aletheic pluralism, logical consequence, and the universality of reason. *Midwest Studies in Philosophy*, 32 (1), 122–40.

Lynch, M. (2009). *Truth as one and many*. Oxford: Oxford University Press.

MacFarlane, J. (2000). 'What does it mean to say that logic is formal?' (Unpublished doctoral dissertation). Pittsburgh: University of Pittsburgh.

MacFarlane, J. (2005). Logical constants. Retrieved 30 April 2020, from http://plato.stanford.edu/entries/logical-constants

Mautner, F. I. (1946). An extension of Klein's Erlanger program: Logic as invariant-theory. *American Journal of Mathematics*, 21 (3), 345–84.

McCarthy, T. (1981). The idea of a logical constant. *Journal of Philosophy*, 78 (9), 499–523.

McDowell, J. (1994). *Mind and world*. Cambridge, MA: Harvard University Press.

McGee, V. (1996). Logical operations. *Journal of Philosophical Logic*, 25 (6), 567–80.

McKeon, M. (2004). On the substitutional characterization of first-order logical truth. *History and Philosophy of Logic*, 25 (3), 205–24.

Moore, G. E. (1925). A defence of common sense. In J. H. Muirhead (Ed.), *Contemporary British philosophy* (193–223). London: George Allen and Unwin.

Moore, G. E. (1939). Proof of an external world. *Proceedings of the British Academy*, 25 (5), 273–300.

Mostowski, A. (1957). On a generalization of quantifiers. *Fundamenta Mathematicae*, 44 (2), 12–36.

Neurath, O. (1932). Protokollsätze. *Erkenntnis*, 1 (1), 204–14. (Translated in Neurath (1983))

Neurath, O. (1983). *Philosophical papers 1913–1946*, R. S. Cohen and M. Neurath (Eds). Dordrecht: Reidel.

Payette, G. & Wyatt, N. (2018). Logical particularism. In J. Wyatt, N. Pedersen & N. Kellen (Eds), *Pluralisms in truth and logic*. London: Palgrave Macmillan.

Peacocke, C. (1976). What is a logical constant? *Journal of Philosophy*, 73 (9), 221–40.

Pedersen, N. J. (2014). Pluralism x 3: Truth, logic, metaphysics. *Erkenntnis*, 79 (1), 259–77.

Peregrin, J. (2001). *Meaning and structure*. Aldershot: Ashgate.

Peregrin, J. (2007). Viable inferentialism. Retrieved 30 April 30, from http://jarda.peregrin.cz/mybibl/PDFTxt/503.pdf

Peregrin, J. (2008). What is the logic of inference? *Studia Logica*, 88 (2), 263–94.

Peregrin, J. (2014a). *Inferentialism: Why rules matter*. London: Palgrave Macmillan.

Peregrin, J. (2014b). *Kapitoly z Analytické Filosofie*. Praha: Filosofia.

Peregrin, J. (2016). Incompatibility and inference as bases of logic. In P. Arazim & M. Dančák (Eds), *The logica yearbook 2015* (157–62). London: College Publications.

Peregrin, J. & Svoboda, V. (2017). *Reflective equilibrium and the principles of logical analysis*. Abingdon-on-Thames: Routledge.

Poincaré, H. (1902). *La Science et L'Hypothése*. Paris: Flammarion. (Translated in The Foundations of Science: *Science and Hypothesis*, The Value of Science, Science and Method. 1913. University Press of America).

Popper, K. R. (1946a). Logic without assumptions. *Proceedings of the Aristotelian Society*, 47, 251–92.

Popper, K. R. (1946b). New foundations for logic. *Mind*, 56 (223), 193–235.

Porello, D. (2012). Incompatibility semantics from agreement. *Philosophia*, 40 (1), 99–119.

Priest, G. (1995). Etchemendy and logical consequence. *Canadian Journal of Philosophy*, 25 (2), 283–92.

Priest, G. (2006). *Doubt truth to be a liar*. Oxford: Oxford University Press.

Priest, G. (2014). Revising logic. In P. Rush (Ed.), *The metaphysics of logic* (211–23). Cambridge: Cambridge University Press.

Prior, A. (1960). The runabout inference ticket. *Analysis*, 21 (2), 38.

Punčochář, V. (2010). Carnapova modální logika C. *Organon F*, 17 (2), 163–84.

Quine, W. V. O. (1936). Truth by convention. *Journal of Symbolic Logic*, 1 (1), 77–106.

Quine, W. V. O. (1948). On what there is. *Review of Metaphysics*, 2 (1), 21–38.

Quine, W. V. O. (1951). Two dogmas of empiricism. *Philosophical Review*, 60 (1), 20–43.

Quine, W. V. O. (1960). *Word and object*. Cambridge, MA: MIT Press.

Quine, W. V. O. (1986). *Philosophy of logic*. Cambridge, MA: Harvard University Press.

Quine, W. V. O. (1990). *Pursuit of truth*. Cambridge, MA: Harvard University Press.

Restall, G. (2002). Carnap's tolerance, language change and logical pluralism. *Journal of Philosophy*, 99 (8), 426–43.

Restall, G. (2014). Pluralism and proofs. *Erkenntnis*, 79 (2), 279–91.

Russell, B. (1923). Vagueness. *The Australasian Journal of Psychology and Philosophy*, 1 (1), 84–92.

Russell, G. (2017). An introduction to logical nihilism. In H. Leitgeb, I. Niiniluoto, P. Seppälä & E. Sober (Eds), *Logic, methodology and philosophy of science: Proceedings of the 15th International Congress*. London: College Publications.

Russell, G. (2018a). Logical nihilism: Could there be no logic? *Philosophical Issues*, 28 (1), 308–24.

Russell, G. (2018b). Varieties of logical consequence by their resistance to logical nihilism. In J. Wyatt, N. Pedersen & N. Kellen (Eds), *Pluralisms in truth and logic*. London: Palgrave Macmillan.

Scharp, K. (2018). Aletheic and logical pluralism. In J. Wyatt, N. Pedersen & N. Kellen (Eds), *Pluralisms in truth and logic*. London: Palgrave Macmillan.

Searle, J. (1969). *Speech acts: An essay in the philosophy of language*. Cambridge: Cambridge University Press.

Sellars, W. (1953). Inference and meaning. *Mind*, 62 (247), 313–38.

Sellars, W. (1974). Meaning as functional classification. *Synthese*, 27 (3), 417–37.

Shapiro, S. (1991). *Foundations without foundationalism*. Oxford: Oxford University Press.

Shapiro, S. (1996). Second-order languages and mathematical practice. *The Journal of Symbolic Logic*, 50 (3), 714–42.

Shapiro, S. (2014). *Varieties of logic*. Oxford: Oxford University Press.

Shapiro, S. (2015). The meaning of logical terms. In C. R. Caret & O. T. Hjortland (Eds), *Foundations of logical consequence*. Oxford: Oxford University Press.

Sher, G. (1991). *The bounds of logic: A generalized viewpoint*. Cambridge, MA: MIT Press.

Sher, G. (1996). Did Tarski commit Tarski's fallacy? *The Journal of Symbolic Logic*, 61 (2), 653–86.

Sher, G. (1999). Is logic a theory of the obvious? *European Review of Philosophy*, 4, 207–38.

Sher, G. (2008). Tarski's thesis. In D. Patterson (Ed.), *Alfred Tarski: Philosophical background, development, and influence* (300–39). Oxford: Oxford University Press.

Strawson, P. F. (1950). On referring. *Mind*, 59 (235), 320–44.

Sundholm, G. (1981). Hacking's logic. *Journal of Philosophy*, 78 (3), 160–8.

Švejdar, V. (2002). *Logika: Neúplnost, Složitost, Nutnost*. Praha: Academia.

Tarski, A. (1936). O pojeciu wynikania logicznego. *Przeglad Filozoficzny*, 39, 58–68. (in English published as On the concept of logical consequence (1936), in *Logic, Semantics, Metamathematics*, Oxford University Press, 1956.)

Tarski, A. (1981). What are logical notions? *History and Philosophy of Logic*, 7 (2), 143–54.

Tennant, N. (2018). Core logic: A conspectus. In J. Wyatt, N. Pedersen & N. Kellen (Eds), *Pluralisms in truth and logic*. London: Palgrave Macmillan.

Turbanti, G. (2017). *Robert Brandom's Normative Inferentialism*. Amsterdam: John Benjamins Publishing Company.

van Benthem, J. (2002). Logical constants: The variable fortune of an elusive notion. In W. Sieg, R. Sommer & C. Talcott (Eds), *Reflections on foundations of mathematics: Essays in honour of Solomon Feferman*. Urbana: Association for Symbolic Logic.

Varzi, A. (2002). On logical relativity. *Philosophical Issues*, 12 (1), 197–219.

Waismann, F. (1945). Verifiability. *Proceedings of the Aristotelian Society*, 19 (1), 119–50.

Williamson, T. (2017). Semantic paradoxes and abductive methodology. In B. Armour-Garb (Ed.), *Reflections on the liar*. Oxford: Oxford University Press.

Wittgenstein, L. (1921). Tractatus Logico-Philosophicus. *Annalen der Naturphilosophie*, XIV (3/4), edited by Wilhelm Ostwald. (English translation in Wittgenstein (1961).)

Wittgenstein, L. (1953). *Philosophische Untersuchungen*. Oxford: Blackwell.

Wittgenstein, L. (1961). *Tractatus Logico-Philosophicus*. (Translated by D. F. Pears and B. F. McGuiness). New York: Humanities Press.

Wittgenstein, L. (1969). *On certainty*. (Translated by D. Paul and G. E. M. Anscombe). Oxford: Blackwell.

Wittgenstein, L. (1984 [1969]). *Über Gewißheit*. Suhrkamp: Frankfurt am Main.

Wrenn, C. B. (2018). A plea for immodesty: Alethic pluralism, logical pluralism, and mixed inferences. In J. Wyatt, N. Pedersen & N. Kellen (Eds), *Pluralisms in truth and logic*. London: Palgrave Macmillan.

Wright, C. (1992). *Truth and objectivity*. Cambridge, MA: Harvard University Press.

Zardini, E. (2018). Generalized Tarski's thesis hits substructure. In J. Wyatt, N. Pedersen & N. Kellen (Eds), *Pluralisms in truth and logic*. London: Palgrave Macmillan.

Index

Aristotle   105
arithmetic
    Kantian account of arithmetic   26–7
Austin, J.   39, 118

Beltrami, E.   25
Bolzano, B.   50
Bonnay, D.   83
Brandom, R.   43, 118, 146
    expressive rationality   120

Carnap, R.
    tolerance   28, 152
charity, principle of charity   57
consequence   75, 79
criteria
    for correctness of logic   16–20

definition   140
demarcation of logic   92–4
    bijection invariance   66–8, 82, 87–90
    expressivist demarcations   147
    homomorphism invariance   85–7
    of logical constants   53–4, 59
    model-theoretical   48, 61
    proof-theoretical   133
Descartes, R.   97
determinacy
    of rules   3–5
development
    of concepts   19–20
Došen, K.   138
Dummett, M.   35–6, 56

Etchemendy, J.   74–81
    Tarski´s Fallacy   78–81

Feferman, S.   74, 83–7
formalism   35–6
formality of logic   48–9, 66, 107
foundations, of mathematics   29, 90
freedom   120

Frege, G.   16, 26, 45, 65, 82, 89, 115

generality of logic   80, 105
Gentzen, G.   133
geometry   122
    affine   63
    Euclidian *vs*. non-Euclidian   24–6
    Kantian account of geometry   22–4
    permutation/transformation
        of space   62

Hacking, I.   135, 140
Harman, G.   111
Helmholtz, H. v.   25
Hlobil, U.   147–8
holism   33, 98
    about logic   45

identity
    of rules   3–5
inferentialism   34, 40–1
interpretation   5

Kant, I.   49, *see* under geometry
    as a logical monist   21, 30–1
knowledge
    change of framework   31–3
    logic as expanding knowledge   104
    synthetic a priori   24

language
    formal   5–6
    language game   114
    natural   6–7, 158–9
Lindström, P.   69
logic
    alternative logics   53
    applicability of logic   106
    change of logic   122–7
    as constitutive for rationality   99
    exceptionalism   160–3, 170–1
    as expanding knowledge   104

formal 5–9
  as management of beliefs 111
  necessity of logic 129
  revision of logic 130
  second-order 83
  topic neutrality 138–9
logical constants 50, 59, 63, 133, 156
  in natural language 51–2
logical dynamism 2–9, 173
logical expressivism 29, 113, 146, *see also* under demarcation
  ludics 150
logical form 64, 75, 167
  categorematic *vs.* syncategorematic expressions 64
logical monism 157–8
  Kantian background of monism, *see* Kant
logical nihilism 168
logical pluralism 151, 157–8
  aletheic pluralism 163–6
  the variety of Beall and Restall 151–6
logicism 26–7, 47–8, 82, 89, 98
  reversed logicism 49

McDowell, J. 42
MacFarlane, J. 49, 65–6
McGee, V. 66, 68, 72–3
mathematics 32
  in relation to logic 45–7, 72, 82, 90, 98
meaning 39
  in holism 34
  implicit 37, 40
methodology
  for dealing with the plurality of logics 13–15

Neurath, O. 125

paradox 161–3
Peregrin, J. 39, 41, 113, 116–18, 143, 163–4
plurality
  of logics 15
pragmatism 36

revision of belief and logic 111
role of logic 96, 159–60
utilitarism about logic 127
psychologism 26–7

quantifier
  generalized 68–71
Quine, W. v. O. 32–6, 54–6, 153, 161
  Translation arguement in logic 56–8

relativism 17–19
rule 2, 166–8
  constitutive *vs.* strategic 116
  expression of rules 6–8, 43, 117
  identity of rules 3–5
  implicit 3–8, 41–2, 44–5, 114
  inferential 113
  modification of rules 7
  prescriptive *vs.* restrictive 118
  structural (*see* structural rules)
  vagueness of rules 4–5

Sellars, W. 122
semantics 76
set-theory 83–4
Shapiro, S. 59, 83, 91, 155, 174
Sher, G. 69–71, 80, 85, 90, 105
society 6
space 23
speech act 38–40
Strawson, P. F. 168
structural rules 135–9, 144, 149

Tarski, A. 61–3, 66–7, 75
topic neutrality of logic, *see* logic
truth
  pluralism about truth (*see* logical pluralism)

vagueness
  of rules 4–5

Waismann, F.
  open texture 59
Wittgenstein, L. 22, 97–8, 114–16
  certainty and scepticism 102

www.ingramcontent.com/pod-product-compliance
Lightning Source LLC
Chambersburg PA
CBHW061832300426
44115CB00013B/2341